A Chiel Among Them

The time must surely now be overdue for a full literary appraisal of the work of David Toulmin. Whilst we can only wait impatiently for this to be achieved, we are pleased to present *A Chiel Among Them*, Toulmin's latest literary endeavour, fully convinced that it will serve to amplify his place in the forefront of the North-east literary tradition.

Since the publication of his first book *Hard Shining Corn* in 1971, David Toulmin has been compared at each subsequent venture with Lewis Grassic Gibbon. And whilst this comparison is justly made and accords Toulmin the literary status he merits, every comparison additionally serves to heighten the difference between these two barons of Scottish literature. Grassic Gibbon composed the scenario of the Howe of Mearns from the suburbia of Welwyn Garden City. And whilst the savage landscape he evoked as the setting for his powerful fiction is not diminished in its artistic merit for this distancing, his vision was that of an observer, viewing from afar the kith and kin characters of his youth that appear in the pages of *A Scots Quair*.

Toulmin, however, has always remained a part of the landscape he paints, a participator in the events that he transposes with only a thin veil of literary disguise into his fiction. The intense sympathy and affinity that he has with his characters, the deep interest in local folklore and history, is that of an author who lives and works on the land and with the people that he immortalizes in his writing.

Here we have a sequel to his previous miscellany, *Straw Into Gold* (1973) again affording the reader a view of the many facets of Toulmin's interest and abilities.

In the fiction of Shift One, Toulmin the author gives us four superbly constructed short stories. The brilliance of his craft, witnessed so many times over the last decade, is strongly in evidence again, catching our emotions and sympathies. We feel the tormented despair of Sinclair Boad in Dark Encounter, we are elevated by the ecstatic rise to new-born faith of Fergie Mann in the One-Armed Bandit.

In Shifts Two and Three, we see Toulmin in the role of social historian, an avid relater of the local history of Buchan. But again his voice is authenticated by the fact that he has himself been involved in all that he speaks of. The feeing markets were an integral part of his working life; he knows of the agonies that are described in Farming on Ball-Bearings because he has suffered the physical pain himself. Toulmin the researcher is at work in one of the most remarkable tableaux of Shift Three, in which he recalls the forgotten airship base at Lenabo.

In Shifts Four and Five, Toulmin becomes the biographer and journalist, presenting for us but a few of the characters of Buchan who have influenced his life, his schoolmistress Miss Henderson having her place alongside Bob Boothby and Johnny Ironside. His retelling of the tale of Jamie Fleeman, the Laird o' Udny's Fool, gives yet new life to this well-known story of local folklore.

Shift Six shows us Toulmin as a reader himself, with not a little ability at literary appraisal. His panoramic view of the Literary Associations of the North East will be of particular interest to all followers of the North-east tradition.

And, almost as a bonus, in Shift Seven, Toulmin turns to auto-biography, allowing us for a moment to have a direct view behind the disguising veil he normally draws over the events in his life. And the origins of his deep fascination with the cinema, which occur time and again in his writings, are shown for us at their conception. We have a glimpse of the 'movie-buff' in his youth.

But it must be said that it is in his fiction that Toulmin's immortality will lie — and no less here than before is his superb literary talent exposed. Take for example only this small cameo of descriptive flow in the One-Armed Bandit:

... *The family sat on one of the long varnished seats that stretched from the centre aisle to the ochred walls and the gothic window that looked over the fields and farmsteads. Kinsourie was about two miles away with its bourich of twisted trees, like withered arms in the raw dreich wind that swept up from the sea. The sunlight was fitful, darting shafts of light through the smudge of smoke cloud, spot-lighting the barren fields with a deceitful glare, while the wind carried the rain squalls across the sky like quiffs of loosened hair* ...

Taken in isolation it is a superbly constructed piece of descriptive excellence, evoking the scene with intense clarity. Put into the context of the One-Armed Bandit at the time of Fergie Mann's first visit to the kirk since his accident, it assumes a dramatic power which intensifies the sharp emotional climax that Toulmin builds in the story. It is written by an author who must have witnessed and studied the same type of sea-blown storm so many times during his daily labours. Burns' own eulogy so perfectly transposes to David Toulmin, writing from the heart of Buchan:

A chiel's amang you takin' notes,
And, faith, he'll print it . . .

Angela J. Johnson
30th June, 1982.

A Chiel Among Them

A Scots Miscellany

by

David Toulmin

Gourdas House, Publishers
Aberdeen
1982

To my grandchildren this work is dedicated.

First published by Gourdas House, Publishers
5 Alford Place, Aberdeen. October 1982

Reprinted April 1983

ISBN 0 907301 06 1

Printed in Great Britain by
Compass Print Ltd., Aberdeen
and bound by
Hunter & Foulis, Edinburgh

Contents

SHIFT
*A traditional agricultural term applied
to a rotational cropping system.*

DARK ENCOUNTER

THE old woman in the kitchen box-bed was in her eighty-ninth year and totally blind from cataract. Twenty years earlier, when the infection first troubled her, an operation could have saved her eyesight, but Liza Boad wouldn't hear of it, and lived out her life in total darkness. Worse still, she had lost the use of her legs, but for a few steps at a time, holding on to somebody for support, and now lay in bed day and night. She knew each member of her family by their voices, by the feel of their hands — even to biting into them gently to feel the knuckles on their fingers, and kissing and fondling each hand as a way of expressing her pleasure at having their presence by her bedside. The smaller, softer hands of her grandchildren were also familiar to her, and smaller still the hands of her great-grandchildren, presented to her from time to time over the bed, still in the arms of their mothers, Liza's grand-daughters, while her seeing hands caressed the baby's face and head, until she got the shape and size of it. "So that's little Bella than," she would habber, "my but she's growin'," and the baby's cheek would be held up to her withered lips for a kiss.

Liza's own childbearing had extended over a period of some twenty years, which gave an extreme of ages, from the oldest to the very youngest of her offspring. Some of her family were dead, while others were abroad, and seldom home, and some of her grandchildren she had never seen. She had outlived her husband by nearly twenty years at Stonelairs, the small farm now worked by Sinclair Boad, her youngest son, the only one of her four sons still a bachelor, and he had been on the farm since the day of his birth nearly fifty years ago. It had even been settled by the family that Sinclair would get the farm when his mother died, since he had given most of his life in looking after her and keeping the home together, and maybe denied himself a wife in the process.

Since her husband died there had been only Liza and her son on the farm, Sinclair doing all he could for his failing mother, which hadn't been so bad so long as she had the use of her limbs, even in her semi-blindness, but had got steadily worse with her fading eyesight, and worse than ever now that she was bedridden. Sometimes Liza's married daughters spent their holidays at Stonelairs, which was a

1

blessing for Liza and a godsend for Sinclair, since their menfolk helped him in the fields, while their wives caught up with the housework. In the long winters of their absence Sinclair managed on his own, even to dish-washing and laundry, besides cooking a spartan diet and carrying his mother to the earth-closet in the garden, all after a day's work in the fields and attending to the cattle in the byres, relieved at times by one or other of his sisters or a niece who came at a week-end to tidy up and cook a proper meal.

The most frequent visitor was Thelma Rae, Sinclair's oldest sister, and sometimes she brought Effie with her, her eldest daughter and niece of Sinclair, relieving him from a lot of his household chores; and field and stable duties also when Effie was there, for she was a sonsie limmer and worked like a horse beast. And all because Liza said she couldn't afford a kitchen lass, though her real reason was that she was afraid Sinclair would take up with a serving quine; especially if she was a bonnie lassie, and since she couldn't be sure of engaging an ugly one in her blindness she wouldn't take the risk. Not that any woman is that ugly in the eye of the male, but that wasn't Liza's way of looking at things, and a word like 'unattractive' for her simply meant ugly.

But the day came eventually when Sinclair told his mother he simply couldn't go on doing a double job and she would just have to engage a servant lass for the kitchen work. He wasn't getting any younger he insisted and was sore tired out at the end of a day without having to do housework. His other complaint might have been that he had no relaxation, no social contacts; never a dance or a concert to break the monotony, where he might meet a woman he had a fancy for, who might become his wife, something his mother would just have to accept, though most of it had passed him by and he thought less about it as he grew older. But Sinclair never discussed these things with his mother, though each suspected they knew each other's thoughts about it and left the fly on the wall. Not that Sinclair didn't have his feelings about sex, and his liking for a dram, which was mostly confined to market days, or the occasional Saturday night in town when he could leave his mother in the care of one of his visiting sisters; and these were the only occasions that Sinclair came home the worse of drink, raving a bit about his old mother being a tether about his neck and him not having a chance to look for a kitchiedeem, though he never went as far as calling her a wife. But as the effect of the drink wore off Sinclair settled down again to his old routine and listening to the wireless, which was about his only diversion from the grindstone in his daily life. But even his sisters had a soft spot for Sinclair in his dilemma, and not a little of their sympathy, in a quiet sort of way; never hostile in their mother's presence, especially Thelma, who had sons of her own she wouldn't like to see in the same position, tied to her mothering petticoats.

Liza pondered the problem and turned from one side to the other in the darkness of her prison bed. During the long lonely days when her son was in the fields, and the quiet sleepless nights that had no ending in light, Liza pondered, till finally she had the answer, and she told Sinclair he could fee a kitchen maid on condition that she slept with her in the box-bed. It was a crafty thought, and the full force of it nearly knocked Sinclair sideways when she told him, for it had never dawned on him that she was afraid he would take up with any lass she fee-ed for kitchiedeem. But he raised no objection, glad of her consent, and at length between them a maid was engaged to look after her.

But it didn't last long, for Liza gave the quine such a heckling from the box-bed while Sinclair was in the fields, that she soon left them, scarcely leaving her imprint in the box-bed. Another girl was found but again Liza harried her from daylight till dark, hounding her from chore to chore, and even in the box-bed, till the quine told Sinclair she couldn't put up with his mother and left them. They had no better results with a third maid, though she stayed a bit longer than the others, with some remonstration from Sinclair, reprimanding his mother for her behaviour in front of the girl, who was sometimes in tears, because she didn't like sleeping in the box-bed, and in her absence Liza said it wasn't like him to let a quine come between him and his poor blind mother, but that she knew all along this would happen. Sinclair began to wonder if he wasn't worse off with a serving quine than he had been without one, and in the solace of the thought he wasn't all that disappointed when the third lass never returned from her Sunday off to sleep in the box-bed.

There had been moments of bliss when Sinclair could whistle at the plough on the thought of it; the new freedom he could enjoy even though youth had left him, with a quine to look after his mother while he did a bit of galavanting — but the prospect was short-lived and he was soon back at his mother's bedside, never sure if he was taken with the quine that had just left, for they were never long enough about the premises to find out.

It was after the third quine had left Stonelairs that Thelma offered her daughter Effie to Liza her grandmother as kitchen help. Effie was out of service at the time and Thelma offered her with the best of intentions, not the least of them out of sympathy for her brother Sinclair, to relieve his dual responsibility, since the alternative of feeing a loon to help him on the grun would have added to their burden, providing bed and board, and was no real solution to the problem. But with Effie on the job Sinclair had a servant lass who stood up to Liza Boad and her blind bullying, and was still on the job at the end of a whole month, though she flatly refused to sleep in the box-bed, and just as well for Liza that she didn't, because for sheer bulk, lying at the back, she would have heaved her frail old grandmother on to the stone floor.

But strangely enough, when Effie Rae came to do the housework at Stonelairs the tyranny ceased, and old blind Liza left the quine alone to do almost as she pleased. Maybe this was what the old woman wanted, an ill-faured creature like her grand-daughter, Effie Rae, who would be no attraction for Sinclair, and being a close relative would also keep them apart. She remembered Effie from the days of her sight, but from time to time, maybe just to reassure herself, Liza would call the quine from her kitchen duties to kneel by the bed, and the old woman would caress her face fondly with her sensitive fingers, which gave the unsuspecting Effie the idea that her grandmother adored her, and she smiled and giggled while the soft feeling hands prodded over her face. Liza in her mind's eye shaped out Effie's big flat nose, wide cheek bones, broad protruding mouth and buck teeth, small piggish eye sockets and tiny ears close to the sides of her man-sized head, then ran her fingers through the floss of dry colourless hair, and over her haunched, masculine shoulders – thoroughly convinced there was nothing here for Sinclair, what though her eyes should gleam like diamonds, her teeth like pearl, because colour was the only thing that baffled Liza. But she was sure there was no enticement for Sinclair her son in such a framework. Then Liza would withdraw her groping hands and the lively Effie would rise up and get back to her housework, her podgy face wrinkled in smiles.

But Effie was not illiterate, for she could read the newspapers, and sometimes read to her grandmother by the bedside in the evenings

4

when the lamp was lit, a service for which Liza was extremely grateful, in that it passed the time for her, besides keeping her in touch with the outside world. Effie even suggested that her grandmother should take up the braille, but Liza said it was too late in life for her to be bothered with it. But Effie had a new portable radio, which she set by the bedside, and Liza could listen to it for hours while Effie busied herself in byre and kitchen.

But Liza had not reckoned with Effie's man hunger, nor her son's moral weakness, and within a few months Sinclair and her grand-daughter, uncle and niece, were sleeping in the same bed and enjoying each other. Nor did Liza know of Effie's illegitimate child, born to her while in former service, now in the care of Thelma her mother, one of Liza's great-grand-daughters she had never caressed with her searching fingers. It was one of the skeletons in the family cupboard that had never rattled in Liza's hearing, nor had Thelma divulged the secret, fearing perhaps that her mother would have rejected Effie had she known of it, though the rest of the family, including Sinclair, had known since the child was born.

Effie wasn't an attractive woman by any standards; almost totally lacking in feminine qualities, with a dull-witted brain and an impudent tongue, thick muscular legs and arms, and yet some lad had thought fit to make her a mother, and a quite capable mother she had turned out to be, though the lad hadn't married her. Now in her thirties she had almost given up hope of getting a man, though her hunger for sex still whittled at her marrow, with any man who thought fit to give her a second look, or who came conveniently within her influence. But she was as strong as the proverbial ox and a willing worker in house or byre, and old blind Liza was satisfied that in her wisdom she had made a good choice with Effie Rae to assist her trauchled son.

Effie wasn't long before she was with child to her uncle, the wife-starved bachelor who had been a willing partner in her wiles of seduction, performed in the old woman's world of darkness. But Thelma's sharper eyes were quick enough to observe her daughter's stoutness, though the build of the quine made it easier for her to hide it from strangers.

"What's this ye've been up till?" Thelma asked her daughter, out of hearing of her own mother in the box-bed, "Ye're gettin' affa stoot."

"Oh naething, mither," Effie replied, trying to put her mother off,

"I'm juist puttin' on a bit of weight; there isn't all that much tae do here and plenty of good meat."

"Weel weel," her mother retorted, not all that sure of her ground, "ye're puttin' it a' on in the same place, that's what puzzles me."

But if Thelma had her suspicions she said nothing at the moment to her brother on the subject, though she might have noticed how he was trying to avoid her searching glances.

"My mither noticed my condition the day," Effie told Sinclair in bed.

"What did she say?"

"Oh, juist that I was gettin' fat in the wrang place, but she's nae sure yet ye see. And when she is sure she'll juist hae tae get used tae things as they are."

"Couldn't ye get rid o't?" Sinclair enquired.

"No Sinclair, I've told ye that afore. I dinna want tae get rid o' my bairn. Haein' a bairn's nae a' that bother for me; it's easier and healthier than an abortion I shid think."

"But the scandal quine: I'm nae ye're proper man; I'm yer uncle."

"Then what are ye doin' in my bed Sinclair Boad? Ye ocht tae be ashamed o' yersel', takin' advantage o' a poor innocent quine."

"Look wha's speakin'. Innocent did ye say? Ye dinna ken the meanin' o' the word. And what if something is wrang wi' the bairn? Ower inbred or something, seein' we're close related."

"We'll juist hae tae tak' that chance Sinclair my loon; there's naething we can do aboot it noo."

"Wheest quine, mither will hear ye!"

"Ly doon and sleep than. Forget aboot the scandal till it comes."

Effie covered herself to the ears with the blankets and was soon snoring. Sinclair lay awake until daybreak.

As time wore on, however, Effie's condition became so apparent that she couldn't hide it from anybody, except her blind grandmother, who had never thought of lowering her hands to Effie's breasts, and if she had Effie would have got on to her feet quick enough; but the fact was that Liza had long since ceased to caress her, convinced of her integrity as a trustworthy grand-daughter. And while others of the family were aware of what was happening a sort of conspiracy was contrived among themselves to hide it from the old woman. To keep the ageing Liza in ignorance of what was taking place under her very nose seemed the most important thing for all of them to do. After all she was still the mistress and Sinclair the heir apparent, and it wouldn't do to disillusion her about her supposedly dutiful son, especially when the will had to be considered, for they couldn't have her changing that. And besides, the shock of the thing might kill her prematurely.

Thelma Rae, Effie's mother, perhaps realising this, did her best as ringleader to get all the others sworn to secrecy, all of her brothers and sisters and in-laws when they came visiting, and their grown-up children besides, each confiding in the other, but mostly with Sinclair as the scapegoat and Effie the innocent victim of his lust. In fact some of them secretly scorned Sinclair as having taken advantage of his dull-witted niece, though they never said as much in his hearing. Sinclair avoided his older sister as much as he could, or stayed in the kitchen when she was about, where she couldn't accuse him in front of their mother. But eventually he had to face her and confess his guilt, with a good swig of whisky to make it easier, for Sinclair was finding solace in drink.

"My God Sinclair," Thelma stormed, "this is a hell of a state of affairs. Yer ain niece! I thocht ye wad of had mair sense, a grown man. If I'd kent this was goin' tae happen I wad never hae latten the lassie come here in the first place. Good God, whatever cam' ower ye man?"

But Sinclair wasn't totally unprepared for his sister's accusation. Worry and guilt and shame had sharpened his wit, and fortified with John Barleycorn he gave her an answer she never expected, nor would have given him credit for in his sober senses; an answer that stunned and surprised her, leaving her almost speechless with anger.

"Maybe ye're nae sae innocent as ye look," Sinclair retorted. "Ye've kent for years that I've been desperate for a wife, and when ye saw yer chance ye sent Effie here tae tempt me, and I can assure ye she was a willin' partner, and she's just as guilty as I am. In fact she led me on, and ye seem tae forget it's nae the first time she's had a bairn ahin the dyke, so she's got good experience.

"I think ye sent her here tae get her bairned tae gi'e ye mair say at Stonelairs than ye are entitled till; maybe even get oor mither tae change the will after ye've had me disgraced, and you bein' the auldest o' the family, if onything happened tae me, or if mither disowned me, ye could be the next in line, with family consent, and I ken that man o' yours has had an eye on the place for years, thinkin' maybe that though

7

ye was a woman body ye was more entitled to it than me."

"Weel weel," Thelma reasoned, "that's all the thanks I get for tryin' tae shield ye. Ye ought tae think shame o' yersel'. How wad I want tae disgrace ye when I'm tryin' hard tae keep a' thing secret frae oor mither . . . tell me that?"

"Maybe it suits yer purpose, or tae shield yer quine . . . bidin' yer time. But whatever ye say it mak's nae difference noo, the harm's done, and it canna be helped. But ye better haud yer tongue for Effie's sake, if ye want me tae treat her weel and bring up her bairn."

Thelma almost spat at her brother, but for the sake of Effie, and perhaps to shield her own conscience, she said no more, but turned and left him, for maybe Sinclair, in his desperation had touched a guilty nerve.

Everybody seemed to hope that old Liza would die before the bastard child was born, or that Effie would somehow lose it beforehand and conceal the crime from her grandmother. It was easy enough to deceive her at the moment, but what would happen after the child was born? How could they stifle its cries at birth? What could they say to the family doctor when he came to deliver Effie? Could they shamelessly take him into their confidence and blame some innocent bystander as the guilty father, leaving Sinclair in the clear, for the doctor well knew they were not man and wife. He had brought Effie into the world from the womb of her mother. Maybe it would be better to hire a private doctor in the toon, who knew nothing about them, but then again he would have to be kept away from Liza in the kitchen bed — unless they used the front door, then he wouldn't have to pass through the kitchen. Still it would be better to take their own doctor into their confidence, by reason of not upsetting the old woman, which he would understand, who ever the father was.

Finally, on Thelma's advice, Sinclair agreed to plead ignorance with their own doctor, swearing blind they didn't know who the father was, Effie stubbornly refusing to divulge who the guilty party might be, even to the doctor — above all to the doctor, whatever his suspicions might be. Not that the doctor might ask, but better be prepared in case he should, for the whole thing was a blatant embarrassment to all of them except Effie, who didn't seem to care who was the father of her child, or what anybody thought about it; or maybe she just hadn't the sense to care, though she wasn't a fool either.

Meanwhile Liza was well content, for up to the very end of her pregnancy Effie had attended well to her grandmother, and the old woman had never seemed so pleased with herself in her blindness for years. The only thing that annoyed her was Effie's sudden craze for playing the wireless full blast in the ben-room, preparing for the day when it would have to be used to drown the cries of a howling infant, just to get Liza used to the occasional sound of it, despite her protests.

When Effie's time was come for delivery Thelma told her mother that Effie had the 'flu or something, and she would be attending to Liza's needs herself for a few days, an explanation that Liza accepted with some concern, enquiring daily at Thelma for Effie's welfare.

Effie's pregnancy was terminated behind closed doors, the family doctor complying with Thelma's earnest request not to disturb Liza in the kitchen, and a fire was lit in the ben-room to provide hot water, all with as little bustle as possible for Liza's sake. Effie stifled her moaning in the pillows when the pains seized her; not that it was all that difficult for Effie, seeing it wasn't her first child, and she had an animal's strength in childbearing, almost scorning the assistance of a doctor, but for the breaking of the umbilical cord, which she wasn't sure about, and the loudness of her mother's protests when she suggested self-delivery. But it was cheap at the price Effie considered secretly, in her craving for sex, and out of good manners or embarrassment the doctor never asked her who had taken advantage of her supposed maidenhood.

And when the bairn cried in the ben-room and Liza enquired about the noise Thelma told her it was a play on the wireless Effie wanted to listen to, and they kept the doors closed to deafen the sound. Within a few days Effie was up and about again and sniggering over her grandmother as if nothing unusual had taken place, while her infant daughter slept soundly in the ben-room.

Visitors were a problem, especially a neighbour body who wanted to see Sinclair about a stray stirk or the loan of a farm implement, and expecting to be asked inside to enquire for his ailing mother, for nowadays Sinclair held them at the back kitchen door or talked to them in the middle of the close, wondering how much they knew or suspected, or if their visit was merely curiosity. Effie had kept out of sight of most of the neighbours during the latter stages of her pregnancy, but sometimes when Sinclair wasn't about she had to go out to the vanman for groceries, bread or meat, and he was bound to notice her condition. There was also the postman on his bicycle, when she ran into him unexpectedly at the corner of the milkhouse; and what the vanmen and the postie told them the neighbours tried to confirm, though they found it difficult to pierce the screen of secrecy surrounding Stonelairs. But whatever their suspicions it would be a long time or they saw Effie's bairn running about in the close, though the time would surely come when the little girl would reveal herself, though Effie considered there was little sense in worrying about that for the present. She would think of some likely story when the time came. Meanwhile she kept the infant securely in the ben-room, drowning her cries with the wireless, and dried her nappies at the peat fire, right in front of her grandmother's bed, though Liza was none the wiser; no more than the neighbours from what they spied on the clothes line.

But as the months flew by and the child grew bigger it wasn't so easy to deceive old Liza. When the creature wailed in the dead of night, cutting a tooth or because of a colic, too late for the wireless to be blamed, Sinclair held a pillow over its piteous little mouth, tempted to leave it there longer than was necessary, to stifle this awful spectre that now haunted his conscience day and night. He had no love for his child that was born of lust, and but for Effie's hysteria, and her powerful arms, he was sorely tempted to suffocate the child with the pillow. How could anybody know what had caused its death — or so he imagined — so long as he had the will to do it. But Effie got out of bed in the worst of cases and walked the floor with her bairn, soothing it with a dumb-tit, until the child fell asleep and lay quietly beside her.

Effie had registered the birth and gave the child her own maiden name of Rae, with Nina as a christian name, and soon they would have to get it vaccinated to comply with compulsory law. Secretly Sinclair wished it would die, for it gave him no pride as a father, rather the opposite and degraded him. But Nina was a hardy wee girl who took after her mother constitutionally; and not a little in looks, with strong mongolian features, and throve every day forthwith, sucking at her mother's breast, sometimes staring at her reluctant father with his own blue eyes in reflection, which sort of reconciled him to his fate and he smiled in spite of himself.

But Sinclair was restless in his sleep and brooded at his work over the evil that assailed him, indulging himself strongly in whisky to drown his sorrows. And all the time he felt that the eyes of his neighbours were

10

upon him, wondering why both lums were now reeking at Stonelairs, both but and ben, kitchen and ben-room, when only one had smoked before, unless he had flitted his mother ben the hoose. But Effie insisted that she must still have a fire in the bedroom to keep the bairn warm, whatever the neighbours thought. What could the neighbours think of him having a bairn by his niece? Some of them were bound to suspect he was the guilty father. But he had been wrong about Thelma — presuming she had been hatching a plot to undermine him with his mother, and he could see now she had been doing her best to cover up for him, and maybe to protect Effie.

Sinclair tried sleeping in his own bedroom again, off the kitchen where his mother lay, but within a week of celibacy Effie was tempting him back to the ben-room, hungry for sex, for it was something you could hardly speak of as love. He was torn between guilt and desire, good and evil, but between Effie's hips again he forgot the consequences, ecstasy stronger than will. For a time they practised evasion, but eventually in her passion Effie clung to him until he spent himself in her child-hungry womb. For Sinclair it was a glorious moment of forgetfulness, but in the aftermath he almost cried out in despair, his thoughts a pin-cushion of guilt and foreboding, blending his sleepless lids with the light of day, while Effie snored at his back.

Out in the lonely fields by day, with God as his witness, castigating his guilt, Sinclair would reform his principles, resolving that when bedtime came he would be steel-willed and unyielding; but as the hour approached, and his mother fell asleep, temptation seized him and he yielded, stealing along the passage to the ben-room, where the bed was warm and Effie was waiting for him, elation setting caution at defiance. She now had Nina in a crib, loaned by one of her sisters, which seemed more civilised and natural; more like man and wife Sinclair thought, mitigating his guilt and making his crime seem more legitimate, like God had winked almost, and turned his back on sin, a compromise with the devil. Now they had the bed to themselves again, and when Effie opened her great hips to him Sinclair was powerless to resist. For a glorious half-hour he enjoyed her amorous convulsions; oblivious to everything but the thrill of the rapturous present, and in the elation of the moment he spent himself in the heat of her desire. Even the aftermath seemed more congenial and he fell asleep delightfully exhausted; until the grey of morning brought the devil to his window, demanding the wages of sin, doused in the rim of the whisky glass or the day could be faced.

How long could it last? How long would it be or the devil had his soul completely? How long would it be before Effie was pregnant again? Oh God! And what would be the consequences this time? Thelma had made it clear that if it happened again she would take Effie away from Stonelairs, and but for her helpless mother would have done so in the first place. It wasn't a threat that worried Sinclair; rather the opposite if his sister was going to relieve him of a dual burden — temptation and its consequences, God and the devil at the keyhole of his soul.

But the problem was getting too big even for Thelma, for how could she harbour Effie and her two bairns by Sinclair — if there was another one — besides the one she had already? In which case Sinclair thought maybe he could defy his sister and claim his right to Effie as his wife; not lawfully of course, nor in the eyes of the neighbours — and then the fear of incest frightened him. Even the Law had business in what you did in your own home when it came to that, and there was also the thought of imprisonment. All of which made Sinclair reach more often for the whisky bottle, though it brought but temporary relief. Nearly a bottle a day he was now consuming and it wasn't enough, and even Effie was getting concerned over his drinking, perhaps without realising she was partly the cause of it.

But Sinclair reached a stage when he realised he couldn't exist without Effie; at once his torment and his salvation, even though her very presence overshadowed him with guilt. His life seemed worthless in either case, overwhelmed by sex and drink, and he was losing interest in the farm, neglecting the work that had formerly been a sense of pride in his life. And what if Nina should prove to be imbecilic? He had heard it said that even cousins could have bairns that were malformed or mentally defective, or both; too inbred, so what could he look for with his niece? Nina wasn't old enough yet to see what she was going to be like, but if she turned out to be a slivering idiot he would go for his gun.

Within nine months of her delivery Effie was pregnant again. She reasoned with Sinclair that they had managed last time and they would manage again. What the hell did it matter how many bairns they had, especially if they were all as healthy and sturdy as Nina was, and physically at least Sinclair was bound to agree with her on that score. Effie insisted that so long as she looked after her bairns properly it was nobody's business about Sinclair and her being uncle and niece. And besides, old Liza couldn't live all that much longer to know anything about her illegitimate grandchildren, though 'ill-gotten' was the hyphenated term that Effie used. She sometimes thought Liza was a bit dottled already, the things she spoke about, her thoughts far away in the past, and speaking in her sleep to folk that were dead. Effie was callous in her reasoning Sinclair thought, and the ethics of law never entered into it. Incest was a word she scarcely understood and when Sinclair spoke of going to prison she giggled in disbelief, merely asking what was going to happen to her and the bairns while he was away. But to be fair to Effie it must be said that she performed the role of wife and mother admirably, almost with grace and capability, belying her rough exterior, but she had got hold of the wrong end of the stick.

By the time old Liza died Effie was big with her second child to her uncle. And Sinclair couldn't face his sister in the open nowadays unless he was drunk, while Thelma and her man both stared at him speechless; merely shaking their heads and almost hissing in anger, while Sinclair hiccupped over his whisky bottle and leered at them from the armchair beside his mother's bed. They dare not say anything in the hearing of his mother, and Sinclair clung to her for protection, determined not to leave the kitchen while his sister and her man were in the house. The others he could abide once in a while, his brothers and sisters who came in by to see their mother; none of them as brazen or outspoken as Thelma, and because the affair didn't concern them so closely they never mentioned it, whatever they said among themselves in Sinclair's absence. Nor could they afford to snub Effie, who now assumed the part of mistress at Stonelairs, none daring to challenge her flagrant authority; least of all her mother, who now fitted into the scene where Sinclair had imagined her to be, accusing her of usurping his claim as rightful heir to the farm, an insinuation she had denied bitterly. An atmosphere of tension pervaded in the family, a smouldering collaboration teetering on flame and fused with explosive, subdued in the presence of approaching death, when Liza had a stroke that robbed her of speech.

And while her great-grandmother-cum-grandmother lay in deathly silence Nina began to lisp her first syllables of speech. Her blubbering

13

efforts while she stood in her crib, her mongolian features strong in resemblance of her mother, were mistaken by Sinclair as the first symptoms of what he dreaded, that she would turn out to be a mumbling, half-witted monstrosity, a conjecture enlivened by his intake of alcohol and the inflamed condition of his thinking. Yet he had the sense not to mention his suspicions to Effie, perhaps fearing her reaction, if she understood the full implication of his fears. Strong though she was in her womanhood Sinclair reckoned that the shock might be too much for her while she was still carrying his second child, and whatever it might turn out to be there was no need for making matters worse. He would say nothing about it until after the birth, if even then, but perhaps would let her find out for herself, if Thelma didn't forestall him, for Sinclair felt certain his sister would notice it first. What his second child would be like worried him even more, raising his consumption of whisky to a full bottle a day, which kept him running back and forth on his bicycle to the emporium, and the way things were going the day would come when Effie would have to fetch it for him, to satisfy his craving, and even now she complained about his drunkenness, especially when he was in such a stupor that he couldn't perform at bedtime.

Sinclair found his mother stiff and cold in the box-bed when he came through one morning from the ben-room. She had died peacefully in her sleep it seemed, without fuss or mute farewell; her sightless eyes closed forever on his guilt, though Sinclair found no solace in the thought, rather the opposite when he visualised the funeral and all the staring eyes. His crime was getting out of doors, beyond his control, with little consolation in the thought that he wouldn't have to use a pillow to silence the second child of their lust; nor turn up the radio when it yelled in the evening, nor stop Nina from crawling through to the kitchen, dreading the day when he would have to pretend to his mother that it was the dog squeaking under the table. But still in the horrors of drink he dreaded the funeral, when he would have to face a barrage of relations; their searching eyes prying into his affairs and glowering at a tearful, bloated Effie, swollen with his sin, blubbering over her departed grandmother.

Sinclair took another look at his mother, all these thoughts struggling quickly through his fuddled brain, then staggered back to the ben-room to tell Effie what had happened. Effie raised herself from the

14

bed that creaked when she left it and went hurriedly through the passage to look at her grandmother. Then she went into hysterics, falling with her great bulk by the bedside and sprawling her arms over the dead woman, weeping in supposedly uncontrollable grief, while she took one of her grandmother's lifeless hands and rubbed it against her own tearful face, biting into the fingers that felt no pain in death. Sinclair somehow knew she would act like this, and standing behind her he also knew she could just as easily be switched off, for her grief was superficial and not of the heart. He pulled her away from the bed and got her on her feet, then told her to dress and run for somebody to get the doctor, and while Effie sat on the room bed, pulling her Cashmere stockings up to her thick sturdy thighs, Sinclair poured himself a glass of whisky and dashed it against his aching throat, the bite of it hitting his palate in a quenching shower, enabling him for a moment to think more clearly.

Effie flew for a doctor, her coat fastened loosely about her, a scarf round her head, in her bauchled shoes, scrambling over the frosted furrows, nearly a mile to the nearest neighbour who had a telephone. Then Sinclair knew that his hour of triumph had come, the final chance to free himself from his burden, once and for all. His last sane thoughts were for his mares in the stable and the cattle in the byres, all waiting patiently for breakfast, duties that he used to perform before touching his own. But what he had to do now was more urgent than anything he had ever done in his life before, and it had to be done quickly and correctly while Effie was scouring the hills for a doctor, before she could return to thwart his purpose. And it wouldn't take long for the sobbing Effie to raise the dire alarm.

Sinclair threw the cork in the window sill and poured himself another glass of neat whisky. It would be his last but it would steady his jaded nerves for the final achievement. And while he gulped it down his eye caught the infant Nina still asleep in her crib; her mother's heavy, almost mongolian features clearly evident in the relaxation of sleep. Then he remembered the pillow and how easy it would be to suffocate her now and save her from a lifetime of misery, besides rubbing out the surviving evidence of his crime; this helpless creature that would carry his guilt into another generation. With a sudden stride he reached the bed, grabbed a pillow and stared down at his sleeping daughter. But indecision stiffened him in the act, drink and the devil striving with

15

reason, the pillow hovering an inch or two from the baby's mouth, trembling in his hands, awaiting the pressure of his mighty arms. It wouldn't take long. He reckoned about three minutes to be certain, for he couldn't have the child reviving after he had gone. A few moments of convulsive consciousness, a furtive bundle struggling in his hands, then all would be still at last, while the panting Effie came stumbling over the fields.

It would be so easy to take the child with him, into oblivion; away from prying eyes and incestuous tongues. Under the sod she would be out of sight, an insubstantial memory that would eventually die, whereas alive she would restore his posthumous guilt with every day that dawned. Then he remembered the other bairn still in Effie's womb, and the only way to destroy it was to destroy Effie and wipe the slate clean. It was the master plan. But why hadn't it occurred to him sooner? So much killing in so little time. It was more than he had intended; and even with the demon whisky dancing in his veins he shrank from the prospect, this working for the devil.

First he would have to choke Nina, then load the gun and wait for Effie at the gable of the milkhouse, where she sometimes ran into the postman, only this time it would be the postman from hell; and she would come upon him unawares, unexpectedly; with no time to think poor bitch, and he would fire both barrels into her heaving belly. The rest would be easy in comparison.

But it was too much in so short a time, and making up his mind was hindering him, wasting precious minutes. By now Effie would be on her way back and he would have to hurry. Maybe this was how the devil worked; in the heat of passion, coming upon you unawares, with little time to think before the deed was done. Then the child awoke and broke his resolve, brushing away the pillow with her little hand and smiling in his face. She smiled up at him with quite lovely blue eyes, almost like his own, and he just couldn't do it ... not now. Nina stood up in her crib and reached out for him and he threw away the pillow. This time he tilted the whisky bottle into his mouth and poured the fiery liquid down his burning throat, then dropped the bottle and ran to the kitchen, Nina crying after him.

He took a last fond, yet almost careless, look at his dead mother and then burst into his bedroom. He snatched the polished, double-barrelled gun from a corner and opened the breach, held the weapon in the crook of his arm, reached up to the shelf for a box of cartridges, inserted two in the barrels and slipped a few in his pocket — in case he should change his mind and wait for Effie — then closed the gun with a snap and bolted for the back kitchen door.

There was no sign of Effie, but he could picture her coming over the fields, panting, from the nearest neighbour, and he opened the safety catch on the gun and pulled back the dogheads. Back in the house he could hear Nina yelling from her crib, crying for her mother. It would be so easy to go back into the house and blow her into kingdom come, but those blue eyes deterred him.

The collie dog eyed him from his kennel and came whining to the full length of his chain, wagging his bushy tail, expecting that Sinclair would release him for a rabbit hunt when he saw the gun. Then he barked loudly, so Effie couldn't be far away. But he must not weaken, though looking at his mother had almost broken his resolve, until the thought of all those staring eyes at the funeral restored his will to die. It was better than a lifetime of shame and guilt.

The dog was still barking, Nina still screaming from the ben-room and Sinclair's heart was beating fast. He walked in the other direction from the milkhouse, towards the gig-shed at the other end of the steading. The farm close was full of singing hens, scraping at his feet, and the barn cock stood up in the midst of them, flapped his wings and crowed "Cock-a-doodle-doo," all looking for breakfast, and the cooing pigeons flapped up to roost on the byre tiles, afraid of the gun.

Sinclair swung the wooden bar from its catch on the tarred door of the gig-shed, opened one half of the door and walked inside. The stable was just through the stone wall and the horses nickered friendly-like at the sound of the creaking door. The light was poor inside, for there was no window in the building, only a small skylight curtained with cobwebs, and the old gig stood at the further wall, slung from the rafters by the shafts.

On the work-bench Sinclair cut a length of binder twine from a ball, tied it in a loop and hooked it on to the triggers of the gun, then made another and bigger loop on the string for his foot. He set the butt of the gun on the earthen floor and set his right foot in the loop. He tried it for tension, making sure that the gun would go off before his foot touched the ground. He balanced himself on his left foot, holding on to the bench with his free hand for support, while he held the gun firmly upright with

17

the other. The hens were squaking and scattering in the close, and from the corner of his eye Sinclair saw Effie running to the kitchen door, likely when she heard Nina screaming, a neighbour woman at her heels, which hadn't occurred to Sinclair, and would have blundered his other plan. He put the barrel of the gun securely in his mouth, biting into it with his teeth, held on to the bench, tramped down his foot and blew his brains into the crosstrees of the old tiled gig-shed.

Effie had scarcely reached the ben-room when she heard the shot, and snatching up her bairn she ran outside. The dog was barking and the hens were cackling and the cattle lowed in the byres. Effie knew it was past milking time, but the gig-shed door was open, and the two women looked at each other and ran towards it and peered inside, through the blue smoke.

"Oh Sinclair," Effie cried, handing her bairn to the neighbour, "what's this ye've done to yerself?" She threw out her arms and fell beside him, careless of the spattered blood, and sobbed her heart out on his slightly quivering body, until her neighbour bent down with her free hand and pulled her away, while the mares nickered again in the stable.

The doctor's car purred into the close and the neighbour woman took him to the gig-shed, old Liza quite forgotten in the excitement, though the doctor got round to her in time.

So they had a double funeral at Stonelairs, and they buried Sinclair with his mother over her husband in the same grave. And nobody pointed a finger nor ventured a stare upon poor Effie, everybody being too much appalled by the tragedy.

So maybe Sinclair hadn't died in vain.

THE WINDMILL

WHEN I was a loon in short breeks I often used to meet the Oyster King on the face of the brae under the cottar hoose. I might have been on the way to Scotstoun for messages with my hurlie, or I would be pulling grass by the roadside for my rabbits when I met Mr. Royston. But in Buchan you didn't bother with real names, for if you had mentioned 'Mr. Royston' to somebody they would have said "Oh aye, the Eyster Keeng," thinking that you were being pan-loaf and trying to imitate the gentry. In fact you would have been lucky if you weren't laughed at and taken the size of, ridiculed and intimidated.

Mr. Royston was a big broad shouldered man in a dark blue suit, grey hat, white shirt, tie, black boots and walking cane; always dressed the same, the only thing that was sometimes different was the tie, nothing else, and as he was never untidily dressed he must have had a stock of these dark blue suits, with accessories to match, except for gloves, for he was always bare-handed, his big knuckles sticking out when he closed his hands over his staff. Except for a slight grey moustache he was clean shaven, a man in his early sixties, with a large stern face, stone grey eyes, big ears, and always chewing black sugar, so that his strong teeth were always stained, his breath smelling of liquorice.

When you met Mr. Royston the first thing he did was to put his hand in the small left hand pocket inside his jacket and gave you a few lumps of black sugar; hard, strong stuff like coal, not the soft liquorice kind that you got in straps, or in sherbet bags at the shop, and it had a bitter-sweet pungent taste that hung about your mouth for nearly an hour afterwards. Some of the farm workers chewed tobacco, but mostly they spat out the bree; but Mr. Royston never spat, in fact he was a gentleman, clean, good-mannered and English spoken, though he was a Scotsman just the same.

But though Mr. Royston gave most of his acquaintances a lump or two of black sugar when he met them on the road, some of them would have gone across fields a mile out of their way to avoid him. Mostly he asked at the grown-ups if they wanted black sugar, but as most of them

19

didn't like to refuse they put it in their mouths while they spoke to him, whether they liked it or no, man or woman, well aware of its potency as a gentle bowel laxative, and hoping they would be home before it took effect. Folk thought Mr. Royston must be bothered himself with the dry-darn when he chewed that stuff all the time. Others thought it was an antidote for smoking, for he never smoked, and never drank that was heard of, though it was whispered that he had an eye for the women, especially the cottar wives round about though he always left a half-crown on the mantelshelf when he visited them, mostly during the day when their menfolks were at work in the fields, and the bairns at school, the only thing that made it look suspicious. Otherwise the women swore out that he was a proper gentleman in *that* respect, and never laid a finger on them disrespectfully, but always left something for the bairns.

Those with a guilty conscience gave Mr. Royston a wide berth, because they were afraid of his staff, for he had already clobbered a few rascals of the parish, and those he spared from the rod got the sharp edge of his virulent tongue. Oh you didn't need a minister with Mr. Royston in the parish, nor a bobby either come to that; but those who behaved themselves had nothing to fear from meeting Mr. Royston on the road, except for the black sugar, though in time the most respectful of his neighbours learned to refuse it politely and Mr. Royston took no offence.

He was the equivalent of a laird in the parish, and since he owned and worked three farms and lived in the biggest one he was entitled to that distinction, though actually his neighbours were not his tenants, except for a couple of crofters on the fringe of his small estate. Most of his neighbours were owner-occupiers, while the rest of the farms were leased from a Landowners Syndicate down there in Edinburgh.

But though the Oyster King wasn't the recognised laird he dominated the community in baronial style, and farmed his own land with such proficiency and thoroughness as to set them all an example. Barrabrae was a laird's toon to perfection, even with a glass roof over the farm close and a clock tower on the steading; a walled garden in front of the farmhouse and a belt of trees encircling it, the farmyard laid with causey blocks, most of which had been supervised by Mr. Royston himself since he came home from abroad. There were even brass nameplates on the horse carts, polished by the grieve every Saturday, after he swept the close. Most farmers just had tin plates on their carts, with their name and address painted on to them in small lettering, and if a lad had fee-ed to a place in winter, and wasn't sure where it was, arriving in the dark he would crack a spunk to let him see to read the cart signs, as there were no signposts at the road-ends, and by this means he could make sure he had come to the right place, and then he would look for the chaumer. But the cart signs at Barrabrae were etched out on the brass, like the carat stamp engraved upon a wedding ring, and the flash of a match merely brightened it into a glitter, so that the lads couldn't read the name-plates on the carts at Barrabrae.

Mr. Royston also had first-class harness, and the lads took some pride in keeping it bright and shining, both for cart and plough, and their sturdy Clydesdales filled their collars and were well fed and groomed. Even the roots of the fencing posts were tarred or creosoted before they were driven into the ground, to preserve them against rot, and the heavy wooden gates into the parks were also painted regularly, and all the doors and windows about the house and steading, sometimes changing the colour from year to year. The copings on all the stone dykes round the fields were pointed with cement, to prevent the cattle from knocking them down, and every park had a watering trough, or one built into the dyke that served two parks, and fitted with ball-cocks to save water, the one scarce commodity at Barrabrae.

Mr. Royston had been a man of the world, well travelled, and had brought back souvenirs from his journeys abroad: paintings and antiques, which were hung and displayed in the farmhouse, treasures from Australia, New Zealand and the East Indies, where Mr. Royston had amassed a fortune in pearl fishing, having been inspired as a boy by the voyages of Captain Cook, and that was why the folk called him the Oyster King. He had grown up as a barfit loon in Scotstoun, a whaling port on the north-east shoulder of Scotland, but instead of joining the whalers in Greenland waters the boy Royston sought the warmer climate of the South Seas, embarking on a China Clipper when he left school at fourteen. He learned the art of pearl-fishing and became one of the richest merchants in the trade. At one time he owned three luggers, manned by native pearl-divers, and a sixty-ton schooner, which he captained himself, for carrying stores. He lost the schooner when she hit the Pender Reef, when he and his crew just had time to clamber into the rigging before the boat was awash, and they later escaped in the small boat to Freemantle, on the mainland of Western Australia, where Mr. and Mrs. Royston resided at the time. When he retired from pearl fishing the Roystons returned to Scotstoun, when he bought the estate of Barrabrae, where he had herded cattle as a barfit loon, and was now the most respected farmer in the locality.

Folk in the Bogside said he whipped his native pearl-fishers when they refused to dive and fed them on handfuls of rice, and that was why they feared his cane when he settled at home, because he was an adept hand at using it, as Jock McGee could well testify, when Mr. Royston caught him leathering his mother. Jock couldn't sit down for days afterwards, and he hid himself under the straw in the barn when he saw the Oyster King coming to visit his mother. The croft was on the Barrabrae estate, and Jock and his mother carried it on after her husband's death. Jock was a 'Coon' to Mr. Royston, as was everybody else who offended him, and they said that was what he called his pear-divers in the South Seas, 'Bluddy Coons'.

But for all that Mr. Royston was kind to his cottar folk, and anyone who called at the farmhouse never departed empty-handed, but was always treated to a bag of biscuits or sweeties from Mrs. Royston, herself a Bogside quine, and if you worked casual on the farm, like harvesting or gathering potatoes, after supper in the farmhouse Mr. Royston was always standing at the back kitchen door when you left and slipped a half-crown into your hand, over and above your wages.

Besides the farms Mr. Royston owned property in the town, and every year at Christmas time he sent a horseman with a cart loaded with a sack of potatoes and a chicken for each of his tenants. Now it so happened, in the year of which I write, Mr. Royston's potato crop was a failure, and he had to buy potatoes from one of his neighbours for his tenants in Scotstoun. He bought the potatoes from Geordie Sang, a bit of a scoundrel who farmed in the Reisk of Dams, and he told his foreman to weigh out some second-rate orra tatties for the toonsfolk, and he kept his better samples for a steeper price in a scarce market. Some of his tenants complained to Mr. Royston that their potatoes had been poor quality this year, and a great many of them rotten, and though it had been a poor year for the tubers Mr. Royston had paid for the best, and there were good fresh potatoes to be had if you paid for them. It was then he realised what Sang had been up to and he told Mrs. Royston he would thrash that coon within an inch of his life, and though

22

the woman was worried she knew it was useless trying to stop him. So he went after his cheating neighbour in a great rage, his silver-mounted stick swinging in the air.

I met Mr. Royston on the brae at the Reisk, and that day he never offered me the customary lump of black sugar; in fact he hardly noticed me pulling clover for my rabbits, but walked straight past, slashing his stick on the long grass by the roadside, his face like the sky before a thunderstorm, his step brisk and lively.

He came upon Sang in the farm close and without question or parley he thrashed him to his knees, the great stick flicking the air in sword play over his victim, the chaumer chiels afraid to interfere, despite Sang's cries for help, and his wife wringing her hands in supplication for mercy on her offending husband. "Treat my tenants like swine you would," cried the pearl-fisher, "and feed them rotten potatoes, while I pay you the market price for the best. You bluddy coon," he cried, "that'll teach you a lesson, and if you don't call off that dog this minute I'll smash his snout so bad he won't be able to eat or bite another living creature in his life. And furthermore," he yelled, "if you send for the police I'll have you to court as a swindler, and I've got plenty of witnesses in the toon, waiting with their sacks of rotting potatoes." And then Mr. Royston straightened his hat and stamped out of the farm close, one of the workmen holding on to the dog, growling at his departure, while the rest of them ran to pick up their master, and his wife prepared a soft seat for him in the kitchen.

"My God he'll pay for this yet," Sang muttered, as they helped him to the kitchen door; "I wunna get the bobby but I'll hae my revenge some day!"

Now it was a fact that despite his wealth and great influence in the district, Royston was dependent on Sang for every drop of drinking water on the Home Farm. Maybe that was why, when he returned from thrashing Sang he stopped and looked at the windmill in Sang's field. Then it occurred to him that he should have thought of this before his onslaught on Sang, but in the heat of anger it had escaped him. Now the reality of the thought stopped him in his tracks and he stared at the windmill, revolving slowly on the face of the brae. But 'the mistakes of wilful men must be their schoolmasters,' as Shakespeare says, and Royston realised the truth of it, for he was now in a predicament that walled him in all round. What if Sang should stop the windmill and deprive him of his water supply? Royston was more afraid of this than he was of Sang going to the police, though even there Royston would have been punished for taking the law into his own hands. Yet this didn't worry him so much as what might happen with the windmill, and he cursed himself for his rashness and lack of foresight. But maybe it wouldn't occur to Sang that he had his enemy by the throat; that by putting the brake on the windmill he could have his revenge on Royston, thirsting him into submission, or at least an apology. Royston went home with his brain on overtime, striving for a solution to his problem.

A day or two passed, and as nothing happened to the water supply at Barrabrae, Royston realised that the vital stroke of genius hadn't yet occurred to Sang, nor apparently had anyone suggested it to him out of sympathy in his quarrel with the Oyster King; maybe because they feared Royston more than they disliked Sang, for Sang wasn't popular with his neighbours, and most of them would have given him his own way just to get him hanged, if he was foolish enough to put his head in a noose. Royston was respected, thereby gaining a point over his adversary. The neighbours knew that Royston was honest, upright and generous, whereas Sang was a cunning cheat, something that Royston had just discovered in his potato deal. Sang would have stoned you out of his parks looking for teuchats' eggs, or sent the dog at you, or he would have cheated your father out of a week's pay if he thought he could get away with it, especially if your father couldn't count money and your mother had stuck up for him and reminded Sang of the deficiency. On the other hand, if anybody was in serious trouble they consulted Mr. Royston; even running after him if they saw him on the road with his stick, when he would lean with both hands on the silver-mounted tip and listen to the tale of woe from crofter or cottar, and sometimes even by the bigger farmers, and then he would set his lawyer or an estate agent or whoever was required to deal with the problem, and in the worst cases paid the expenses from his own pocket. It wasn't unknown for him to send his horse carts to flit a poor cottar who was in straits and couldn't afford to pay for it, so the poorer folks had a lot to thank Mr. Royston for.

So you could say that Royston had more friends in the parish than Sang had, but though you listened to their talk about the potato affair in chaumer or at market, or even at the kirk on a Sunday, you couldn't really make out whose side they were on — but one thing was sure, nobody had mentioned the windmill. Maybe because they weren't dependent on it, or directly affected by its use, the thought had never entered their easy-going minds — a factor which gave Royston a breathing space to prepare for the day when it did, and whispered it in Sang's ear, if he didn't think on it first himself.

Royston looked a long time at the windmill that evening as he came down the road from Sang's place. It stood in the middle of Sang's park, a latticed structure of steel about twenty feet high, with a pump house at the base and a giant wheel on top, fitted with blades to catch the wind, and a huge tail to vary direction if the wind should change, like the vane on a weathercock, but much larger, with the name of SAMSON printed across it in great white letters. On windy days the bladed wheel spun rapidly, while the great tail darted back and forth like a kite on a string, vibration rocking the latticed pylon supporting the mechanism, the driving shaft down the centre working up and down feverishly, while in the shed at the bottom the pump churned the excess water to foam as it gushed down the overflow, and when the drain spilled over it flooded the pump-house floor and ran down the field, a fearful waste of precious water in a dry spell and a danger of wrecking the windmill. On windy days like this Royston walked up to the mill and applied the brake, tightening the rope on a wall bracket that slowed the wheel, or stopped it completely in extreme cases, reducing the risk of damage. Royston was so much concerned for the safety of the windmill that he looked after it himself, never trusting it to Sang, and this they had agreed upon when the structure was built.

Then there were days of calm when the windmill scarcely stirred; long hot days of summer sunshine that dried up the ground and drained the reserve cisterns so that everybody at Barrabrae had to save their water. At a lower elevation this never troubled Sang. He had the bottom half of the main cistern at his own steading and it was never empty, while Royston had the top half to give him gravitational flow. At the last gasp Royston would come storming up the brae and stare at the motionless windmill like the Ancient Mariner at the copper sea, then he would clamber over the dyke and walk up the footpath to the pump-shed. This year the field was in grass, but when corn or turnips were growing, Sang left a clear path for Royston. Inside Royston would stare at the stationary pumping-rod and the rusting pump into which it was

25

inserted, and the oily, stagnant water dripping back into the main supply well under the building.

But for all his genius in planning and laying out the water scheme Royston wasn't a god; even though he was by now a town councillor where he had once run barefoot he couldn't bid the wind to rise or divert the supply of water. Years ago he had laid the supply pipe deep underfoot across a quarter of a mile on Sang's farmland, and there it must remain. He paid Sang a rent for the half-share on the stance on which the windmill stood, and the same for the site of the main cistern at the top of the brae, and for the pipeline, all settled in a land court and duly signed by both parties, and by witnesses at law, a contingency which might deter Sang from cutting off the water supply, or from interfering with the windmill, though Royston could by no means be sure of this. Now he realised fully how this incidence had placed him at Sang's mercy in a quarrel. Every time a cottar wife at Barrabrae filled her kettle; every time a cattle beast drank from a water trough; every time Royston himself took a glass of water from the kitchen tap, Sang was now staring at them all as from a mirror on the wall, his eyes hateful, his face set, licking his dry lips in a lust for revenge.

So far Royston had never found sufficient water on the Home Farm, only ditch water on a neighbour's boundary, which supplied some of his fields, and in dire straits he had been forced to cart water from one of his outfarms for his thirsting cattle beasts, though the thought of carting water for everybody about the place appalled him, and he searched his mind for some alternative.

Shortly after his quarrel with Sang, Royston kissed his wife on the cheek and said he was going for a long walk, though he didn't tell her where he was going, just as he had played down his report to her on how he had reprimanded Mr. Sang, not to give her concern, so she merely cautioned him, and told him to put on a cravat in the cold wind, though he refused to wear an overcoat. Then he took his hat and cane from the hall-rack, put a lump of black sugar in his mouth, and set off down the farm avenue.

It was mid-January and bitterly cold, but Royston was accustomed to having the elements about him and the wind in his face; good for the circulation he said and kept the blood going in a walk. Rich as he was, he never had a motor car, preferring rather the exercise that walking gave him, and he phoned the town for a horse-cab on longer journeys, though he frequently walked to Town Council meetings in Scotstoun. Sang had a motor car but Royston snubbed him on the subject and regarded it as an insubordination on Sang's part, muttering that the creature could ill afford it, adding under his breath that Sang had probably swindled somebody to get it, and after the potato affair he was more convinced of this than he had ever been.

He walked to Craigie Simpson's croft, on the edge of the heather on the Berryhill, the man who had divined for water the last time Royston had tried it. Craigie was owing payment to Royston for three loads of turnips he had bought the previous spring, and no doubt that's what he would think the big man was after, to settle the account. It was in Royston's mind, but when he saw the poverty of the place he decided he would settle it in a different manner; especially when the two urchins opened the door to his knocking, only half clad they were and without shoes on their feet in midwinter, and what Royston could see of the kitchen was bare and comfortless. If money was all he wanted here Royston felt he should turn on his heel and depart, for he remembered the days of his own poverty and his heart went out to the bairns. One of them said their parents were out in the byre and went over the close on her bare feet to fetch her dad. There was no smile on Craigie's face when he saw Royston, for he remembered his debt, until Royston told him he wanted him to divine for water again, and that he could forget about the price of the turnips before he even started. Craigie's face lit up. "All right Sir," he said, "but as I told you last time it would be thirty feet down and under rock, you're better with the old windmill for all its bother."

"Never mind about that," Royston snapped, "when can you start?"

"Tomorrow if you like."

"Right, tomorrow then, and bring your assistant," and Royston left five shillings for the bairns, for he knew there were more of them somewhere and departed.

Next day Craigie Simpson cut a fresh broom twig in the shape of an oversize catapult, and holding the twin ends in his hands, knuckles uppermost, the point of the stick before him, he walked slowly over the spot where he had formerly divined water at Barrabrae. As he approached the central area the point of the stick began to rise, and directly over the water vein the elevation was stronger, so that he couldn't force the stick down again, but yet it wouldn't rise to face level,

27

as he had expected. He stopped and kicked a hole in the ground with his heel. "There it is Mr. Royston," he said, "same as last time; the vein hasn't shifted, and we'll have to blast the rock to get the water."

"This time we'll blast," said Royston, remembering the last time he had refused, rather doubting Craigie's genius with the divining rod, though he believed what Moses had done for the Israelites.

Craigie and his assistant took off their jackets and with their spades they threw the earth aside from a wide area. They dug for days with pick and spade until they were underground below head level, then further and further until they had to shore up the crumbling walls, one of them filling the bucket at the bottom and the other pulling it up with a rope to empty it on the surface. At the end of the week they were down twenty feet in hard core but still no sign of water, and every day Royston paid them a visit to see how the work was going.

Twenty-five feet, thirty-five feet and still as dry as dust; not even moisture, a deep frightening hole where oxygen was getting thin and the men had to take shorter spells down in the well, scrambling up and down the ladders and criss-cross of planks supporting the walls. It was exhausting, nerve-wracking work, and even though Royston had given them one of his own men to help, Craigie and his man were tiring. Lack of oxygen was crippling them, now so scarce that a match wouldn't burn at the bottom of the hole. When they struck rock at last Royston lost patience however and cried out to Craigie: "Dammit man, you'll have to give me stronger proof of water there before we blast; it doesn't look like it to me!"

Craigie came up the ladder, panting for air, and looked Mr. Royston straight in the eye. "You want more proof, Mr. Royston?" he gasped.

"Aye," said Royston, "how can ye be so sure there's water down there in that dry hole?"

"Have he got an oil paintin' Mr. Royston?"

"Aye, I've got a whole room hung with them man. Come to think of it I've got one of Moses striking the rock with his rod to provide water for the Israelites."

"Then, Mr. Royston, tak' that picture into another room where there are no other oil paintin's and set it against the wall; then blindfold me, and give me my twig, and let me gyang into the room and I shall find the picture; and when I do, will ye be convinced there is water here?"

"We'll see," said Royston, still doubtful, but after dinner that day,

THE WINDMILL

Craigie Simpson wiped his boots on the mats in the big hoose — he wouldn't take off his muddy boots because he said the ironwork on the soles had some attraction for the mineral he was looking for in the painting — and Mrs. Royston tied a thick cloth round his eyes and handed him the broom twig, which led him straight to the picture of Moses hanging on the wall.

"Now," said Craigie, still blindfolded, "lead me to the lawn, and throw a copper penny in the air; not a silver one, but a copper penny, and wherever it lands I shall find it."

So they led Craigie through the front porch on to the lawn and Mrs. Royston threw a penny in the air and Craigie searched for it in the grass with his twig outstretched before him. In about three or four minutes Craigie found the coin and stood over it between his leather boots, the stick pointing up in his face. Mrs. Royston untied Craigie's blindfold and her husband picked up the penny.

"We'll blast the well," was all he said.

The blasting had to be controlled, so as not to dislodge the scaffolding supporting the walls, yet strong enough to split the rock and release the water. Royston employed an explosives expert from the Department of Public Works, equipped with a compressor and pneumatic drills, and he supervised the blasting.

The first detonation was a sharp crack that awakened the district and threw stones a hundred feet out of the gaping well, but all the neighbours saw was a puff of brown smoke drifting over the field. News had got around though that Craigie Simpson was digging a new well for the Oyster King and they had a fairly good idea of what was going on.

Sang heard the bang and saw the puff of smoke and in a flash he realised what Royston was up to. He looked at the windmill on the face of the brae, and just as quick it came to him that this was the weapon with which to fight his enemy. Why hadn't he thought of it sooner? And yet if Royston didn't find water it could be his trump card after all. He didn't go to the police because he feared the scandal, but this was something that could be done on the quiet; on the sly, behind somebody's back, which suited Sang's nature, and he gloated over his brainwave. Immediately his own cistern was full he would stop the windmill, thus depriving Royston of a flow of water from a higher level. In this manner Sang imagined he could humiliate Royston and bring him begging for water; either that or it would develop into a war between them, Sang running to brake the windmill and Royston to release it, and likely they would clash and Sang remembered Royston's stick and the thrashing he had endured and decided he would be better prepared next time, armed with a knife, or maybe even the shot-gun; after all, the most they could charge him for would be manslaughter, and he would plead self-defence. Then he changed his mind about the shot-gun; at least for the present, for with that they could maybe charge him with murder.

The blast in Royston's well had not brought them water, so after the mess had been cleared up another charge was set for the following day, round about noon, when the horse beasts would be out of the plough, not to frighten them in the furrows. Meanwhile Sang had shut off the windmill and Royston's cistern was falling fast.

The second blast was no more successful than the first had been, and when the taps ran dry at Barrabrae Royston ran up the road to see what had happened to the windmill. He couldn't see it from the farm, only from the top of the road that ran over the hill, and by the time he reached the summit he was out of breath, his heart hammering and pulsing in his throat, wild with rage. The windmill was stationary, even with a fair breeze going, and Royston realised that Sang had turned it off; that the blasting had given him away, and that Sang had had the brainwave Royston suspected would come to him, sooner or later, only it was sooner than he would have hoped and their private war had begun.

Royston was not a young man, and he had another quarter of a mile to walk before he reached the windmill; yet he struggled on, his walking stick at a swift pace beside him, until he reached the small hinged door into the shed at the base of the windmill. Inside he released the rope from the pegs that held the wheel in check, and the great vane swung round until the wind caught the wheel and set it whirling, the interior shaft plunging up and down driving the pump, a small spurt of water escaping the valve at every thrust, the wooden shed trembling in the vibration set up by the mechanism. There was only one thing for it: stand guard over the windmill; at least until nightfall, when the cistern at Barrabrae would have gathered some water, and by heaven, if Sang appeared he would split his head open, and Royston fingered the silver-mounted end of his staff to reassure himself.

Mrs. Royston became aware of her husband's absence and sent her maid to look for him at the well. Craigie Simpson was hauling up pailfuls of shale and splintered rock, while two men filled the buckets in turn down in the well. He told the lassie her master had gone to look at the windmill, though he himself of course knew little of the feud that existed between Royston and Sang, except for the gossip he had heard about Sang getting a thrashing, and considering the reason for it Craigie thought he deserved it, though Royston shouldn't have flouted the law.

So Mrs. Royston got the grieve to send one of the farmhands to look for her husband at the windmill, where he found his master pacing round the structure like a Serjeant-at-arms. Royston thought of leaving the man on guard a while to relieve him, while he could nip home for a cup of tea; then changed his mind, because he didn't want to involve his men in a quarrel which was strictly his own, perhaps invoking strife and ill-will where it was quite unnecessary; and besides, he was doubtful whether the man would be a match for Sang if he appeared, for Sang would merely order the man to get off his land, and in all fairness he was quite entitled to do so. He sent the man home to tell his wife simply that the windmill needed attention and he would be home by nightfall.

Darkness fell, and Royston shivered in the cold another hour but Sang never appeared, so he left the windmill whirring merrily and set off for home. He had to confide in his wife at this stage and told her everything, and she cautioned him to be careful, and Royston said he wasn't so old but that he could still look after himself with that Damned Coon Sang, whatever his tricks. All the same, his wife said, Sang might have one of his men with him and maybe he should do the same, just in case, but Royston reasoned that this would only spread the quarrel, and he wouldn't involve the servants.

Sometime in the night or early morning Sang had stopped the windmill again and Royston set it going in the forenoon. All day he watched with a flask of tea and just about dinner time he heard another blast from the well, and saw the puff of smoke, hoping every minute to see Craigie or his assistant come running up the road to tell him they had struck water. But nobody came near him, and as darkness closed in again in the short winter day, he closed the shed door on the windmill and walked briskly home.

"You'll catch yer death of cold," his wife warned him, pouring a hot toddy for her man before his evening meal. But Royston ignored her, merely to say he was sticking to his guns; that no bluddy coon of a rascal

31

farmer was going to frighten him; he who had faced far greater dangers in foreign countries (which she well knew), and Royston resolved to get up earlier in the morning and maybe catch Sang at the windmill.

"But that won't be the end of it," said his anxious wife, fearful for the consequences if there should be another confrontation with Sang.

Royston reassured her. "All right woman, give me another couple of days, and if we don't strike water in the well by then I'll go to law. I'll promise you that, but in the meantime I've got to keep the windmill going for our own supply of water. There is no other way."

But Sang wasn't to be seen in the morning, though the windmill had been stopped again, until Royston undid the rope. All day he sat or paced around the structure, just to let Sang see he was on the job, for he had no doubt the scoundrel would be watching him from a skylight somewhere, or from a tree about the steading. At noon again there was another blast from the well; muffled it seemed and deeper down, and surely this time they had loosed the spring of water. But as the afternoon wore on Royston stopped watching the road, and stuck another lump of black sugar in his hungry mouth.

On the morning of the fourth day of his vigil, while it was scarcely daylight, Royston caught Sang running away from the windmill. Royston waved his stick at him and gave chase, catching him a whack with his stick before he reached the field gate. Another blow crumpled Sang's right arm, and the long knife he was carrying slipped out of his hand. But he ran on and Royston still gave chase, until Sang turned suddenly at the gate and grabbed Royston's stick with both hands. Now it was a struggle for the stick, each wrestling with the other and trying with their feet to trip each other up. They twisted the stick this way and that, each trying to get possession of it, until Royston tripped and fell and Sang wrenched the dreaded stick from his hands. And then he laid on Royston, the older man rising to his feet against the onslaught, taking most of the blows on his arms, until he caught Sang by the jacket and threw him on the ground, the pair of them rolling over each other and Sang holding on to the staff. Each punched and struggled and rolled on the ground until the stick was lost and they went for each other with bare fists, wallop for wallop, wherever they could get a blow in, each trying to rise to his feet, until he was pulled down again by the other, both panting for breath, but Royston being the older man was likely to go out first. And even while they fought an early morning detonation from the well failed to distract them. They swore at each other with bated breath, and the blood flowed freely, and yet they tore at each other like wild beasts, each determined to last it out, and now that Sang had got started his cowardice left him, and he swung at Royston with renewed vigour. The older man was losing his strength, unable to stop Sang reaching for the stick, and in the final tussle Sang got hold of it again; then up on his feet, slashing at Royston, who rolled this way and that, avoiding the blows, and holding his hands over his head to protect his face. Sang's face flared with rage, his eyes bloodshot, saliva at his mouth, trying to crack Royston over the head with the silver end of the stick, until Royston caught his foot and threw him on the ground again. Both men were now exhausted, their blows more feeble, their breath expiring, their wrestling a mere embrace, until they fell beside each other, nonplussed, their bodies heaving, gasping for air.

Craigie Simpson came upon them at this final moment of capitulation, jumping from his bicycle and running into the field, when both men sat up and stared at him. "For God's sake, Mr. Royston, we've found water, gushing so fast the well is near half full ..." But then he stopped and stared at the two figures on the ground, soaked in blood and their clothes torn, now staggering to their feet again, Royston laying first hands on his staff, then his hat, which had gone early in the fight, while Sang staggered about searching for his knife. When he found the knife he put it in an inside pocket and came back to the gate, intending to styter past the two men without a word, until Royston held out his hand. Sang stopped and looked at him in a softer gaze, the hate seemingly gone out of his eyes, then at Craigie, who was still puzzled by the pair of them, and their behaviour; and then Sang took a step slowly forward and held out his hand to Royston. The two men shook hands in a mutual clasp and parted, Sang going up the hill to his farm, while Craigie took his bicycle and walked down the brae with his master.

"Dammit, you were right, Craigie," Royston was saying, "we've got water you say."

"Aye, we have that, Mr. Royston; that last bang broke the seam. But it won't run by gravitation to the fairmhoose; ye'll have tae get an engine tae pump it — far mair reliable than a windmill, always at the mercy o' the weather.".

"But you were right Craigie after all, that's what puzzles me. You see ..." Royston gurgled, "that wasn't a real oil painting; it was an imitation print, the only one I've got that isn't real. How the hell did you manage it man?"

"But there was water in it," Craigie protested, "and that was enough!"

"Aye," Royston laughed, "and holy water at that." And he fair roared with laughter.

"But the penny was real, wasn't it?" Craigie persisted.

But Royston was still roaring with laughter. And normally he didn't often laugh.

ONE-ARMED BANDIT

FERGIE Mann had filled his hoose with dothers trying to get a
loon. You could remember a blacksmith who had fathered a
football team trying to get a quine, and had managed it at the
twelfth arrival; but Fergie wasn't so fortunate and his wife drew the line
when the sixth quine made her appearance, for maybe she had had
enough of her own sex and wouldn't risk another try. But though Fergie
Mann was also a football fanatic he hadn't a loon of his ain to kick a
football in the close, though that wasn't the proper reason why he
wanted a loon at his heels. Quines could play football come to that, and
all manner of ball games; in fact Fergie got great amusement watching
his dothers stotting a ball at the kitchie gable, throwing it against the
wall and kicking up a leg to catch the ball under it on the rebound. Some
of his quines could even stot two balls, catching them alternately in
perfect rhythm as they bounced off the wall, like a juggler on a stage,
higher and higher and never missing a catch.

But Fergie Mann's desire for a loon in his family had a deeper
purpose than playing football, for it was to help him with the wark at
Kinsourie, the sixty acre place he owned and worked on the bents at
Pittenheath, and maybe a loon could take over when he was too old for
the chauve of the place, and maybe under the sod at Bourie kirk.

Aye faith, and that reminded him that next Sabbath was the autumn
sacrament and he would have to attend, a bit of a scutter when he was
haggled with the wark at the end o' hairst, but he would just have to go
for the look o' the thing and to please the wife. He hadn't been to the
spring communion and it wouldn't do to miss two of them, though the
wife and one of the married quines had been at the last one. You never
knew when you would need a minister and you had to keep in touch
with the kirk for fear you offended him.

All of his six daughters had grown up now, four of them married,
one in service in the toon, and Babee the eldest helping her mither with
the hoose wark and sometimes on the grun, gaitherin' tatties and sic
like, that were a fair profit when ye could catch the early market, and
they grew fine here in the sand aff the bents, better than the corn that
was mostly strangled in knot-grass.

Babee would have been married too, but that she fell with a bairn to
the son of a big farmer who had jilted her, maybe thinking she wasn't

good enough for the likes of him, though she was good enough to take up with. So Fergie gave his quine shelter at home and in reward she had given him a grandson. A grandson! It was a Cup Final Day in Fergie's life when that loon was born. It was a blessing in disguise that wiped all the shame from his conscience of his dother having an illegitimate bairn. What did that matter? He had been denied a son and heir to Kinsourie but now he had a grandson who would bear his name and serve the same purpose.

Fergie was cheerier at the marts and roups than the neighbours had seen him since the Dons Football Club won the Scottish Cup, beating Hibs by 2-1 in 1947. He was like a cock on the sharn midden after the moulting and had been crowing ever since the loon was born. And he diddled that bairn on his knee with an affection that made his other daughters jealous that he didn't take so much notice of their kids, his grandchildren that had been born in honest wedlock. He had two loons among his town-bred grandchildren, and they were all right for a game of football in the calfies' park, but they had no interest in the farm work and they were fear't at the beasts and wouldn't go near a horse, or even a stirk that was chained in the byre. But he would bring up young Fergie differently, and as soon as he could speak he would teach him the farming ways.

Little Fergie he was called, after his grandfather, who insisted upon it, and as the father hadn't married Babee she had to give her son the family surname as well, which suited old Fergie just grand. He wasn't concerned about the father, so long as he paid for the upbringing of the loon. Babee could keep the money, it would make up for the wages he couldn't afford to pay her as a kitchie-deem. And if looks were anything to go by the father could have denied young Fergie on the spot, for by the time he went to school he was the spitting image of his old grandfather, and seeing that the chiel had married another deem by then he wasn't likely to be interested.

Babee's loon had no fear of the nowt beasts; a sturdy nickum who could corner a calf or hold a ewe in a pen or his grandfather got a look at her foot growth. With every year that passed the loon became more and more interested, until he lived and breathed farming ways, and apart from his days at school he was always with the old man, even to sharing his football enthusiasm, and never missed a match at Pittodrie.

Mechanisation was beginning to bite in the Bogside, as it was all over the country, folk selling their work horses and buying a tractor, and the necessity caught up with Fergie Mann and he sold the pair of work beasts and bought a Massey-Ferguson, one that started on petrol with the gear handle but ran on paraffin once it was heated up. He sold the horses for dog meat because nobody wanted them. It was sad to part with the petted creatures but he didn't have much choice. All the farmers in the Bogside were doing the same thing and nobody wanted horses. They were sold cheaply for whatever use could be made of them, and it was mostly for tins of cat or dog food or as meat for the circus lions.

The sawmillers bought horses to drag fallen trees out of the forests, and that reprieved some of them, while others were sold in Europe for barge pulling, but it was all a mere drop in the ocean compared with horse redundancies over many years.

Fergie carted his harness down to the beach and threw it into the sea: saddles, collars, hames, britchens, backbands and theets and bridles, because nobody wanted that either, and but for the saddletrees and collar pegs still sticking out of the stable walls you would never have guessed there had been a horse beast at Kinsourie, and where there once had been the sweet scent of hay there was now a stink of paraffin.

He also got rid of most of his horse implements, mostly for scrap, but as some of it could be adapted for the tractor on a small place it wasn't such a loss, except that it broke your heart to see a fine long-board plough or a drill-moulder carted away to the scrapyard. Harrows, rollers, bone-davie, binder, reaper, and tattie-digger could be used with the tractor, once you had added a hitching-bar, and the same with the horse carts, fitted with motor tyres. Sparkie Lowe the blacksmith at Bourie did most of that sort of work, now that he had a welding plant; in fact he was almost obliged to do it, because in a year when he had shod about three hundred horses he was now down to a mere dozen, and these also would soon be gone.

Without the horses Fergie had a surplus of hay, enough to keep a puckle extra stirks in the stable, which added to his income at the store cattle sales, and helped to pay the balance he was owing for the tractor. It was a handy little machine that could be whisked about anywhere without ill-usage, and could work for long hours on subsidised paraffin, which couldn't be said for the hay that fed the horses.

A CHIEL AMONG THEM

Things were looking up for Fergie Mann, especially since that loon of Babee's came on the go, and it wouldn't likely be long or you saw the scamp seated on the tractor thing, him that had cried all night when the horses were taken away, but now had forgotten about it with the sight of the tractor and all the things it could do on the croft and the hurls he got in the cart. It was plain to everybody that the loon had put new life into old Fergie; not that he was ever lacking in spirit, but he doted on the bairn like he was his own first-born, and his mother had a quiet safe seat in the leith of it, and had even gotten another lad, though that was nobody's business and the thought never troubled her father, so long as she left him with the loon. Babee had given her father something her mother had never given him, and though Fergie knew this wasn't his wife's fault and never hinted as much it was plain that Babee got her own way in everything, though she wasn't a quine to take advantage of her father's generosity.

But now it was the autumn sacrament at Bourie kirk and Fergie had scarcely a straw in his barn to bed the nowt. He should have thrashed on the Saturday but there had been a football match at Pittodrie and he couldn't have missed that for all your sacraments. He told his wife he couldn't go to the kirk because he would have to thrash a load of sheaves for the nowt. She said he had neglected this on purpose as an excuse for not going to the kirk; but he had managed to go to the football. But it didn't matter she said, Babee could take the car and drive her down; though folk would be wondering what had become of him, and so would the minister, seeing he hadn't been there last time, and if your tokens weren't handed in the elders knew you hadn't been there, and they stood in the porch to make sure that nobody else handed them in for you.

"It's your money they want woman, nae the tokens."

"Aye, but ye're supposed to be there tae hand in the envelopes yersel'!"

"Is ony o' the quines comin' oot frae the toon?" Fergie asked.

"No. Ye ken fine that was never arranged and it's owre late noo. You and I was to go and Babee would bide at hame wi' the loon."

"Ah weel wuman, but I'll hae tae thrash onywye. We canna hunger the beasts, kirk or no kirk!"

"Ye should hae thocht on that afore yer fitba'."

"But mighty, wuman, the Lord himsel' stripped the ears o' corn on

Sunday tae feed his disciples."

"That's nae excuse. Ye're a proper heathen. An' fa will help ye tae thrash onywye? Ye canna manage yersel'."

"Och, the loonie will gie me a hand," said Fergie, "he's big enough noo tae throw inaboot a pucklie sheaves. Awa' tae yer kirk wuman and we will see that the tatties are on the boil or ye come back."

"See that ye put salt in them than," and with that Mrs. Mann powdered her nose and got ready for the kirk with Babee.

"You and yer damned kirk," Fergie taunted, though half in jest, "If I had my wye I'd have the place burned doon!"

Now the mill was humming, but in his excitement Fergie hadn't left the heating lamp for long enough under the nose cone, so that the engine was back-firing like a regiment of Home Guards at rifle practice, the sky alive with croaking rooks, alarmed at the gunfire, and folk that were passing for the kirk thought that Fergie had gone fair starkers. But at length he had the engine heated up and chooking away right cheerily while he lashed the sheaves into the hungry stripper drum. But the loon wasn't fit to keep him going, struggling with every sheaf from the load that had been toppled on the barn floor. Fergie was in a bit of a fluster and excitement was one of his failings, impatient with any niggling thing that hampered his progress. The mill was whining in idleness between the mouthfuls of corn, impatient for the food that filled the riddles in its belly, for the straw that danced on its delivery shakers, the corn that spewed into the elevator cups speeding up to the grain loft, and the chaff that was blown into the cattle court; for though Kinsourie was a small place Fergie had kept abreast of modernisation.

Fergie came out of the feeder box once or twice to grab an oxterful of sheaves, the loon doing his best to supply him, when Fergie slipped and fell into the stripper drum, the ravenous mouth mincing off his left arm to the elbow, bones and all, spewing the wet red flesh and blood into the corn riddles, all in a flash, before Fergie even realised what had happened to him.

"Stop the engine!" he cried to the loon, and his grandchild sped to the engine hoose to stop its clamour, choking off the paraffin that was its life blood, for Fergie had taught him every move.

Old Fergie staggered from the barn and slouched round the corner to the kitchen door, the dog yelping at his heels, the blood from his elbow stump spouting in the air. "My God," he murmured, "How long can I last?"

He collapsed on the kitchen floor, writhing in pain and shock, his warm blood squirting over the furniture, while he grasped the shattered stump in frustration. "Give me a cushion, quick, Fergie loonie," he cried. His grandson gave him a cushion from the settee and he thrust the raw stump into its folds on the linoleum, stifling the flow of blood from the severed artery. He calmed himself to give the loon instructions, flaying his excitement with pressure on the stump, while the oozing blood seeped into the cushion.

"Go to the phone loonie," he cried, "get Doctor Bilson's number in the book; ring him up and tell him it's urgent, that I've lost an arm in the mill. Hurry loonie, before I bleed tae death!"

'Loonie' was his pet name for his grandson, and now he used it with compelling urgency. "Tell him to send an ambulance as weel," he cried as an afterthought, while little Fergie thumbed through the leafy bulk of the directory.

It was a credit to Fergie's constitutional strength that he never lost consciousness, and he heard every word that his grandson told Doctor Bilson, or whoever was at the other end of the line, for maybe the doctor would be at the sacrament. He was seized with a violent trembling and he struggled to keep his throbbing stump on the cushion, now soaked with blood and spreading over the floor. When the full extent of his injury had filtered through to his shocked brain he was transfixed with a sudden fear. A fear of death. A fear of the Lord. "Oh my God," he muttered, "I wish noo I had gone to the kirk."

"Dinna leave me Loonie," he cried in his vexation. "Dinna leave me. Somebody will tell the folk at the kirk. Maybe you could 'phone the Mullart's folk, they're nearest the kirk, if they're nae a' at the sacrament." Loonie complied, anxious for the safety of his grand-father, though the tears were running down his cheeks and he spluttered into the mouthpiece between the sobs in his throat.

Fergie was dazed by now and a thick glaur of blood had gathered round the beating stump, congealed on the cushion, and he dared not move it for starting the flow of blood again, an expediency that was saving his life. He just lay there, silent, staring at the walls, trembling, cold from loss of blood, the dog sniffing at the cushion, until little Fergie shooed him away. Then there was the noise of a car in the close and the loon ran to the door. Doctor Bilson was just getting out of his car, and

40

further up the farm road an ambulance was approaching.

There had been no dinner for Babee Mann and her mother that fateful Sunday. They got the fright of their lives when the miller's housekeeper sneaked into the kirk during the sermon and told an elder what had happened, who whispered it to the minister, bending over the pulpit to hear it. The minister then came up the stairs in his long black robes and whispered softly to Mrs. Mann at the end of her pew. On returning to the rostrum the Rev. George Fiddes muttered a prayer for his wayward parishioner, beseeching the Lord to grant his safe return to the fold.

Meanwhile Mrs. Mann and her daughter were speeding on the road to hospital in Aberdeen. They had called in past at Kinsourie but found nobody there; only the dog in the close, wagging his tail furiously, and a blood-soaked cushion on the kitchen floor.

II

But now it was the autumn sacrament of the Lord's Supper again at Bourie kirk, almost a year to the day since Fergie Mann lost his arm in the threshing mill. And if you were sitting on the gentle slope of the gallery, behind Fergie and his family, you could see that his wife sat next to him, on his right side, ready to help him turn the pages of the hymn book she shared with him, while the sleeve on his left side sheathed an arm of shining steel. Babee and two of her sisters sat with their mother, their husbands on Fergie's left, out from the toon for the sacrament, though they didn't always come, but this was a special occasion — Fergie's first return visit to the kirk since his accident.

The family sat on one of the long varnished seats that stretched from the centre aisle to the ochred walls and the gothic window that looked over the fields and farmsteads. Kinsourie was about two miles away with its bourich of twisted trees, like withered arms in the raw dreich wind that swept up from the sea. The sunlight was fitful, darting shafts of light through the smudge of smoke cloud, spotlighting the barren fields with a deceitful glare, while the wind carried the rain squalls across the sky like quiffs of loosened hair.

A CHIEL AMONG THEM

The congregation rose to sing 'Come, Ye Thankful People, Come,' and you couldn't say what Fergie's thoughts were: whether they were a torture of regret that he hadn't come to the kirk that fateful Sunday, or whether he was just thankful that the gluttonous mouth of the mill hadn't swallowed him completely, and that his minced remains weren't rotting under a tombstone beneath the window that looked out on his croft.

The thought of his wife as a widow brought tears to his eyes, though the hand that shared her hymn book was steady in her sight. "You and yer kirk," he had said jeeringly that Sunday, "If I had my wye I wad burn it doon!" But she had never reproached him, or hinted that the Lord had punished him for his transgression. The only obvious difference was that she had to look up the place for him in the psalms and level out the pages, otherwise he brought up the steel shaft from his side, awkwardly at first, with a socket square in it that fitted the knob on the steering wheel of his car.

At work he fitted the robot arm with a sinister looking hook, or with a clamp attachment for the shaft of fork or hoe, or a pincer like contraption for picking up sheaves or holding out his newspaper, a mechanical existence that contrasted badly with his eager and compulsive nature, impatient with a handicap that distorted his anxious progress in the scheme of things. But his courage and cheerfulness in facing his deficiency had already earned him the nickname of the 'One-Armed Bandit,' which was really a compliment to his indomitable spirit in facing his disablement. There were men in the parish who would have lost heart; who would have given up the struggle on a croft in the face of it, their spirit crushed in the effort to adapt themselves, but Fergie soldiered on with a smile, his bright eyes undimmed by fate, his thirst for life unabated.

Of course it was disheartening at first, especially when he got up in the morning and couldn't put on his clothes, the healing stump hanging uselessly by his side, throwing him off balance when he tried to hitch up his trousers; and it was nerve wracking trying to fasten shirt buttons with one hand and fumbling with his bootlaces. But he was a chiel of independent spirit and wanted to manage on his own; to carry on the work on the farm, but on those desolate mornings, with tears in his eyes, tears of desperation, his nerve-shocked body in a tremble, he was forced to turn to his wife for assistance. She was the only one who saw him on the floor like a frustrated child, struggling with his infirmity; to the outside world he was always on his feet and fighting. But he soon learned to leave his braces on his trousers and to sling them over his shoulders, and got a zipper on his flap for going to the bathroom.

But if you had expected any serious change in Fergie Mann that first Sunday back at the kirk you would have been surprised at his composure. His eager eyes were still as bright and cheery as windblown skies in harvest time, and men folks who enquired of his wellbeing were reassured that he was still his same old self. They got a poke in the belly with his steel encased limb that had them bowing before him as if they were doubled up with laughter, and for the women he held out the spike for a handshake, making the excuse that he had to use his right hand to remove his cap.

But sometimes in the kirk he felt the eye of God upon him, an apprehending eye, which hitherto he had scarcely been aware of on his conscience. Now in the face of the whole congregation he felt rebuked, and a fit of claustrophobia seized him, an urge to bolt for the door; that he was an outcast imprisoned with his guilt, much as he had repented his defamation of the kirk and wished to be back in the fold. His salvation was not to be found sitting brooding at home, however, torturing himself with regret; he had to be up and doing, and coming to the kirk he felt he was trying to make his peace with God. And if a tremble seized his body his wife would take his healthy hand in hers and squeeze it reassuringly, and a smile of relaxation would spread across his face.

But Fergie was an impatient Job, and his penance would be long before the Lord relented. He couldn't perceive that he was being tried in the fire, and that yet another sacrifice would be required of him in contrition for his waywardness, a parting that would bring more tears than he had yet shed; for the Isaac of this Abraham would yet be demanded of him before the Lord was satisfied.

In the meantime Fergie was thankful it was his left hand that had been severed, otherwise he would have been doubly smitten, for with his right hand he could still do many things, like holding a pen to fill in his football coupon, or spreading jam on a slice of bread; or even in turning the pages of the bible, wherein he sometimes found comfort in his distress.

But it was in the byres and fields where he felt his infirmity most keenly; stumbling like a bairn with a fork or a hoe, tethered to the shaft with the clamp on his steel arm, like a prisoner chained to a ball, tears of frustration welling in his eyes, while a rolling turnip evaded his capture, or a wisp of hay blew away in the wind. His working day was half as long again as it used to be and stretched into nightfall, when he fell exhausted into his armchair, which beforehand he had scarcely needed. Were it nor for Babee and her help in the fields and byres, and little Fergie when he came home from school, his world would have been a shambles.

But he never lost interest in the Dons Football Club. Just as the kirk was a reassurance the football matches were an escape. Even before he got the knob for the steering wheel of his car he was at the road-end waiting for the bus, his grandson by his side, Babee left at home to feed the cattle. And when the Dons scored a goal he held up his steel arm and cheered them to victory. In the old days he held up both arms, but in the steel arm there was a defiance of fate, a challenge with adversity that kept him in the stream of life.

Little Fergie mastered the tractor before he left school, and while he ploughed and harrowed his grandfather stood in the field and gave directions, blowing on a whistle like a referee on a football pitch, and the loon learned the signals and obeyed like a sheepdog, on a code arranged between them, so many blasts for each command, and long into the twilight you could hear the shriek of Fergie's whistle.

From where Fergie sat in the gallery he could see everybody that came into the kirk from the door in the gable facing the road. They came in from the porch where two elders stood by the collection plate and took the token cards from the communicants. Except for those in the back seats everybody had to come up the centre aisle wherever they sat down, and those who came right under the gallery were in full view before they disappeared to take their accustomed seats. This being communion Sabbath the elders were gathered under the pulpit, in the very centre of the church, behind the lectern and in front of the organ, with the choir on either side, and such was the design of the building that this focal point could be observed from every angle, and today was a full house.

His sermon over the Rev. Fiddes came down the stair from his box and seated himself among the elders, where he partook of wine and bread with them as the Master with his disciples, and having blessed the trenchards of bread cubes and the glass thimblefuls of wine on the varnished trays, the elders would distribute themselves about the kirk, passing the victuals along the pews, each member taking a cube of bread and a thimbleful of wine, and when they had swallowed of the body and blood of the Saviour they deposited the tiny glass in a small bracket under the desk in front, where their bibles and psalm books rested.

This was Fergie's greatest embarrassment, when he couldn't pass the trenchard of breadcrumbs and the tray of wineglasses as formerly, and though he managed to put the cube of bread in his mouth, his hand trembled violently when he lifted the glass, while it rattled against his teeth, spilling the red liquid on his shirt front, the red blood of Christ. Worse still, while his wife took great care to place the silver handle of the tray securely in his hand, his neighbour on the other side, his son-in-law, had scarcely grasped it when Fergie in his excitement let go, and the tray and glasses splattered on the floor.

There was a great stir around Fergie, and the folk in front stood up when they felt the glasses birling round their heels, rolling down hill to the front of the gallery. But apart from the spilled wine it was quickly tidied up and another tray of wine was brought forth, though Fergie was flustered and went almost to pieces in his embarrassment. It was as if the blood of Christ had been denied him; as if he was unworthy at the table of our Lord, like an Escariot in the midst of the faithful, rebuked and ridiculed in the house of prayer. In one terrible moment he felt the presence of the Almighty.

But even as Fergie faltered on the steps of rightousness the eye of the Lord was upon him. For this prodigal son the fatted calf had yet to be slain for his homecoming. For this Doubting Thomas the Lord would yet stir up great waters, even as the commotion in parting the Red Sea; yea, even as great as the delivery of Jonah from the whale's belly would be the stirring of waters, and a strange new wonder would come up out of the sea for this present day Saint Fergus, which would bring him great riches and deliverance from evil, and would bring him forth among the Lord's annointed, in the way of the Lord, and he would go forth as Peter before him as a fisher of men. Thus, from the most unlikely sources, and by the most unusual circumstances, He chooses his disciples, even as fine metal that has been tempered in the forge of life.

A CHIEL AMONG THEM

Then Fergie felt the comfort of his wife's hand in his own grasp and the strength of her body seemed to flow in his veins, and she soothed him into calm. The scene passed and the fluster on his face subsided, and the beating vein in his neck resumed its former normality.

There was a long interval while the elders continued their work, and Fergie watched and envied their fitness and capabilities in the face of his own disablement.

But when Benzie Wurrell of the Muckle Ward stood in the lower aisle with his tray a smile crossed Fergie's face. He remembered the story that had been told of Benzie when he picked up the prostitute in Aberdeen. He offered the randie quine thirty shillings for his fun but she would have nothing less than a fiver. But Benzie grudged a five-pound note that Friday in the toon and let her go. He wouldn't budge a penny, and when the quine left him she cried out: "Ye wunna get muckle for thirty shillings!" Next week Benzie was back in the toon, but this time he had his wife by his side, her with her lang bit neb and her bleary een and her claes thrown on wi' a graip. And they met this same quine in Union Street, and she glowered the pair of them up and down in passing, and over her shoulder she cried to Benzie: "I tel't ye that ye wouldna get muckle for thirty shillings!" But of course Benzie's wife didna ken what the quine was havering about, or what she meant, and blissfully she was none the wiser.

It wasn't a thing to be thinking about in the kirk, but some of Fergie's rampant spirit returned with the thought of it and he almost laughed outright. At least it showed the colour of the elder's coat, and yet he was here unscathed regardless of his transgression. It made a bit of a sham of Christian justice Fergie thought, for his own desecration of the kirk had been no worse, and yet he had been maimed for it.

But from that day forth Fergie was a marked man, singled out from the multitude to carry the cross for Jesus. He was the chosen one of a hard Taskmaster who had tried him in the fire and found him worthy, and in the years to come the truant elder wouldn't be fit to untie the bootlaces of His disciple, so far would Fergus rise in favour with the Lord.

When all the elders had returned to the lectern with their trays and glasses the Rev. Fiddes went back up the steps to the pulpit and called the final hymn. After the singing he gave the benediction and everyone left the building and the fading organ music, and a lot of friendly folk crowded round Fergie and his wife to ask for his wellbeing.

III

The sacraments came and went and the years rolled on and things went well enough for Fergie Mann. During that time his daughter Babee got married and left the household, leaving her son with his grandparents. But to the neighbours Fergie had changed: gone was the rumbustuous extrovert, and in his place a serious minded gentleman of refinement; one who read books and studied theology and the lives of the Saints, spending hours in the town libraries and at college classes when he should have been at home helping young Fergie with the farm work. He had even stopped swearing and went to church every Sunday, and all you could get out of him was religion. He still went to the football matches occasionally, but not nearly so often, and lads like Benzie Wurrell said he was going clean off his head with religion, but if he didn't land in the asylum most likely he would be enrolled as an elder of the kirk; in fact he said it had already been suggested, and the minister had put forward his name, but that they thought he would be a bit awkward with the trays on Communion Sundays.

But Fergie was not dismayed by what the neighbours thought of his changing personality and his new outlook on life. Religion had added a new dimension to his perception of life; had given grace and beauty to what had formerly been mundane and commonplace, especially in nature and the changing seasons in relation to farming, something he had scarcely realised in his former existence. The Parable of the Sower had a new meaning for him, and he could identify with Joseph and his Brethren during the famine in Egypt, and what had previously been a boring sermon now transpired as almost an incantation on the elegance of Hebrew poetry. He had always loved the land and farming from a practical and commercial angle, but this new appreciation of scripture enriched his thoughts with something that went beyond physical culti- vation; a soaring of the mind to meet the challenge of the infinite, to hold court with the unseen power of life, the spirit of growth, the unfathomable source and reason of being alive. Living by bread alone now seemed inadequate for Fergie, and seeking a fuller life became an inspiration, a mission that filled his thoughts with a divine purpose, that others might share his enlightenment. It was as if his physical disablement had been replaced with a mental faculty which had been repressed in his former masculine existence; a sort of staff to lean on which had become a torch in his hand.

Little Fergie had left school but still worked with his grandfather, ploughing with the tractor on neighbouring farms to make up his wages. He couldn't understand the change in his grandfather but accepted it as a sort of reaction to his accident in the threshing mill. And besides, his mind was on other things, like emigrating to Australia with one of his pals, but for the thought of leaving the old man on his own. But of course the neighbours had other ideas, and they said that Fergie had scunnered the loon with his religion. And who else would put up with Fergie saying grace at mealtimes and his bible readings in the evenings? If his ain loon had tired of it there wasn't much chance of a stranger putting up with it.

When Fergie heard of his grandson leaving, he thought of Abraham and Isaac, and that perhaps it was the will of God to do his bidding, to make it impossible for him to continue with the farm, and to embark upon the path of righteousness in a training for the clergy. There was one big snag — he couldn't afford it. Even though he sold Kinsourie at its present value it would scarcely keep him alive for the five years required for a scholarship in divinity, even with grants considered, and he would have to buy a house to live in.

Things were brought to a head in the hay time when Fergie lost his balance and fell off the horse rake that was yoked to the tractor. He fell in front of the long row of sharp prongs at the back, like a dancing portcullis between the wheels, and he was rolled forward on the hard ground like a wood log, while he yelled to the loon to stop the tractor. He was bruised and badly shaken when his grandson pulled him out, trembling all over, and he had to go home until he recovered.

The accident decided his wife that it was time she had her say. She insisted that they lease out the farm to someone else for cropping, on condition that they themselves remained in the farmhouse, though at the same time she knew that her man would eat his heart out with nothing to do. Nor would it bring in enough money to carry him through university, with enough to spare for their daily wants, for she knew what was in his mind and what he wanted to do, however daft it might seem to other folk.

All the same she had her way. Things couldn't go on as they were once young Fergie had left them, and they couldn't afford to pay for outside labour at the present high level of wages.

Then all of a sudden their grandson made up his mind finally to go abroad. He and his pal got a job with an Australian firm of earthmoving contractors, driving the big bulldozers on high bonus pay, far more than he could ever hope to earn with his grandfather, even on contracting work on outside farms.

Parting with his grandson was like the offering up of Isaac for Fergie Mann. He wept openly by the fireside, but the loon wouldn't be dissuaded. His passage was already booked and he was leaving with his friend in three months' time for Australia. Fergie lay awake at night wondering what he would do, and when he fell asleep he rolled onto his arm stump, which stung him wide awake again. His wife had little rest with him, and begged him to take her advice and leave farming, especially now that their grandson had gone.

It was eight years since Fergie lost his arm and he was now fifty-three; not too old yet for the ministry he considered — if he could afford it. Meanwhile they leased the land to a bigger farmer who also filled the steading with pigs, paying Fergie to look after them, and it looked like this was how he would end his farming days; a paid servant on his own premises, little better than the Prodigal Son of the bible.

He held a roup and sold off his livestock, tractor and implements and most of the hand tools, because it didn't seem likely he would have any further use for them, and the money would eke out his income.

But the fatted calf had yet to be slaughtered and there was a great stirring of the waters offshore from Pittenheath; a great commotion in the North Sea where oil and natural gas had been discovered, and the surveyors for British Gas and Total Marine were casting about on the coast for a suitable landfall for their product. One of them tripped over the steel crup of a saddle sticking out of the sand, where Fergie had thrown it all those years ago, and when he looked over the bents his eye lighted on Kinsourie, where Fergie was feeding his pigs, unaware that Divine Providence had relented and that his penance was about to be rewarded with a crown of gold, the Light of the Morning Star and the

Keys of the Kingdom.

When the surveyor set up his direction finder he discovered that the saddle prow was in a direct line between Kinsourie and the Frigg gas field some two hundred miles north-east in the sea between the Shetland Isles and the coast of Norway. He called his companions in the search, and after some discussion they decided to put forward a suggestion that Pittenheath was the ideal place to bring the gas pipes ashore, with Fergie's farm bang in the centre, where they could install the thermal storage tanks and the buildings for processing plant and extraction of chemicals.

Fergie was glad he had always resisted his wife's persuasion to sell the farm, because the price he was now offered was far in excess of what the most enterprising farmer could have offered him. He told the Land Commissioners they could have the growthy bitch, and they assured him they could handle the couch grass, and when you saw these giant earth scoops sweeping up the dirt for the foundations of the gas buildings you could believe them. The sad thing about it was that Fergie's grandson had gone all the way to Australia for a job driving one of those bulldozers, tempted by the lucrative pay packets, when he could have started on the beach at home. But such are the ways of the Lord, Fergie concluded.

He got such a stunning price for Kinsourie that his neighbours called him the 'One-Armed Bandit' to his face, and said that he had hit the jackpot. But Fergie merely smiled and poked them in the belly with his fish-hook, which could have torn their ears off, had he not now been a man of God. Some of them who thought they knew him better said that the de'il was aye guid tae his ain, but in this case they had hold of the wrong end of the stick, and they might have said that the sun always shines on the righteous.

Fergie bought a bungalow in Aberdeen, where his fellow elders said he would be much nearer the Dons and the football stadium at Pittodrie. He did attend a game or two but that was not his main purpose in the city, for he had already completed a two-year course on evening class bible study at King's College, and had graduated for a further full-time three-year training scholarship on theology and divinity studies. He matriculated as a Bachelor of Divinity, a licensed minister of the gospel, enabling him to preach in the parish churches, but until a charge could be found for him he became a sort of priest in limbo, standing in for ministers who had fallen by the wayside.

He eventually returned one Sunday to stand in for the Rev. Fiddes at Bourie, who was indisposed with pneumonia. It was standing room only to hear the Rev. Fergus Mann deliver his sermon, a bigger crowd than he had ever seen on Communion Sabbaths, with chairs brought in from the church hall for people in the aisles, while he stood there by the lectern in his long black robe, the steel arm of God hidden in its folds, gesticulating with his right hand, while he spoke in a hard clear voice that hushed the kirk to silence.

He lifted his text from the First Book of Corinthians, 15-50: 'Now this I say, brethren, that flesh and blood cannot inherit the Kingdom of God; neither doth corruption inherit incorruption. Behold, I shew you a mystery; We shall not all sleep, but we shall all be changed, in a moment, in the twinkling of an eye, at the last trump; for the trumpet shall sound, and the dead shall be raised incorruptible, and we shall be changed. For this corruptible must put on incorruption, and this mortal *must* put on immortality. So when this corruptible shall have put on incorruption, and this mortal shall have put on immortality, then shall be brought to pass the saying that is written, Death is swallowed up in victory.'

As a basis for his sermon he went back to Kinsourie, which no longer existed as a farm, but had been swept from the face of the earth by the will of God. He didn't speak of the loss of his arm or about his conversion; nor even of the couch grass which strangled his crops, even as the darnel in Palestine, but he dealt at length with another weed that had troubled him over the years as a farmer. He had ploughed it down every winter, hoping to get rid of it, but in the following summer it always appeared again, mostly in wet sour land; which was maybe how Kinsourie had got its name from our forefathers. In summer he attacked the weed with shim and hoe, at a time when it was mostly in flower, before it podded seed, and although he killed the parent plant there was always more to take its place. It was not a very troublesome weed but a very persistent one, determined to survive every form of persecution. Even weed-killers had not subdued it, for in the earth heaps thrown aside by the bulldozers he had seen it again in flower.

This plant was known as the Redshank, probably because of its pinkish flowers and sharing the habitat of these birds, and the botanical name was *polygonum persicaria*. It was also known as the 'Blood of

51

Christ,' because of one solitary crimson spot on each pointed leaf, like a spot of blood. Like the Passion Flower with its crown of thorns and its ring of crosses, the Redshank was supposed to have been growing on Calvary, under the cross, and that the blood of the Saviour dropped on its leaves during the crucifixion. That may be hearsay, Fergie said, but what concerns us here is the virility of this persecuted plant, and its determination to survive in the most adverse conditions.

The Rev. Mann was not surprised that the couch grass survived, because it had roots everywhere in the soil, like the root of evil, but the Blood of Christ was an annual with an individual root and stem like any one of us in the wilderness of life. Each leaf had its spot of blood that signified this plant above all others in the field, just as each one of us has his spot of sin; and just as each generation is ploughed back into the earth another appears with its spots, for the process of life is eternal, and the presence of Christ immortal, and would remain with us like the spots on the leaves.

Now the Rose of Sharon, known to gardeners everywhere as *hypericum calycinum* is a plant of similar structure, with a lovely yellow flower which has earned for it this biblical name, like the lily growing on the banks of cool Siloam's shady rill, with visions of a land flowing in milk and honey. But not for the Rose of Sharon these spots of blood on the leaves, which you might say was an omission on Nature's part, because the *hypericum* is a domesticated plant growing in gardens, protected and nourished by garden lovers everywhere, which would have ensured a perpetual reminder of the crucifixion. But the wisdom of God shines through even in Nature, for garden cultivation is not the theme of Christianity; rather it is a fight for survival in the midst of persecution and anarchy, with the flower of the fields and boglands as its emblem, exposed to the elements and the plough and the hoe. Even the Passion Flower was denied this divine privilege, not so much because it was a hot-house plant, but because it blossomed but for a day and died with the sunset. Such an emblem was not for religion, which isn't for a day but for all time, though its life in bloom marks the duration of Christ's suffering on the cross.

The silence in the church was uncanny. Surely this was not the Fergie they had known in the past; the worthy who swore freely and cracked foul jokes at roups and mart; the football fanatic who waved a steel arm to cheer his favourite team to victory; the Peter Pan who went on the rampage with a tin-whistle in the gloamin', now in his flowing robes and decanting on the glories of Christ and religion. But their ears had not deceived them, and his strident voice kept them awake with an inspired urgency they dared not ignore.

The actual reappearance of the defiled Redshank plant did not really surprise him, Fergie said, because there were always some stray seeds left in the ground; what puzzled him most was what took place under the earth to make it sprout — this rejuvenation in the seed during the spring months that sent the plant forth again. This is an unseen resurrection that is almost spiritual in its infinite mystery. Science may try to explain it in botanical terms; they may even analyse it in a practical sense, but we remain mystified. The biological chemists will tell us that a teaspoonful of God's earth contains more organisms than the entire human race — but that does not explain the miracle of life.

This invisible transanimation is something of the spirit of nature and yet as tangible as the air we breathe, just as so many other things are hidden from us and yet we have to believe in them. It is a life force that even death cannot destroy, for it breathes life into death in perennial resuscitation, as witness the young tubers on the stem of the old rotting potato, for even as the old plant dies the younger is already alive. It is an inherent stimulus in disembodied nature, one of her hidden mysteries which science is at pains to describe for us. 'No human thought can imagine what is that transformation by which this corruptible shall inherit incorruption, and this mortal put on immortality. We sow a grain, we reap an ear, a corn. Likewise we bury a corruptible body; but it is not a corruptible body that we look for as the harvest.'

Fergie's voice showed not the least sign of self-consciousness, and he spoke with a conviction that compelled wrapt attention, even among the scoffers, dispelling doubt in the minds of those who wavered. Why then, he cried, if Nature can perform such miracles — why should we despair of our own spiritual resurrection? It is no more inconceivable than the infinity of space, which is without end or border line, and in this we believe, because we must, there is no alternative. Was it because of lack of evidence that we are sceptical of an afterlife? Nobody had come back to reassure us. Nobody but Christ, who had risen temporarily in the flesh for the benefit of the chosen few. In that assurance we must have faith; even though it be a blind faith, faith in the things which are hidden from us for a divine purpose we cannot understand, unless it be to give us a choice in dispelling evil to become Christians and achieve salvation, both in this world and the next which is to come.

There was a great sighing and coughing into handkerchiefs when Fergie had finished, and some were in tears, for they knew this man's background, and they just couldn't believe in the change that had been worked in him; a transformation which was even more striking than his theme on the Redshank plant, a weed in their fields that would now have their closer attention.

Fergie's wife didn't go back to her old seat in the gallery. On an occasion like this she felt that her rightful place was on the floor of the church with her husband, facing him from the front pews, where she sat with her daughter Babee and her man. They had come out from the city by way of encouragement for Fergie, but they were not long seated before they realised that he wouldn't require it. All the inspiration he needed was in the response of his congregation, in the earnest faces of the men and the tear-washed cheeks of the women. The reception overwhelmed him, for he had not sought to bring his old friends to tears. He had been apprehensive of his welcome but now he was almost ashamed of the composure their emotion had given him. After all, he had not dwelt on an emotional theme, but their hearts had gone out to him in his new found strength and faith; a man who had been struck down in their midst and was yet whole again, an encouragement to all who faltered on the treadmill of life.

And if his wife had felt embarrassment in their midst it soon slipped away in the encouraging smiles of her old neighbours, warming to her humility in the circumstances. Concern for her husband's welfare was nearer her heart than any feeling of triumph or pride and her old friends acknowledged it. Babee choked back the tears of pride for her father and shyly avoided the assuring glances of her old acquaintances.

Fergie raised his arm of steel and called all to prayer, and with bowed heads they listened to him. He prayed for the sick and the weary and for those who were close to death; for the bereaved and those afflicted with sorrow, for those who were parted over long distances, and for those who were in distress over worldly affairs. He prayed for the welfare of our present Queen and her household, and for the divine guidance of our rulers in the affairs of state, and for the preservation of peace in the world. For the lonely and the weary he had a special word, and for the Rev. George Fiddes, that by the grace of God he would

54

recover his health and rejoin his congregation.

But there was no mention of his own infirmity, or whereby he had found his new strength to come amongst his old friends as an ambassador for the Most High and Mighty One.

'We plough the fields, and scatter the good seed on the land,' was the closing hymn and it filled the church like a crescendo. The average clergyman may have derided Fergie's sermon. But as a son of the soil he said what was in his heart among farming folk and they understood and were proud of him.

There may have been those who came to scoff but now they stayed behind to shake the hand of the One-Armed Bandit of Bourie.

TWILIGHT VENUS

IT was four years since Jeck Knowles had come to work at
Kinchurn, and now here he was sitting by the bedside of this dying
woman. Tina had suffered a stroke, and now he watched over her
unconscious body in the living room of the old farmhouse. The maid
who was looking after her wouldn't stay the night when she thought her
mistress was going to die, though she promised she would be back the
next day.

It was a dark March evening and the window curtains were closed,
and now that there was electric light on the place a white globe in the
ceiling shone down on Christina Smith, known to almost everybody in
the parish as Tina, spinster sister to Jason Smith, Jeck's employer.
Jason had asked Jeck to look after her until midnight, when he himself
would be free to come over from the Homefarm — or the 'Muckle
Toon' — to relieve him.

Jeck Knowles was a youngish man and fairly good-looking, though
a bit narrow in the shoulder blade to be much admired by women.
When women looked at him he felt sure they felt as he did when he saw
a woman with spindly legs — uninspired and emotionless. For all that
he had got a bit wife and had three bairns and lived hardby in the cottar
hoose along the main road from the farmtoon.

Being an outfarm he worked mostly alone on the place, especially in
the winter months, looking after the cattle in the byres, except when his
barn was empty of straw, when the lads from the Muckle Toon would
come across the parks and give him a bit bum of a thrash. Pulling
turnips was his main job in the fields in winter. In the summer, when his
cattle had been dispersed to pasture he joined with the squad in the orra
wark, like hoe, hay and hairst.

Tina had taken a dwam in the morning and the quine that was
looking after her had found her mistress lying unconscious at the back
of the bathroom door. She was only a temporary maid because Tina
was an independent woman and managed on her own. But she hadn't
been well this last fortnight and Jason had advised her to engage a maid
to look after her. But when the quine found her mistress collapsed in the
bathroom she ran to the byre for Jeck Knowles. She wouldn't have
done this if the telephone had been working, when she could have
phoned Jason, but there had been a batter of snow in the night and the

wires were down, so she had to run for Jeck. Between them they managed to trail Tina through from the bathroom to the front room and laid her on the couch and happed her with blankets from her upstairs bed to keep her warm.

Syne Jeck put on his army greatcoat — the chiel had been in the Home Guard — and left his nowt howlin' for maet and set off owre the parks for the Muckle Toon. It was still dark and the morning stars sparkled like golden pinheids in the frosty sky, while the crunch of Jeck's welly boots broke the crust on the snow. It was heavy going and the wind whipped at his cheeks with an icy thong, while he snuggled his face deeper in the raised collar of his khaki coat.

There were lights at the Muckle Toon, winking through the naked trees, mostly from the byres, where the cattlemen were busy with the morning feed. Jeck knocked on the back kitchen door and the face of Jessie the maid keeked out at him in the mirk.

"What brings ye here Jeck at this time o' mornin'?" she speired him.

Jeck explained his urgent errand and the lassie ran upstairs to the bedroom of her mistress and Jason phoned the doctor from his bedside. Fortunately the phone wires to the main road were still intact and he got through.

That was nearly twelve hours ago and now there wasn't a mirror small enough in the room that Jeck could use to see if Tina was still alive, nor a feather that could be stirred with her breathing. But he thought he could just feel it on his cheek when he went close enough, so he refilled the hot-water bottle and replaced it at her feet. The doctor had said that the most important thing was to keep her warm, so he heaped more coal on the fire and soon had the place like a hot-house, despite the icy draughts from doors and windows.

Over the years Jeck had been quite a favourite with Tina, washing and polishing her car, cleaning her upstairs windows and looking after her garden in his spare time, and sometimes she'd take him into the house for a cup of tea and a blether, and maybe she'd give him the loan of a book to read, or play over the latest record she'd bought on her braw new radiogram. But there was nothing unusual about this, for there wasn't a tradesman working about the place, or a vanman who called, or a piano tuner who didn't have his cup of tea with her and a hearty chat in the living-room that had once been the kitchen in the old farmhouse.

Tina never tired of telling them the story about the time one of the old farm cottages was empty, and Jason her brother had decided he wouldn't use it again, because it had been condemned, and he would have it pulled down. For a time, however, Jason had allowed Tina to keep her hens in it, after the great gale when her two portable hen-houses had been wrecked; collapsing like a pack of cards, her hens flying like birds to a far corner of the field, carried by the wind, and she herself had escaped serious injury, having left one of the sheds a moment beforehand.

So Tina filled the empty cottage with her laying hens and fed them twice daily, and Jason sent a man occasionally to clean it out. The cottage was close to the main road, and one day when Tina was in the cottage a gentleman came out of his posh car and tapped on the door, which was always closed to keep the hens inside. He wanted to know the road to some strange place, but Tina said you should have seen his face when she opened the door in her apron, with hens in the windows and standing on the shelves at her back, all clucking and singing away merrily as if poor Tina lived with them permanently. And she could hardly keep a solemn face to direct him on his way, far less explain her predicament; and she couldn't imagine what the poor man thought when he went back to his car, for he was off in a moment, no doubt in amazement, hardly believing the sight of his eyes.

Before that she had kept a tame pig that spent a lot of its time in the farmhouse, lying on a rug in front of the fire, grunting away to itself when it wasn't asleep. One day a deaf mute selling books called at the door, gesticulating with his fingers. But before he really got started the pig sprang forth from the kitchen between his legs and down the farm close, and the poor man got such a fright Tina said, that if anything would ever make him talk that pig should have done it.

Meantime Jeck could hear the traffic faintly on the main road out at the front of the house, across the lawn, about thirty yards away, muffled in the snow that slowed their speed; and there was the occasional gust of wind at the windows, thudding the glass, a fresh wind that would soon dispel the snow. Otherwise the room was as quiet as a mausoleum, and Tina like an effigy under the woollen blankets, just as the nurse had left her.

TWILIGHT VENUS

Jeck lifted the lid of the piano and tinkled a few notes, not that he could play anything but he hoped forlornly that the familiar sound might waken Tina; that perhaps she would move her limbs under the blankets. After all, she was a music teacher and took in pupils for piano lessons to help out with the housekeeping money, for apart from the interest on her bank account she had no other income. People had lived for years after a stroke, Jeck reflected, and the doctor hadn't given up hope for her. He would be back in the morning as soon as it was light and the snow had cleared away on the roads.

Tina was a middle-aged, genteel woman, with a bit of refinement and culture, far above Jeck's standard of living, and yet he managed to talk to her in his own off-hand sort of way, with the little learning he had to keep up with her. She wasn't bad looking either, though getting a little plump and her hair was grey, with the slightest hint of a double chin. In the dark winter evenings she was all alone in the farmhouse. When the windows were in darkness and the garage door left open Jeck knew that she was away in the car. She would be off to play the piano at some local concert, or having a game of whist at the club; attending a sale of work or a guild meeting in the church hall, or at organ practice for the church on Sunday. She was always on the go, but always returned alone, put the car in the garage, closed the door and went up to the house in a brisk walk, fearless in the darkest night. But if Jeck came out of the byre about this time she would wait for him, and the two of them would walk up the brae together, talking about the stars, the weather, the phases of the moon, and what Jeck had missed not being at the concert. Sometimes they got on to politics and even religion and would stand half-an-hour together, especially if it were a clear calm night, and Jeck's patient wife would be wondering what had kept him so long in the byre, when he had only gone along to see that the cattle were safely bedded down for the night.

But besides being fearless in the dark Tina was also courageous in adversity, refusing to take life all that seriously, or even death itself come to that; joking with her doctors when they diagnosed her serious illness, holding death at arm's length; living for the present, one day at a time, heedless of tomorrow. Perhaps she knew instinctively that she didn't have long to live. But whatever her fear of death it never reached her lips. She was defiant and strangely insensitive to his presence over the years, and even as he cradled her now in his cold arms there was the shadow of a smile at her slightly twisted mouth.

Jeck put more coals on the fire and replaced the guard, while Tina's dead parents in their Edwardian clothes stared down at him from the papered wall, wondering what he had to do with their daughter. Another picture of Tina's that Jeck liked was the inside of a kirk with a young man playing at the organ and two angels looking in at the window and not a soul in the pews. Jeck thought the best time to look at this picture was in the early summer mornings when nobody was about, and he used to keek in at the window where it hung on the opposite wall before Tina was up, just as the angels were doing, spying on the young man at the organ, and the sight of it in the quiet secret light of the morning made him feel creepy all over.

Looking at it now wasn't quite the same. He wasn't spying any more, but the thought occurred to him that the angels might be keeking through the blinds at him now, watching him with Tina, before they came to take her away. He looked at Tina and he could have sworn her eyelids flickered. Maybe he just imagined it but he watched her intently for a while, then touched her cheek with the back of his hand, but she was still soft and warm.

He sat down in the armchair again and tried to read the daily paper but he couldn't anchor his thoughts. He got up again and took the blind aside but there was nobody there; nothing but the black sky and a white mantle of snow on the ground. Even the traffic had dwindled away and a sad moaning wind moved the naked arms of the trees. The mantel clock chimed ten and settled down again to its quiet ticking. Two hours yet before Jason would arrive.

Jeck was hungry. It was now over four hours since he had supper and Jason had told him to make himself at home. He could have helped himself to whisky from Tina's cabinet but he was not in the mood. Tea would be fine and he knew where Tina kept her caddy and her home-baked shortbread, scones and queencake. She did a lot of home baking and Jeck knew where she kept her tins in the pantry.

Jeck boiled the kettle on the cooker ring and brewed himself half-a-pot of tea. After tea he sat and smoked, helping himself from Tina's cigarettes on the mantelshelf. It was warm and cosy in such richly furnished surroundings, with a lush carpet on the floor, and after such a long day on his feet he felt drowsy, almost on the verge of sleep.

Jason had engaged Jeck Knowles as a stockman in this very room, after showing him round the premises and introducing him to Tina. She had lived here with her late mother since Jason took over the Home-farm. Formerly Jason and his wife had lived here with their family, but when their father died Jason became manager of the family estates and moved to the Homefarm, changing places with Tina and their widowed mother, who had since died and Tina now lived here alone.

TWILIGHT VENUS

When Jeck first shook hands with Tina, Jason remarked to him that she had never been married — "though she's had plenty of lads," he added, jokingly: "and if ever ye get tired o' yer wife ye can come along and sleep wi' her:"

Tina said nothing to this but smiled blandly, accustomed apparently to her brother's blustering jokes; perhaps half expecting that the chiel would accept them in a spirit of frivolity, though her white face coloured notably in the lamp light. But Jeck thought she must have turned forty and must by now have realised she was most likely to be left on the matrimonial shelf.

Over the last four years however, from occasional remarks by Jason, and some from the neighbours, a body could gather that in her youth the ebullient Tina had been something of a tomboy; more likely to be seen on the roof of the steading than in her father's parlour, or playing with the cottar loons in preference to the quines, and later with the chaumer chiels rather than with the females of her own age group. In fact Tina had established quite a reputation for herself with the youths of the parish, from farmers' sons and budding auctioneers to tradesmen and seedmen's agents, with the occasional bank clerk thrown in and the odd clergyman in passing.

But not one of them had managed to pin Tina down to domestic bliss, maybe because she was too particular in her choice of a husband — 'Owre ill tae please,' as Jason put it — or because she had always preferred her freedom to being tied up with a man and his bairns. By the time her father died Tina must have known she was at the end of her romantic tether, for her life was then devoted to looking after her ailing mother.

But Tina made no boast of her romantic conquests, nor explained to anyone why they hadn't led to marriage, and if she referred to the subject at all it was in a jocular manner. How she became a spinster was a topic enjoyed by Jason, who made a big joke of it and seemed to delight in making fun of her in front of strangers, a prerogative derived from the fact that he was himself happily married, as were their brothers and sisters, all except Tina, and she became the butt for his flagrant, boisterous, tantalising humour, which poor Tina, as the wayward black ewe of the family accepted without rancour.

Whatever the reason for her spinsterhood Tina still liked the company of menfolk, as Jeck could well testify, though he'd never breathed a word about it to anybody, not even to his wife, for fear he created ill feeling between her and Tina. Jeck minded on that time she had cornered him in the little milkhouse under the water cistern, across

the driveway from the back kitchen door. He was filling the cottars'
flagons just before supper time when she went in after him and closed
the door at her back. There was barely room for the two of them
standing between the shelves, and with Tina between him and the door
Jeck had no escape. The window was a mere peephole in the gable,
covered with gauze, so that nobody could see them, nor open the door
while Tina stood behind it. She had chosen the time and the place
carefully, with about fifteen minutes to spare before the cottars
collected their milk flagons. Jeck was defenceless, with a milk flagon in
one hand and a measure jug in the other, so he just stood there while
Tina kissed him softly on the cheek, her brown eyes searching his face
for some reaction or response. But he just stood there, mystified,
surprised and a little shocked that the sister of his employer could
become so intimate with him. She was so tactful, so tempting, so bold;
and though not really beautiful quite a woman in her way, with quite a
lot to offer a lad of little means if he were anywise inclined to play the
love game with her. With so rich a bait, so much to offer a poor cottar,
Jeck was tempted for a moment to replace the utensils on the shelf and
embrace her. Och it wouldn't matter for a bit kiss in the sly, nobody
would know about it and her lips were rich and ripe, her eyes chasing his
own in a futile orbit.

But where did these things end? This was how they began but the
results could be wretched, and if Jason got wind of it he might sack him
on the spot, in spite of all his buffoonery. And Jeck was a happily
married man with little excuse for yielding to a lovelorn spinster, and
though he tended Tina's garden he was no Lady Chatterly's Lover.

Tina was disappointed and her eyelashes fluttered in her dis-
pleasure. "Are we too old for courting then?" she asked, her hands
itching to lay hold on the tactful Jeck. "I'm sure you're not amiss to a bit
of love-making, even though you are married." Jeck could have said he
thought she might be past it, and how unfair it would be for his wife; but
he just stood there, nonplussed, scarcely knowing what to say to
appease her. "Oh I suppose so," he managed to say at last, thinking of
the risk she was taking and rather sorry for her besides. Tina turned her
back on him and opened the door, then stood for a moment watching
him, perhaps hoping for a snap change of fortune, then left abruptly and
skipped over to the house. Since then she had treated him more
casually but things went on much as before. The odd cup of tea when
Jeck was in the garden, a book to read, a chat on current affairs, the soft
brown eyes watching him always; then a swish of skirts and she would
leave him to his own torment and self discipline.

TWILIGHT VENUS

Since then Tina had been dogged by ill-health: first by a heart enlargement and the removal of two ribs to allow for expansion, and her only lament on this occasion, after extensive surgery, was that she now had a rib less than the menfolk, which hadn't happened since Adam and Eve, and she joked about the loss of her 'Woman's Rib,' which she said had formerly given her a feeling of superiority over the male sex.

She then developed an abdominal cyst which extended her girth prodigiously, when she joked with her friends about being 'in the family way,' and every male who had been enticed into her parlour was whimsically referred to as the father, though Jeck Knowles wasn't included in her catalogue. But those who paid a sympathy call, or out of curiosity, stayed to marvel at her courage in making fun of such a sinister misfortune.

By medical decree Tina was obliged to carry her growth for an allotted period, wherein the doctors deemed it ripe for surgery, a circumstance which enriched the humour of her pregnancy hoax, when Tina would hold her bulging waist line in both hands and laughingly predict the month of her delivery, saying she wouldn't have long to go now, and folk marvelled at her brazen stoicism and lively spirits.

When the surgeons removed the cyst at the infirmary they showed it to Tina and said it weighed twelve pounds, and she added relish to the story by saying it actually had hairs on it, and that she felt no pride in being the mother of this monstrosity — delivered, she joked, by Caeserian means. Fortunately her growth was not malignant and Tina came back from hospital slim as a teenage girl, boasting that the devil himself would be her next male conquest.

But Tina was laid low again, this time by cerebral haemorrhage, and the anxiety was that though she lived she would never be the same effervescent Tina, but more likely a liability to her family, and knowing Tina a body knew she would rather have died.

Again the clock chimed, eleven musical staves and Jeck got up from his chair once more to look at his charge. She still lay motionless in the single bed and the memory of his wife's dream came into his mind. Early that morning, while Jeck was at his brose, his wife told him the alarm clock had awakened her from a strange and rather embarrassing dream, and this would have been about the time that Tina collapsed in the bathroom. His wife said she had dreamed that she was in bed with the farmer, Jason Smith, and though the details were a bit hazy in her mind, she remembered that Jason had behaved in a most respectful and apologetic manner, the two of them trying to figure out how it was that they had come to be in the same bed; whereupon she was awakened by the clock, but determined to tell Jeck about her dream while it was still fresh in her mind. Jeck made fun of it at first and wondered he said what the devil would have got up to if the clock hadn't gone off.

But his wife didn't think it was funny, and neither did Jeck before the day was done, because Jason came to him in the byre just before dinner time and asked if he had a single bed to lend that would hold Tina in the living room, because the doctor didn't want her moved upstairs, and it would save them a lot of trouble in taking her own double bed downstairs.

Jeck went home to consult his wife and told her the riddle of her dream had been answered, and that it was a good thing she told him her dream beforehand or he wouldn't have believed her. He called her a witch, though a pretty one to humour her, and then the two of them set to thinking how they could lend Jason the single bed. Two of their loons had a bed each while the little nipper still slept in a crib, so they would put the two big loons in the double bed and Jason could have the single one, and Jeck said in fun that he didn't deserve it for sleeping with his wife. She slapped his lug for him and said if she had known he was going to make fun of her dream she wouldn't have told him about it, and she warned him not to tell Jason.

Jeck went back to the farm and told Jason he could have the bed and mattress, though he didn't tell him about his wife's dream. Jason went along to the cottar house to collect the single bed and mattress in the boot of his car, and when Jeck's wife saw him she could hardly look at him because of her embarrassing dream.

Jeck looked at the clock again and it was thirty minutes from midnight. He began to yawn from weariness waiting for Jason and sat down in the chair again. He had had a long day.

Then he must have dozed off in the armchair and the reality of the moment took the form of another drama. Somehow he knew Tina was dying and he had gone over to kiss her goodbye. Surely he thought in his dream there could be no harm in it for a dying woman. But it had become a kiss of life and she came alive in his arms, sitting up in bed and staring around her, whereupon Jeck ran to the phone and was reporting her progress to Jason. He was excited about her miraculous recovery, while he watched her from the hall, shouting into the phone:

"Now she has thrown off the blankets. She's coming out of the bed. She's on her feet, a bit shaky but she's holding on to the bed. She's coming over to the phone. You'll hear her in a moment. Here she is ..."

Jason was shouting from the other end of the line. "You've fallen asleep," he cried, and he shook Jeck vigorously into wakefulness. "It doesn't matter anyway, Tina's dead!"

"Poor Tina", was all that Jeck could say, and he got up and looked at her still in the bed, his mind jumbled between a dream and wakefulness.

"I was dreamin' aboot 'er," he told Jason, "I could a sworn I saw her oot o' the bed. It was so real like when ye woke me up."

"Weel maybe she just got up tae go tae heaven, poor soul," Jason said; "she's just newly dead 'cause she's still warm. Ye hav'na neglected her and ye're fair done for want o' sleep. Awa' ye go hame tae yer bed. I'll tak' owre noo but I couldna come sooner."

Jeck took a last look at Tina, bade Jason goodnight and departed. Half-way along the avenue he glanced back in the darkness at the farmhouse, for he was now fully awake in the cold. Jason must have gone upstairs because there was a light in Tina's bedroom. Maybe he was replacing the blankets on Tina's own bed. She wouldn't need them now. The he suddenly wondered: How close was a dream to the supernatural? Had he actually seen Tina's spirit leave her body in the minutes that he slept?

On his way home he had to pass the old cottage where Tina had kept her hens. It was empty now and the windows in darkness but a car was stopped on the road and a man was knocking on the cottage door, a loud hollow knocking that made Jeck's hair stand on end. In the darkness he looked like a man in black, with a Quaker's hat on his head, and long flowing robes like a priest.

But Jeck had seen enough, and he took to his heels and ran to the cottar house where his wife would be waiting. Should he tell her his own dream?

A CHIEL AMONG THEM

WILLIAM ROBBIE

WILLIAM Robbie was born in the parish of Old Deer, in the farming heart of Buchan on August 20th, 1887. He was the seventh of thirteen children born to a farmworker in a three-room croft house. At the age of three he got a box of crayons from Santa Claus and began colouring a menagerie of farm animals. These later developed to cut-out models for a Noah's Ark lay-out, but none of his brothers or sisters shared his enthusiasm. Any artistic talent that the young Robbie may have inherited is said to have come from his mother's side of the family. Moving to Whitehill he attended school at New Deer, where Gavin Greig was headmaster, and between his folk-song collecting he observed the fine art work of his young pupil. He consulted the boy's parents and tried to persuade them to send Willie to art school. They were too poor for this however, and even though dominee Greig offered to help financially they wouldn't accept charity. So Willie slogged on with his own inclination, winning prizes at various Buchan schools for his art work.

On leaving school he had to fee as an orra loon on the farms. Progressing to his first pair of horses he began sketching and painting them in water-colour from the live models. He spent whole week-ends and most evenings at his hobby in the farm chaumers, sometimes by oil-lamp, and when he married he enjoyed the privacy of a cottar house and a public demand for his pictures, by now done in poster colour.

He worked a six-day week of ten hours, besides stable time and relief work on Sundays; holidays were few but those he got were spent at the local agricultural shows, where he developed an undying fascination for the prize horses, especially the Clydesdale breed, which were then the supreme champions on the Buchan farmlands. Ploughing matches were another attraction, but though Robbie was himself by now an expert ploughman he did not participate in the competitions. While most other lads expended their spit and polish in harness rivalry Robbie absorbed himself in getting it down on canvas board.

The Clydesdale for Robbie became almost an obsession, and to the end of his long life he lamented the coming of the tractors that robbed him of the apple of his eye as models for his painting. At the shows these

67

animals were sometimes in full harness regalia, and this was how Robbie painted them; never with a cart or lorry behind them, but always dignified in Sunday dress and paraded in holiday spirit. "My hairt's aye in the Clydesdale horse yet," Robbie mused in later life. "It's a peety that they're dyin' oot. It's a damned shame. The tractors have juist clean spoil't the landscape a'thegither. What wis bonnier than a fairm toon an' twa, three pair o' horse pullin' the ploo, their tails a' tied up?"

But Willie didn't always practice what he preached here, for this was just the picture he seldom indulged in, for the prize Clydesdale had taken possession of his soul. And it was almost purely art for art's sake, for he had been known to say he would have done it for nothing, which he did for a beginning, giving his pictures away to friends, until the demand got on top of him and his materials got more expensive.

"I wid hae deen't supposin' I had niver gotten rid o' one o' them. I had tae paint a Clydesdale horse, simply because they were the finest draught horses in the warld. There wis naething tae beat them."

If Robbie had been asked for a signature tune he would have given it in a snatch of a poem he had by heart from his youth:

> *Captain McDougall has blawn on his bugle,*
> *The Clydesdale he tries tae play doon,*
> *But there's nae a guid callant*
> *Fae Hieland or Lowland*
> *Will rise and dance tae his tune.*

It was the era of horse pride and the harness boom, which became a status symbol on the Lowland fairmtoons at the close of the nineteenth century. Harness had done nothing for the plough-ox, but cart harness on a prize Clydesdale was magnificent, especially when embellished with martingales, rosettes and bunting, and there was great rivalry among the chaumer chiels to excel in this mode of decoration. Married horsemen sometimes took their saddles and horse collars home in the evenings for beetling and polishing, and there is the story of the foreman who was so obsessed with harness cleaning that he had his wife crawl across the kitchen floor with a 'family bible' saddle on her back to see how it looked after a shine.

Ploughing matches were another excuse for burnishing leather and nickel-plate, but as the outfit in plough harness was far less extensive, with less opportunity for exuberance, Robbie seldom adopted it for his pictures. The annual ploughing match was much more a workaday affair compared with the prize-ring at the summer shows. It was a winter exercise with leafless trees and colourless fields and without the sun sparkle to glitter the harness, the antithesis of Robbie's ideas in painting.

Second to the horse, Robbie's theme was the harness, and his styling was magnificent. And with the harness mania thus prevailing it isn't surprising that a Robbie painting got pride of place on the walls of the farming fraternity, and for the cottars to have a picture was almost as urgent as for the farmer to have the real thing — the finest horses and the best harness for miles around. Even in 1980, where old stables still existed you could see the prize certificates where they had been proudly tacked on to the beams above the stalls where the animals stood that earned them. This was the attitude that carried Robbie to success in painting, something that wouldn't have happened if he had attended art school. There was a folk-art about his work that expressed the do-it-yourself- tendency of the farm workers, something that an art training wouldn't have bargained for, and would have glossed over it entirely.

A paradox in Robbie's life is the fact that despite his love for horses he gave up his ploughman's lot in middle life for casual work: ditching, draining, fencing and dyke-building, content to watch the horses from a distance, detached and free as it were to form his own perspective. During the First World War he worked as a railway navvy at Lenabo, but apart from this he had been all his life on the Buchan farms. He had lived a great many years in the farm chaumers, but at the age of forty-one he married Williamina Mundie and went to the cottar market looking for a job. But he resented the purely cottar existence with the tied cottage and preferred to pay a rent, which gave him a better sense of security and more freedom for his art work. Casual work gave him more spare time to paint, especially in his own home, where he could have more privacy than he had in the chaumers; free weekends especially, and in rainy weather he could take a whole day off to paint without much loss financially.

Robbie also disliked the incessant May Term flittings which prevailed with the cottar life. In a rented cottage he imagined that he could stay longer in one place, but as things turned out he moved house quite frequently, perhaps even more often than he would have done as a cottar, whatever the reason, and this is important in Robbie's life because he never dated his pictures. The only way we can ascertain his progress and development as a folk-artist is to know where he lived at a given time, because he always gave the address where the picture was painted under his signature. His first cottage was at Glendaveny, near Tortorston, where he and Mina went to live in 1928, then Cairnhill of St. Fergus, Easterton Barnyards, Howe o' Buchan, Thunderton, Hayfield and Smiddyhill, in that order until his death in 1967.

I first met Willie Robbie in 1935, when I was myself cottared as second dairy cattleman on the farm of Newseat, near Peterhead, farmed at that time by the late Mr. Robert Davidson. Mr. Davidson had just gone in for tuberculin tested milk, one of the very first in Aberdeenshire to do so, and considerable alterations required to be done on the existing byres, such as deepening of the urine channels and the installation of tubular stalls, mostly concrete working, and a new dairy had to be erected adjoining the steading.

A local contractor completed most of the byre work, but Mr. Davidson employed Willie Robbie to build the new dairy, and as the portable cement mixer as we know it was not then in general use he mixed it all by hand, or with a shovel rather, which he did with untiring energy and great dexterity, until he was sure the mixture of cement and sand and water was of the right consistency for brick-laying, or for reinforced concrete and floors.

That was how I met Willie Robbie, in the odd moments between milking times when we had a word with him on the job, me and my workmate, the late Frank Cadger, the head cattleman, who told me that Willie was the man who painted all the horse pictures that were hanging in the cottar houses and the farm mansions.

I went to see Mr. Robbie at his home, a rented cottage on the farm of Easterton Barnyards, near Tortorston, leased from Mr. Tommie Cunningham, as he did not require a worker in it.

I was immediately attracted to Willie's art form, and by his inspired dedication at this period half-way in his career as a folk-artist. I feel almost ashamed to call him an amateur, and yet, considering that he was entirely self-taught it is difficult to pin him down as a professional, although he was earning money from his hobby. I could scarcely

70

believe that this tireless, conscientious labourer could so transform himself from his day's work to the delicate and intricate task he now had before him on the kitchen table, that of putting harness on the pair of Clydesdale horses in his latest picture. He did this by shaping haimes, saddle-crups, hooks, buckles and drag chains from the silver paper he collected from discarded cigarette packets. Willie smoked a pipe and black twist Bogey Roll so he had to look elsewhere for the tinfoil he required. For cutting the silver paper he used a well-sharpened, needle-pointed pen-knife on a glass plate, and as some of these chain links were tiny enough to grace a lady's neck the work was painfully minute. How those work-gnarled hands that grasped a shovel-handle could now relax in such taste and refinement; how they could manipulate the pen-knife with such exactitude on the tinfoil was almost beyond my comprehension. The microscopic silver pieces were picked up with a kirby-hairgrip and gummed on to the harness to simulate nickel-plate and steel dragchains, and in Robbie's painstaking hands the finished mounting had the durability and apparent strength it was intended for.

Robbie did all his painting on the kitchen table. Before that, as one chaumer visitor put it: "His easel was the lid o' his kist, and the room was dimly lit by the flickering flame of a smelly paraffin lamp from the inside of a farm lantern." He never had an easel or a palette and he mixed his pigments in an empty water-colour box. With a talent like Robbie's these refinements are not essential; they are useful but they don't make the artist. That comes from the life-force of the man or woman who undertakes it. His pictures were in great demand, so great I imagined, that had he increased his prices and gone full-time he could have supported his wife and son and thrown away the shovel. But Robbie was the patient, slogging artist, and even though his pictures were selling abroad perhaps he feared that saturation would stifle local demand. This was something he needn't have worried about, for although he lived to be an octogenarian, and was still painting, later in oils, his pictures were still very keenly sought after, especially by visiting tourists.

In 1914 his pictures sold for half-a-crown, later increased to five shillings, then to seven shillings and sixpence in 1924. This was still the price when I met him but he said he never liked to charge a cottar body more than five shillings. They were hanging on the walls all over

71

Buchan, on farm, croft and cottar house, and eventually they were much sought after at roups and auction sales. Nowadays they can be seen in the 'Harness Room' or 'Hayloft' lounges in Buchan hotels and have become more or less collectors' pieces.

On that first visit to Willie Robbie I found his cottage in a state of ordered chaos. There were pictures in all stages of execution, propped on sideboard and dresser, and ben in the 'room' they were stanced on chairs and chiffonier, besides the requisite materials for their completion, awaiting the mood and pleasure of the artist.

I asked Willie for a picture, which he agreed to paint for me, and I got his nephew, Louis Robbie, who was a carpenter at Inverugie, to frame it. But it was a special picture and almost a new experiment for Robbie, that of painting cows along with the customary pair of horses. Because I had just begun work as a dairy cattleman I asked Willie if he could put a cow or two in the picture. This he did with remarkable naturalness, with five brightly coloured Ayrshire cows in the middle distance of my picture, the usual pair of stolid Clydesdales removed slightly to one side to make room for them. This picture now remains unique in Robbie's repertoire, and he said it would cost me the full seven shillings and sixpence because of the extra work involved.

I had great pride in my picture, but somehow I felt it was jinxed, because every time we moved house the glass was broken. After several flittings reframing began to loosen the tinfoil harness decoration and I gave it to a friend who touched it up and restored it better than I could have done. The last I heard of this hallmark in Robbie's career it was hanging in Peterhead Academy art class.

There has been criticism of Robbie's horses in that they lack spirit and mobility. They are perfect in bodily form, in the prime of physical condition; princely, majestic, noble creatures, the pride of the showman's eye, yet too severe and statuesque in presentation, like standing to attention at an inspection parade. Muscle anatomy is apparent in Robbie's later pictures, once he had started in oils, graduating from water-colour and poster media. This is particularly noticeable in his single stallions, which are the epitome of equestrian grace, painted on request for eager tourists, and for members of the Agricultural Societies. Formerly his horses had been strictly two-dimensional, flat on the surface and almost part of the background on which they were painted, an integrated still-life grandeur which robbed them of life and virility.

Strictly speaking Robbie's horses were assembly-line produced from stencils cut out beforehand and laid on the canvas board for tracing, while he sketched in the background accordingly, before he started to paint. He could cut out these stencils blindfold, without any preliminary outline, and he would use them for several months on succeeding pictures. Had the process of print-making been more popular in Robbie's day it would have saved him a lot of repetitive work and because he never employed it every Robbie painting is an original.

Apart from colour the horses were always the same, the stolid mantelpiece ornaments that dominated the picture, though sometimes facing the other way; mostly a pair of dapple-greys, or the dapple-grey in front, the dun or chestnut at the back, but slightly forward for harness display, always in pairs, their heads and legs in symmetrical alignment. This uniformity saved time and effort in supplying demand, because to vary design would have taken longer, though I am surprised that such a painstaking artist made no attempt at individual pose for his animals. But of course everything was sacrificed for the harness exhibition, which demanded regimentation in this shop-window dressing, even to the ribbons and pennants frozen in the wind.

The horses were never seen in the stackyard, which is surprising, because corn-stacking was another art and prestige of the horse era, worthy of Robbie's admiration. Nor did you ever see them at the stable door or over the watering trough, their domesticated habitat, nor in front of the cart-shed pillars. They were always stanced in a position of grandeur, mostly at the entrance of the drive to the Home Farm, or near the garden gate at the front of the house, with the inevitable blocked dyke and pillared gateway and white spiked iron fence, the green lawn showing behind the railings and sloping towards the farm buildings. Robbie liked depth and distance in his painting, but his picture was so full of itself that there was no room for the sky. This was especially noticeable in his earlier work, until he widened his scope, but despite this there was no appearance of crowding and his perspective was always to scale.

Robbie's backgrounds were varied and elaborated in sylvan splendour, the farmhouse and steading always different, though mostly a 'laird's toon' in preference to the pedestrian croft, somewhere worthy of the breeding of the sturdy horses in the foreground of the picture. Robbie had the most luxuriantly landscaped fairmtoons in Buchan, dream-like almost in their serene beauty, with sometimes a mill-dam or a bridge arching a stream. In his later work he was careful to avoid the emergence of the factory farm, the Dutch barns and the electric pylons, though it is surprising that he never gave us a smoke stack or a silo in his earlier work, as these innovations were contemporaneous with the horse era. Nor did he ever paint a horse picture in a russet scene of autumn glory, or with horse footprints in the snow, no budding trees and daffodils in springtime, but always high summer with gilding sunshine and a verdant greenery.

Yet I loved Robbie's backgrounds, and his trees and woods and farmsteads were exquisitely beautiful. What he seemed to fill in from mere necessity was to me his hallmark, warm with his own personality, a vision of horticultural serenity from his heart's desire. For me the horses got in the way of something approaching a Landseer or a Constable in pastel shade. Sometimes I felt that Robbie lavished his talent for too long on the same subject, horses, and this became more evident in his later years when he resorted to landscape work and dabbled in oils and pigments.

You could say that Robbie's horses, splendid as they are, were the price we had to pay for Robbie's backgrounds, yet the background was merely an excuse for painting the horses. Without the horses we would have had no Willie Robbie, because from his earliest years the sight of a show horse had dominated his imagination. Yet in his equestrian greatness there is strength but no motive power. It was only in advanced age that he yoked his horses to a plough, taking the strain of the yoke, with a ploughman between the stilts on a golden stubble field. Previously it had seemed below their dignity to pull a plough or to muddy their snow-white fetlocks, and they had always been standing on a gravel path that revealed their iron heels and toe-bars, almost their shoenails. In this period of his work his world was purely theatrical and artificial, and as this comprises the bulk of his effort, so he will be judged, purely as an amateur artist.

I sometimes wonder if Robbie's regimentation was a workaday lack of imagination or if it was a latent stubborness to conform; to emerge from the showground cocoon of his experience and the prime source of his inspiration. Another thing that surprises me about Robbie was that he never imitated his greatest rivals, the late Victorian photographers. While Robbie was painting his isolated pairs of Clydesdales those gentlemen were setting up their tripod cameras in front of whole teams of horses, three or four pairs at a fairmtoon, sometimes with the odd pair of harnessed oxen, with the horsemen and chaumer chiels in attendance, hand tools and brose caups on display, the kitchie quines sitting on the grass, and maybe the farmer and his wife at the end of the line. This was all in black and white of course, but if Robbie had captured it in colour he would have been the doyen of North-east artists, ranking with James McBey or Joan Eardley, Archibald Edgar or Joseph Farquharson, or even with Spanish Philip in his royal robes. But the human element is strikingly absent in Robbie's painting, and whereas the photographed horses are mostly facing the camera Robbie's horses were always in profile; a side-on view to give full justice to the harness. A full-frontal would have denied Robbie much of the tinsel decoration, which for many years absorbed his genius. The showground Clydesdale in his pristine glory was the embodiment of his art; the Clydesdale on holiday, with no concession to the notions of travelling cameramen, who were also keen on doing binder teams in the harvest fields.

The next time I visited Robbie he was living at Smiddyhill, within whistle-blow of Inverugie station. By then he was an old man and the horse pictures had given way to Highland scenery on the ben-room table, while stanced on the chairs were beautiful vistas with deer and long-horned russet cattle painted in oils. Even then he confessed to me that he sometimes regretted not having gone to art school in his youth, on the grounds that it might have been a short-cut in his experiments with mixing oil colours and pigmentation, all of which he had to learn for himself the hard way. Failing eyesight had forced him to discard the tinfoil in favour of metallic silver paint in harness decoration. In the gradual disappearance of the workhorse he wasn't so interested in country shows. He went more often to visiting circuses, purely for the joy of watching the performing horses and ponies. Equestrian action for Robbie was poetry in motion, that language of the mind that borders on ecstasy, yet it was not until his later years that he transferred this animation to his painting. But though horses still filled his mind they no longer monopolised his painting. His scenic work at this stage was entrancing, and his translucent, flower-petal colouring transported the mind to ecstatic realms beyond mortal bounds. One feels that art training would have helped Robbie to achieve this dimension much earlier in his career, and would have widened his scope materially.

For the sake of argument however, it must be said that the lack of training gave Robbie an originality which can only be described as hymnal; a conception of all things bright and beautiful, with the warm sun directly overhead, casting no shade on horses, trees or buildings. This lack of shadow may have been coincidence in his early work, but fifty years on he was aware of it but didn't change his high noon perception of reality, not even in his pictorial work. By then his method had become an inborn tradition that brightened his pictures, when shadow would have dulled his reputation and perhaps his sales. Buchan life had enough of shadow and his customers appreciated the romantic idealism of Robbie's pictures. "I'm tryin' to give them a bright-lookin' scene. You could mak' it a dull, drab scene ... but the brighter you mak' it, the bonnier the picture." So we may assume that the glamour was an intended impregnation in Robbie's painting; perhaps an introvert McGonagallism which few professional artists would dare to imitate, and I sincerely mean that as a compliment to his excellence. There are several Buchan artists who have copied Robbie's style but none have reached his brilliance, or his idyllic harmony.

Robbie was a shy modest person and he made no attempt to exhibit his work. He was the uncultured, primitive artist who shunned publicity. I tried to persuade him to get his pictures hung in the gallery of the Arbuthnot Museum in Peterhead, but he shied away from my suggestion. Edie Swan, one time art teacher at Peterhead and Ellon Academies and later associated with His Majesty's Theatre in Aberdeen, tried to arrange an exhibition of Robbie's paintings, but this also floundered. Kenneth S. Goldstein, the American folklorist, interviewed Robbie in January, 1960, and wrote an appreciation of his work for Chapbook, Scotland's Folk-Life magazine, and at the School of Scottish Studies, Edinburgh University, we can still hear Robbie's voice on the tapes Goldstein recorded. Otherwise a great cloud hangs over Robbie's life, casting a shadow he never allowed to invade his art work.

Colour television would have done him credit but he died on the fringe of it. He still cycled to town but never drove a car. He resorted to painting lush Highland scenery but he never had the joy of seeing the original of his sites. He was content to have them on colour post-cards and from the glossy travel magazines. He began to substitute the horses with Highland cattle, deer and sheep, and some of these he had from the farming journals. Highland ponies were conspicuously absent from these paintings, and one wonders if Robbie would have considered their inclusion as a retrograde step in his maturity. Had he been a younger man in our modern car-conscious society he may have roamed the hills with sketch-pad and camera, seeking out that which most appealed to him, rather than accept it second-hand from ready-made sources. But Robbie was unique in that the camera never drove him to abstract work; to caricature, the burlesque or the cartoon, for although the farm horse had disappeared he still retained it in memory. But he liked the animal world of Walt Disney, and one wonders just how Robbie would have represented it.

He once told me that he used to complete a horse picture in two evenings, but allowing for his off periods, and he did have these, we would allow him one picture a week in over forty years of painting, in which time he produced something over two thousand pictures. Latterly he raised the price of a horse painting to one pound, average size of twelve by fourteen inches. He did much bigger scenic views by request, and also miniatures, and he still indulged himself in his favourite cut-out horse models in fretwork, and the occasional wall plaque, using wood-putty or plaster-of-paris as moulding in shaping his animals in bas-relief on a wooden base, mostly painted in oils. In his advanced years Robbie preferred oils to water-colouring because working in oils allowed for mistakes. "Ye canna afford tae mak' mistakes wi' water paints, ye canna paint ower them as ye might wi' poster colours or oils." The harnessed porcelain horses now in the shops would have driven Robbie out of fashion, or to stucco or plasticene modelling, but I fear that the very authentic plastic harness and simulated chain work would have beaten him.

Robbie retired from manual work at the age of sixty-eight. Two years later he was persuaded to take up the brush again after a lapse of sixteen years, from the war years in 1942, when he had been so much preoccupied on outside duties that he stopped painting completely, his longest fallow period. In retirement he devoted himself almost entirely to his art; when he wasn't eating or sleeping he was painting, and in this period he achieved a flowering maturity that wasn't observed in his earlier work, especially in his landscape and scenic painting. Visitors to the cottage at Smiddyhill were frequent, either to discuss his work or purchase a painting for framing, for by now he had become a legend and his name a byword among the local students of art. He even had the occasional evening of card-playing with friends and neighbours, probably as a diversion from the intensity of his art study, but apart from this there was no social life to speak of outside the home. It was an Indian Summer close to Robbie's life which was sadly blurred by the recurrent illness of his wife, his devoted partner for forty years, but now in need of his care and attention, so that he frequently laid his brushes aside to look after her and to catch up with the house work.

His beloved Mina died on March 10th, 1967, and Willie followed her a month later on April 4th, at the age of eighty-one, heart-broken it is said, with no desire to continue life without her. He is survived by his son, also William Robbie, but alas without the painting instinct to carry on the work of his father. Robbie the artist was a kenspeckle figure, typical of his work-grained generation, his features lit by a tolerant smile against life and its set-backs, with pleasant eyes that twinkled from a pattern of wrinkles and crow's-feet, a generous moustache and rather protruding ears, slim in build and of average height, and always wore a jaunty, wide-fitting cap, ordinary suit, work-a-day shirt with collar and tie.

William Robbie lies buried with his wife and the daughter they lost in infancy in the cemetery at Longside. He is at rest among the friends and neighbours for whom he painted his beloved Clydesdales, the tinselled pictures which still adorn the walls of so many Buchan homes. The tractors plough to the very dykes of the graveyard, but their chugging no longer disturbs the sleep of the artist who dreaded their coming to his native farmlands.

THE PLOUGHING MATCHES

The winter ice is breakin' up,
The wast wind whistlin' cracks his whup,
An' noo ye hear their "Hi! woa! h'up!"
(Pleasant the hearin'!)
As plooman-lads wi' steady grup
Draw oot their feering'.

J. Logie Robertson

WOULD anybody be sober enough nowadays to take part in a ploughing match on New Year's morning? In the old days of horse ploughing very few could afford to get drunk on Hogmanay, least of all the ploughmen, and if they did they had only one day for a hangover — New Year's Day, the day of the tradesmen's ploughing match.

This was something quite apart from the regular or professional ploughing competitions, and being a general holiday the event was arranged by the farming committees for the convenience of the tradesmen. It was a trial of skill in which the boldest amateur could participate, including the village blacksmith, the joiner, the miller, the saddler, the shoemaker, the tailor, the watchmaker, the baker, the grocer and the butcher, and even the postman; but as the bulk of these men had started their working lives as farm servants, or very near to the land, they weren't exactly amateurs. So the semi-professionals borrowed a plough and horse team from any obliging farmer, and sometimes the foreman to 'set' or adjust their ploughs, a very important factor in winning these competitions. Mostly they had to accept everyday harness, which was dull compared with what the regulars would turn out with, and the teams were less colourful on the plough-rigs.

The regular matches of course were another matter, when harness pride dominated the competitive spirit. The horses on these occasions were adorned with their best Sunday harness: high-peak studded collars and 'Glasgow-Pike' haimes (the steel frame with hooks that fitted on to the collar to hold the drag-chains) and mostly open bridles were used, as opposed to 'blin' or blind bridles with eye-shields, which prevented a spirited horse from seeing what was coming behind it, or what it was pulling. There was no saddle or britchen in plough harness, only a leather strap over the backs of the horses to carry the 'theets' or drag-chains attached to the plough yokes. The britchen was the leather contraption hooked to the saddle and slung over the hindquarters and used as a brake, when an animal could use his weight in holding back a loaded cart on a brae. Town cart horses were mostly docked to prevent the tail stump from being crushed in the locking-bar of a cart when toppled. But a great many farm horses (unless they had been bought in the town) had a full length tail stump, sometimes with the rich black hair tied up in the height of fashion, like the farm wife or the kitchie deem, and bedecked with raffia or coloured ribbon. In one of the bothy ballads it is given the other way round, the kitchen lass being blamed for flirting with the lads;

> *Wi' her hair tied up like my horse tails*
> *Tae charm a' the lads at the Fornet.*

Mane rolling was another fad, again using the tri-colour, red, white and blue raffia to hold the plaited hair in position, and because of the time it took for this accomplishment it was usually done the evening before the ploughing match. Fetlocks were washed in soft soap and brushed dry until they shone like white beards, and hoofs were painted with melted down harness blacking or linseed oil. White ear-muffs, rosettes, martingales, bunting and pennants completed the regalia, and all this preparation counted as points with the judges when they allocated prizes for the best groomed pair of horses and for the best kept harness. Two or three judges presided, experts who were chosen by the committee from outside the parish, men whom they trusted would not be prejudiced against the competitors, either in ploughing or harness rivalry.

Before the days of mechanised transport the plough teams contrived in various ways to reach the field of contest. Competitors from neighbouring farms slipped a two-wheeled skid or 'ploo-hurlie' with a slot for the plough-sock, under their ploughs and took their team on the road to the fields. On reaching the gate they slipped off the hurlie and slid their plough on the share-board over the grass to the plough-rig. Those from further afield loaded their ploughs on a cart, with a saddled horse pulling it, the other plodding behind on a lead. On reaching the field the plough was unloaded and the saddle was replaced with plough harness on the cart horse, the odd horse brought forward, and the pair of them yoked to the plough. Two competitors sometimes shared the same cart, with two ploughs loaded on it, the second ploughman leading his team.

Each man drew a ticket at the gate from Hilly's hat, a slip of paper marked with the corresponding number of a 'rig' or ploughing area, the luck of the draw, which gave fair play to each competitor, whether he landed on a rocky ridge or in a soft or 'spootie howe', or on a rig with a blind summit, so that he couldn't see both ends of his furrows, an obstacle to straight ploughing. Mostly a good level field was chosen, but with charity matches this wasn't always possible, when the committee had arranged a match for some unfortunate brother farmer who, either from ill-health or misfortune had fallen behind with his ploughing. They also afforded the prize money, either from their own pockets or from any existing provident fund, and for the same charitable reasons the scheme was sometimes extended to include hoeing matches in high summer.

The handicaps thus taken care of each man proceeded to 'prop' or tape his 'feering' or first-furrow, so that he could see a straight line ahead of him between his horses, guiding them by the reins accordingly (which was more difficult than steering a tractor) and throwing a shallow guide-line furrow to start with, and setting another light furrow against it on the way back; then ploughing both ways, up one side and down the other until he met his neighbouring competitors on either side, when each would close or 'scale out' a 'midse' or meeting furrow which united the ploughing areas.

It wasn't always possible at ploughing matches, but in ploughing generally, and wherever possible the feerings were raised on old midses, which were unavoidably hollow, and as the feerings were slightly higher than the general level of ploughing, this process over a number of years sustained a reasonably flat surface for subsequent cultivation. The same applied to field verges, when throwing a furrow against the dyke and throwing it away the next year kept down the level of the earth; otherwise, when the field was in grass the cattle would have leapt the dykes. A narrow yoke was used so that a plough horse could get as near the dyke as possible, for there was no wastage on arable land, and corners that couldn't be reached by the plough were dug with a spade. But of course the end-rigs were never ploughed at the matches, but were tidied up afterwards, and 'gushet neuks' or triangular corners were avoided.

The average depth of ploughing was from six to eight inches and prizes were awarded for the lowest feerings and the shallowest midses, or when the first and last furrows were least distinguishable from the rest of the ploughing, and for furrows with ridges sharp enough to cut a crow's feet on frosty mornings. Nowadays of course, with the modern reversible tractor ploughs, which swivel over and plough both ways, these horse-era feerings and midses have been abandoned, though they are still used with the early one-way tractor ploughs.

Each man ploughed on average about half-an-acre, and in the short light of a winter's day he was allowed about three hours to complete his area, with a short mid-break for a bottle of beer and a bap, supplied by the committee. Upwards of twenty teams took part, and if a plough-man hadn't finished his rig when the referee blew his whistle he was disqualified, or liable to be so, depending on the leniency of the judges. The weather of course, had an influence on the state of the ground, and if the match had been preceded by heavy rain or severe frost it could be a deciding factor for the individual, and was sometimes considered by the judges. Postponement because of a snow storm or icy roads was not uncommon, and ploughing matches in lashing rain were not well attended.

Another barrier to the prize list was leaving tufts of grass sticking up between the furrows, and as the competitions were invariably held on old lea this was liable to happen. For this hazard competitors were allowed to 'trail a ball', which helped to bury the grass, and scarifiers were carried on the beam, a sort of miniature plough which assisted in shaping the furrow. Cutting wheels were also permitted, and when properly adjusted on the beam buckle they carried the plough to some extent and maintained a uniform depth.

That the cutting wheel was an advantage can be observed in the bothy ballad THE GUISE O' TOUGH, as sung by John Mearns and the late Willie Kemp.

THE PLOUGHING MATCHES

The new ploo she pleased me, she pleased me unco weel,
But I thocht she wid be better gin she had a cuttin' wheel.
Tum a hie dum do
Tum a hie doo dae
Hie dum doo
Tum a hie doo dae.

Latterly, because of improvement in plough design, results were
judged in two distinct classes, the swing-plough and the longboard
sections. The swing or sock-plough was an improvisation on the old
oxen or wooden plough, while the feather-and-moveable-point long-
board meant less wear and tear and smaller blacksmith's accounts,
besides throwing a deeper and heavier furrow. It was generally
accepted that you graduated from the primitive sock-plough to the
more sophisticated long-board division, but there was a championship
in both classes.

The first prize of five pounds and the championship cup was
awarded for the overall straightest furrow, the best turned furrow, best
feering and midse, with runners-up to sixth position in smaller awards,
and individual prizes for feering, midse and furrow down the line. After
the grooming and harness judging the prizes were then downgraded to
the ploughman with the biggest family, a weekend hamper of butcher
meat, and I have heard of the odd packet of contraceptives. There was
also a consolation award for the best-looking ploughman, a mirror or
shaving kit, and a bar of soap for the man with the dirtiest face, but
would have been more appropriate for the man with the dirtiest hands,
especially among the tradesmen, who were allowed a helper who
padded or shaped the furrow ridges where there were wrinkles or signs
of grass, a practice the judges winked at but didn't disqualify. Another
concession the tradesmen enjoyed was an evening meal and a dram at
the local 'Arms' hotel after the day's work, while the regulars had to be
content with their bap and bottle of beer.

But the biggest ferlie at any Buchan ploughing match was the day
that the tink from nowhere lifted the cup as champion. Nobody knew
where he came from and he gave his name as Donald McPhee. He
arrived with his old sock-plough on a float and did everything himself.
His horses were tatty and unkempt, his harness held together with bits
of wire and binder twine, but his ploughing was of such excellence that

the judges couldn't ignore him. Spectators crowded to admire his rig of polished furrows gleaming in the sunlight, but not a word could they get out of him. He vanished as he had appeared, a complete mystery, and he handed back the cup, accepting only the money as his prize. The only ones who had cause to rejoice were those of the Peter Jamieson brigade, the harness fanatics, nicknamed after a very popular brand of black leather polish.

But not for me the tradesmen's ploughing match on New Year's Day. Not because I was drunk but because I considered it too much of a busman's holiday. I never was a ploughman anyway. I was a stockman, and my New Year's Day off was far too precious to be spent on watching something I saw on a smaller scale every day of the week. So I was off on my bike to the Regal Cinema to see Walter Huston as RHODES OF AFRICA, or Robert Donat as THE YOUNG MR. PITT, as far as I could possibly get from the cow's tail. Yet if I hadn't been like this, with a wider world of interest than the parochial ploughing match, whereby I sought to enlighten myself, I should never have written about them. The world is full of paradoxes, for apart from the prize list in the local press, very few that I know of have ever elaborated on this department of social history in agriculture.

THE FEEING MARKETS

I am often asked about the feeing markets. Were they really like the slave markets of ancient Rome — or those of the African slave traders? Well, of course they were a legacy of the feudal system, instituted by William the Conqueror after the Norman Conquest, but they differed from the slave markets in that the price agreed upon for your services was your own in hard cash at the end of the Term, not paid to an owner-master for the possession of your body. The feeing market was a hiring fair, not an auction mart. The prospective farmer-master paid for your work, besides providing bed and board for single men, houses for married men, and there was no third party arrangement.

Conditions on some of the farms were as menial and sordid as they were for the slaves in the American Deep South; in some cases even worse, barring the use of the whip, with food at the barest minimum of existence, and sanitation non-existent. Sometimes there was an intimacy between the slave families and their masters which was seldom reached among Scottish farm workers and their employers. Married men were less at the mercy of the capricious farm wife (though not all of them were capricious), having their wives to cook for them, but a single man could terminate his dissatisfaction at the end of a six-month Term, while a married man was engaged for a year. And of course, the system worked both ways, as there were faults on either side, and if a farmer wasn't pleased with your services he had to put up with it for the same period.

What I must make clear is that the prerogative of engagement was entirely with the farmer. You didn't ask him for a job — it just wasn't done — he asked *you* if you wanted employment. You didn't go to the feeing markets and badger the farmers for work. You just stood around and waited, perhaps all day, depending on the demand for workers, until one of them offered you a job, and sometimes none of them did, in which case you applied to the advertisement columns in the papers, which was common practice by the time the markets went out.

You could be perfectly satisfied on a farm and have to leave at the end of a six-month Term because the farmer never asked you to stay on, and you never asked him why. To have done so would have been considered the height of bad manners; a sort of unwritten law that was strictly adhered to, and you sometimes left a place with no idea of what you had done or had not done to please your master, perhaps a man you held in good esteem, yet he was not obliged to explain to you the reason for your wordless dismissal.

Sometimes it reached your ears through the staff grapevine, if somebody was in the know, or in the confidence of the farmer, especially the grieve in charge, and if he was open-minded he might hint on the sly why you had to go. But then again he could be the reason for your dilemma, in that he didn't appreciate your efforts; maybe you didn't get up in the morning, or he didn't like your manner or behaviour, or even your looks, in which case he could whisper to the farmer and he would ignore your services at the next feeing time.

Of course the grieves themselves were subject to the same conditions, and could even be undermined or superseded by an informer in the staff, depending on the nature of the farmer, but being slightly further up the scale the engagement of grieves was a more private affair and free from insubordinate interference.

So, if you hadn't been asked to stay on at a farm at the end of a Term you went to the market to seek new employment. You could go in any case, whether you were staying on or not, merely indicating to the grieve or farmer that you would be taking the day off, and you could make a holiday of it and never go near the market, as many did, since everybody was entitled to the day off, if not the market day then any other day of your choice. After all, the farmer couldn't have everybody away at the market and nobody at home to attend to the animals, especially if he was going himself to look for men.

Married or cottar men had only one market day a year, held in early April, whereas single men were entitled to two market days, one in mid May, the other in mid November, two weeks before the respective Term days, on the 28th day of these months, when you began or ended employment on the farms.

Feeing markets were held at places in the centre of agricultural communities, in villages like Longside, Ellon, Maud, Strichen, Turriff, Keith and Alford. There was even a feeing market for single men, held in Aberdeen at the Castlegate and known as Muckle Friday Fair. It was mostly a dual-purpose affair for the farmers. They paid their accounts to the seedsmen and implement agents, who had offices in the Green and Hadden Street nearby and new business contracts were discussed. After or between times the farmers had their dram and canvassed the market for likely candidates to drive their horse teams or attend to their cattle.

As a servant you would mix with the crowd, hoping that some farmer would stop and ask, "Are ye lookin' for a fee, laddie?", in which case you would answer "Aye" or "No", as the occasion demanded, because the farmer had no other way of knowing your circumstances. Sometimes a farmer would recommend your services to another farmer and you got a job that way.

There was never much to spend on a market day. After your bus or train fare you couldn't afford to buy your dinner, and there weren't many farmers who offered you a cup of tea. It was nearly six months since you had your last pay packet, and at the Term you would have accounts to settle with the draper, tailor and shoemaker, and you would have to pay your mother for your washing, though she never asked anything for your weekend keep on your Sundays off from the farm. Married men were paid monthly, but apart from a wee dram and a sweetie for the bairns they never spent much.

About the only money you could spend was the arles you got from a farmer as bargain money, mostly half-a-crown, though the meanest of them would give you a shilling, which was the same as you got from the recruiting sergeant (the King's shilling) if you joined the Army, and they were always present at the feeing markets, on the lookout for dissatisfied farm workers. Some lads got drunk on their arles money, and as the afternoon wore on the markets became more lively.

Between the market day and the Term, if you had heard bad reports of the farmer you had engaged to (and sometimes you did) and you then decided you wouldn't go near the place, either because the food was poor or the grieve was a tyrant, you were supposed to return the arles money, either in person or by sending a postal order, though most lads never bothered and looked for another place unscrupulously. It happened to me only once and I was honest and made it official by returning the money.

One way of getting another chance of employment was to go into Aberdeen on the Friday after the Term, known as Rascal Friday, where the lads (and lasses) who had run away from their new places in the first week could still find employment, provided you were prepared to run the risk of being speired at by a rascal farmer, for the system worked both ways.

A CHIEL AMONG THEM

I never in my time saw women at these markets, though before my day they say it was quite common. The kitchie quines were mostly engaged through the newspapers, when their prospective mistresses had an opportunity to interview the girls personally, and I have never heard of the farmer's wife going to the feeing markets.

The system died with what was known as the 'Stand Still Order', issued by the Coalition Government during the Hitler War to ensure an efficient work force on the land, and only by special permission at tribunal level were you allowed even to move from one farm to another, which made quite a mockery of the old feeing markets.

After the war, when the Order was rescinded, the long-term engagements were never revived. Free engagements with a one month's notice of termination on either side was adopted by all and sundry and it sounded the death knell of the feeing markets. And heaven be praised for that. Men stayed longer on their respective farms, freed from the compulsion of the Term flittings.

Besides the feeing markets there was always the employment registry, where for five-shillings you could have your name inserted for a job. The most legendary of these was Mother Cameron's in Aberdeen's King Street. The farmers consulted Mother Cameron, and if she had someone in her ledger that suited an individual employer she arranged an interview. If a bargain was struck she charged the farmer an equivalent sum. She tried to be fair and forthright with both parties, and from long experience she had an almost intimate knowledge of her clients.

She was still on the job in the sixties, and the last man I remember who got a fee at Mother Cameron's was sitting on a chair when the farmer came in.

"He's nae verra big when he staun's up," she pointed out, well aware that most farmers preferred a hefty chiel. The farmer looked at the lad in the chair, and contrary to expectations he remarked: "Och but that doesna matter sae much nooadays wuman, we've got a' sizes o' them ootby!"

FARMING ON BALL-BEARINGS

PERHAPS the most drastic changes over the last century are to be found in agriculture. In the old days of the horse plough and broadcast sowing of grain, narrow ploughing was favoured on the assumption that 'the mair seams the mair lice', a pun I think that the Scottish soldiers of the First World War brought back with them from the trenches, referring to the lice in the seams of their kilts.

Deeper and wider tractor ploughing, with heavy discs and powerful rotovators to make a deeper tilth for drill sowing has changed all that. The horse harrows merely scratched the surface and the broadcast grain trickled into the sharp narrow furrows, to be covered up by repeated harrowing and a flatten out with the rollers, whereas the modern tractor-drill can complete the operation at one go, except perhaps for a final 'straik' with the light harrows to smooth the surface, and this operation can even include manure distribution, before the final rolling, so that the 'lice' are plentiful without the seams.

The Spring harrowing in the old days was indeed a 'harrowing' exercise for the horsemen in the fields. Some of them dreaded it, because it had to be done on foot, day after day behind the horses, sometimes for weeks on end, on soft ground, a great many acres, so that a man walked hundreds of miles in a season, criss-crossing the fields four or five times, once before the corn was sown and three or four times afterwards. I have heard of a man harrowing until the blood was oozing from the lace holes of his boots, and I myself have walked behind the harrows until my legs were like to crumple under me, and it was a tiring time for the horses too.

But there was an irritation worse than all this that began between the thighs, at the lower end of the split in the buttocks, which eventually became so raw and painful that a man couldn't walk, like bleeding piles (haemorrhoids). In the absence of modern palliatives the old-fashioned cure for this was to smear the irritation with the slime from the inside stem of a docken, that uncivilized member of the rhubarb family, to sooth the inflamation, which perhaps gives the etymology of the humble dock, if not the origin of its botanical name *docce*.

Another remedy was to insert a 'bool' or marble into the groove of the buttocks at the lower end to keep the hips apart. I assure you it was no laughing matter, and of the two remedies the bool was the more satisfactory, with longer lasting assuagement, which was far more important than the embarrassment of inserting it. A man could stride on behind the horse harrows for a whole afternoon without discomfort with a bool in his arse, except from the knowledge that he was on ball-bearings, or lubricated by the juice of a docken.

This is something that our modern tractormen have never experienced, and shows the importance of reduced harrowing methods where the old ploughmen were concerned. But those chiels had no waistline problems, whereas the greatest danger facing tractormen is that of falling asleep in the etherized atmosphere of their cabs, especially while rolling silage pits, which can almost be described as subconscious suicide, moreso when wearing ear-muffs.

Our century has achieved almost the ultimate in revolutionary harvest operations, from the sickle and flail to the combine-harvester, and unless we can supersede natural propagation, which is hardly feasible in widespread field germination, we cannot go much further in this direction. The aim now must be to eradicate the spread of weeds which the combine-harvester has encouraged, and this may be accomplished over a period of time with appropriate weedkiller spray. The old barn mills riddled the ranch seed into a box, which could be emptied on waste ground, where the birds and the weather played havoc with the heap, and some people even burned it. The combine-harvester riddles the seed back on the stubble as it moves along, where the seeds are unavoidably ploughed in for future germination, and this is the problem farmers have to solve.

It is indeed ironic that weedkillers have been less efficient than manual efforts in cleaning the fields, and this has become more evident with continued manpower depopulation over the years. No amount of mechanical spraying has so far matched the hoe in cleaning a turnip crop, which in recent years has become a disgrace compared with the efforts of our grandfathers. But the combine-harvester is the culprit, and a method of preventing the redistribution of weed seed by this machine will have to be mastered. In every other respect the combine is now our best answer to inclement harvests, and progress in this method may remain static for the next hundred years, which was about the period of time enjoyed by the binders.

Emancipation in the purification of milk in our century has been the most beneficial factor in public health improvement ever experienced.

FARMING ON BALL-BEARINGS

Consider that, until I was in my early twenties, as with everyone else in my age group, every cupful of raw milk we drank was liable to be rank with tuberculine bacteria. With every mouthful we ran the risk of contracting the dreaded tuberculosis which was crowding the sanatoriums with incurable cases.

Survival of the fittest was a process of immunisation over the centuries like the emergence of the myxomotosis free rabbit. But the price in human mortality was stupendous, like that of the smallpox epidemics which have now been curbed, or even the plagues of the Middle Ages, terminating life prematurely to millions over the years before pasteurisation, which has emptied the tuberculosis hospitals in our own time.

Those who were fond of drinking raw milk suffered most, while those who preferred it cooked were protecting themselves unconsciously. It was as simple as that, though nobody knew it, and boiling was the answer in killing the lurking tuberculi. Now the daily pinta is delivered in the thermostatically sealed bottle for all to enjoy without risk of infection, thanks to the persevering spirit of pioneering science in the service of suffering mankind.

A crofter with one cow, if she carried the disease, was poisoning his family with every milking. Now he is healthier with a pint at the road end, delivered from the pasteurisation centre in the city, pooled from attested herds scientifically protected from the contagion throughout the country; and the same applies to brucellosis, that other scourge of the bovine world to which man is susceptible.

The cottar was also at risk, supplied with milk from the farm on which he worked; indeed it was part of his wages, with a latent death in every mouthful, depending on the health of his employer's cows. Fortunately there was always a favourable percentage of germ-free cows, probably because the bovine life span is considerably shorter than that of humans, so that the danger for the farming fraternity was no greater than it was for the general public.

Another remarkable transformation in the agricultural scene is the elevation of the cottar family to almost middle-class in the social strata of society. Within the last thirty years, from almost ignominious grossness the cottar is now a highly respected, intelligent, responsible member of the community, and his value becomes more apparent with his growing importance in industry, whereas his former superfluity debased him.

As the value of gold lies in its scarcity so with the modern highly efficient farm worker. If lead was as scarce as gold it would have a similar currency value, perhaps even more so because of its many uses, so the leaden soldiers of agriculture are now moulded in the finer metal, and just as much sought after.

But machinery alone was not responsible for the depletion of the agricultural work force. After every subsequent wage increase over the last quarter century there was an immediate spate of redundancies, until the employers are scarcely left with enough rope to hang themselves, which indeed would be easier than replacing the men they were so anxious to be rid of. The agricultural colleges have done little to redress the imbalance, because the instinctive farmworker is a child of nature, and since his spawning ground has been transferred to the colleges his conception has been squirmed at the roots. A son of the soil cannot be born where the inherent parents of such a breed have been uprooted and dispersed beyond recall.

A great many cottar houses stand empty. Some of those that are occupied contain tradesmen and lorry drivers who feigned agricultural experience to get accommodation, quacks of their trade who are not so easily got rid of as were their genuine predecessors. Farmers are now saddled with men who have little or no qualification for farm work, protected by the reform bill on the tenancy of tied houses, which was initially intended to give security for those who were formerly dismissed. It is a process of rehabilitation which has back-fired on a race of unintelligent men — men whose forefathers were justifiably credited with consummate wisdom and foresight. But sufficient unto the day is the evil thereof.

The crofters too are disappearing, encouraged by the Government's Golden Handshake policy to promote bigger holdings in the interests of mechanical expansion in farming methods. This is a complete reversal of pre-war Government schemes to chop up the bigger estates in aid of the small self-employed smallholders in an era of decadent lairds. But now the lairds have made a comeback, and aided by big business in land speculation are buying back the farms they formerly sold, and closing expiring leases to take over farms from old tenants on their estates.

FARMING ON BALL-BEARINGS

Dykes have been buried and hedgerows uprooted to make bigger fields for the reversible plough and the combine-harvester. Gone are the days when a young married ploughman could lease a croft from the laird and go in for farming on his own. Existing farmers owe it to their forefathers for having done this, and then for hanging on to everything they could get, and grasping all around for further crofts, when the lairds were selling, until they had a sizeable estate now occupied by grandchildren.

Bulldoze farming has now become big business and private and public liability companies are replacing the parochial laird, with offices in the cities and board-room meetings sponsored by the banks. The big cartels are gobbling up the small family farms just as the supermarkets have squeezed out the small shopkeeper, the only difference being that the small farmer has to be consulted and the small shopkeeper ignored.

The Inland Revenue has brutalised farming into amalgamation, unification or disintegration, and since unity is strength it is the only course to survival; but in the case of farming the impetus comes from within the industry, not from outside opposition.

In consequence the croft houses are occupied by aliens, week-end holiday makers from the cities, while the landlords till the soil, with the visiting tourists as a profitable sideline. All of which has radically changed the agricultural scene and completely transformed traditional farming practice.

KINMUNDY AND THE CREESHY RAW

GO anywhere you like in Buchan, or further afield if you like, and you will scarcely find two fairly large farms closer together than Nether Kinmundy and Mains of Kinmundy, in the parish of Longside. Both farms were originally in the two hundred acre class and only the farm road runs between them, and in the old days the stackyard for each farm was on either side of the stone dykes. In fact they were so close together that during harvest the stackbuilders from both farms could 'news' to each other while crawling round their rucks, or the forkers could swap a sheaf of corn by pitching them across the road.

Both farms had water-mills, and one dam fed the other, revolving the bucket-wheels that drove the barn mills. Mains of Kinmundy, being on higher ground got a full dam first, and when they had a thrash the water from their wheel filled the dam at Nether Kinmundy, where the farmer there had to open his sluice and thrash as well, if he didn't want to loose the water; otherwise it spilled over and eroded the dam banks, all of which was very important in a dry season when water was scarce. And one of the best ways to seal a dam sluice after a threshing day was to throw in a shovelful of peat dross to close the seams.

Both farms took advantage of the oil-combustion engines as soon as they came on the market, and sometimes you could hear the 'chook-chook-ity-chook' of the engines on both farms simultaneously when they had a thrash on the same day, though more by coincidence than design, as had been the case with the water-mills. One type of engine, the ALLAN, made in Aberdeen, was first tested on the farm of Aikenshill, in Foveran, which was owned at the time by the Allan Brothers.

Nether Kinmundy (Longside) used to be farmed by Mr. Charles Penny, but when he retired in 1930 the late Mr. John Taylor of Mains of Kinmundy took over the management of both farms, and the family have since added to their territory in the general trend of expansion.

Because of their close proximity when separately owned the twin farms were considered one-sided geographically, with all the land on one side of the steadings, so that the horsemen had a long journey to plough the outlying fields, or in carting dung to them, or driving home turnips, and the foreman had to be a good time-keeper to fit in the number of 'drachts' or double loads he and his team could manage with their pairs of horses in a yoking; and as the hours were strict in those days the second and third horsemen had to see to it that their teams didn't lag, and to be at the watering trough and the stable door at the same time as the foreman at lousin' time.

Where gates were encountered on horseback the foreman had to dismount to open them, the third horseman to close them, while the second horseman in the middle sat still. Tractors have shortened these laborious journeys but amalgamation was the real answer to the problem, since the steadings are now in the centre of the estates.

In 1921, when Charlie Penny, as tenant of Nether Kinmundy, bought his farm at around seventeen pounds per acre he got the Creeshy Raw thrown in for nothing. For this he drew a small rent of something like five pounds a year for each of the eight or ten cottages, with a wee bit more for the one used as a shop and licensed premises by Mr. Norman Davidson, before he became a dairy farmer at Hillhead of Gask in Cruden. In my time the shop at the Creeshy Raw was run by Tammie Beagrie and Mrs. Beagrie, and their red-haired daughter Dolly used to serve behind the counter, until the family moved to Longside.

The Creeshy Raw is something of a mystery, but there is no doubt it was built to house the workers at the Messrs. Kilgour Woollen Mill, which was situated near the steading at Nether Kinmundy. When the mill closed down it is believed that the workers employed themselves making tallow candles, from the fat or 'creesh' of sheep and oxen, thus earning for their row of cottages such an incongruous title.

All that remains of the Creeshy Raw is a stone dyke which formed the back wall of the cottages. They were all thatched, and some had wooden chimneys, and it was a great wonder that they never caught fire.

When old Charlie Penny and his guidwife retired in May, 1930, he had a roup and we had to turn the sharn midden to make it absolutely square for measurement and valuation. The middens were seldom if ever given over to public auction, since carting them away would have been futile and wasteful, so they were evaluated by the square yard for the incoming tenant, in this case Mr. Taylor, just over the dyke.

It was the only time in my farming experience I have ever been employed turning the sharn midden. Fortunately we were finished before the sale, and we got a week's paid holidays until the Term, something unheard of fifty years ago. We had all the crops in except the turnips, a task which again was always left to the incoming tenant, when he could use the sharn midden as fertiliser.

We had the assistance of a retired policeman, a Mr. Thomson I recall, who chewed tobacco all day long and told us he was on duty at the launching of the great White Star liner *Titanic* in Belfast, in 1911. It seemed quite a come down for an old policeman, turning the sharn midden, but he enjoyed it, and we enjoyed his company, a fascinating character who had been well travelled.

All the farm implements had to be cleaned and painted and numbered for the sale, and we washed the horse-carts in the milldam. When I trotted out 'Bud' the orra-beast round the farm close for the farmers she went for a five pound note. 'Prince', the dapple brown pride of the foreman's pair brought bids up to twenty-five pounds, bought by a proud and jubilant crofter in the Kinknockie area.

It was the year after the great depression, following the Wall Street crash in New York, and the reverberations could be felt even at the farm roups down in Buchan yonder.

My fee for the six months was seventeen pounds. And my mother got a shilling a day with perquisites to board me. I was cheaper than the average stirk at the roup, and less expensive to keep — but at least I wasn't sold with them. Yet it was one of the happiest years of my life.

THE WORTHIES

THE white stag deer on Mormond Hill was laid out by the order of
Cordiner, laird of Cortes in 1870, the year of the Franco-
Prussian War. At that time Pitfour house, ancestral home of the
Fergusons of Pitfour was still intact, a mansion house in the palatial
scope of Blenheim Palace in the heart of a Buchan wood. So also was
Slains Castle, baronial residence of the Earls of Erroll, and fictional
inspiration for Bram Stoker's 'House of Dracula' — now both are gone,
Pitfour House completely, and Slains Castle in ruins, within my own
lifespan.

Pitfour or Mintlaw Games, held in the policies of Pitfour, used to
rival Aikey Fair as an annual holiday for the folks in Buchan, when
they flocked in their hundreds by gig or on foot or bicycle to the grounds
of Pitfour, where all manner of athletic and gymnastic entertainment
and display was provided for them by a generous and public spirited
laird. Nowadays all that survives from that auspicious yearly event is
the shrewd remark of a farm servant of the period who was asked about
the quality of the food at the farm where he had started work at the May
Term before the Mintlaw Games. "Och," said he, with his thumbs in
his gallowses, "the table at oor toon is as big as the Mintlaw Games
dauncin' boord but damn all on't!" By which we can assume that he was
but sparcely fed.

But Aikey Fair had its stories too. Take the case of Roch Annand,
George Rough Annand, a Buchan worthy whose best sayings are un-
printable, who had gone to Aikey Fair and bought a pound of bogie-roll
tobacco at a shoppie on the way.

In our modern age of pre-packed goods it is difficult to realise that in
Annand's time everything came loose (or in bulk if you like) and had to
be scaled out in whatever quantities the customer wanted it: a pound of
sugar from a hundredweight bag or a jar of treacle from an equally
heavy cask, and so with tobacco, mostly black twist, an ounce from a
pound roll, thus bogie (Bogie's) roll.

Most shopkeepers had a measure on the counter whereby they cut
off a length of rope tobacco as near an ounce as could be judged and
threw it in the weighing pan, adding or taking away a small slice as
required, but they were never far out. They were also adept at twisting
small squares of paper into cone-shaped containers for sweets, before

97

the days of our scientifically sealed polythene disposables.

But on the day of Aikey Fair George Annand hadn't the time to scutter about with this and he told the shopkeeper he would take the whole pound of tobacco, which was held together with matchstick pegs, and he put in in his jacket pooch.

He was next seen striding through the folk at the fair filling his pipe, with several yards of rope tobacco trailing behind him, having opened out the whole roll, while he whittled a pipeful with his knive from the end of the roll in his hands.

A cronie spied Annand with the rope of tobacco behind him and asked for a pipeful, seeing that Annand seemed in cheerful mood. "Och aye," says Annand, pipe in mouth, "juist tramp aff a daud!" Which gives you a measure of Annand's buffoonery and generous self-assertion which has made his name a legend on the Buchan farms.

But where Aikey Fair was held for hundreds of years on unruffled heather there is now a gaping quarry that would hold the carcasses of all the horses that used to be for show and sale there for a dozen years. The Sunday carnival is now held in the floor of the quarry and around the rim of it, but the traditional Wednesday market has now gone forever.

Aikey Fair was held in late July, by which time the corn was sprouting ears, and although still green you could pluck a stalk of it and fix it in your buttonhole, then the farmers would know you were looking for harvest work, man or woman, which of course, was only seasonal and had nothing to do with the feeing markets, which were for longer term contracts. Artistic minded folk made a sort of harvest brooch with the corn stalk, which served the same purpose.

The story is told of the lad who got a hairst at Aikey Fair but couldn't sharpen his scythe. On the morning he started the farmer took him to the cornfield and sharpened his scythe for him, informing him it was now sharp enough to cut itself. When the farmer left the lad he laid the scythe among the corn and sat down to fill his pipe, but being such a fine sunny morning he sat too long and soon fell asleep. When the farmer returned he was still sleeping, so he kicked the lad on the soles of his boots, informing him that he wasn't being paid to lie and sleep in the cornfield. When the lad woke up he looked at the farmer and then at the scythe: "Wisht man," said he, "ye said the thing wad cut itsel' and ye niver ken fan she'll start!"

Another version of the story is that before the farmer left the field the chiel asked him in which direction he should cut, whereupon the farmer pointed to a crow on a post and told him to "Follow that craw!" But when the farmer left so did the crow, and flew across a neighbour's cornfield, landing on a post at the other side. When the farmer returned the chiel was in the neighbour's park, slashing down the corn. "What the hell are ye doin' there?" the farmer cried, "it's here ye are supposed tae cut." "Weel," cries the billy, "ye tel't me tae follow the craw and ye see faur he's gaen!"

The real art in scytheing is to know how to sharpen the blade. A giant could kill himself trying to keep up with a little man with a scythe if the little man knows best how to whet the blade to the best advantage. The story is told of the wee mannie who was foreman at a place and a great big chiel was second horseman. The grieve sent the pair of them to scythe round a field for the binders, cutting a double bout, one behind the other, not to be so hard on themselves taking one big bout. But even so, every time the foreman looked round the bigger chiel had casten another cloot: first the jacket, then his waistcoat, then his sark and then his semmit, in the heat of the day, hanging them on whin bushes all round the field, and even so the little man had to help him out before they reached the gate. "That'll learn ye," the foreman said, "ye tak' the size o' me at a'thing else but ye canna beat me at this job." And the man was speaking truth.

While still in the Mintlaw area perhaps I should mention Tocher of Yokieshill, the doyen of all the Buchan worthies. He was a man of tremendous strength and his graip (fork) of five prongs was specially made at the smiddy, a thing like a modern hydraulic fork-lift that no other chiel could handle, like the two-handed sword of Wallace. No doubt it is an exaggeration but the story is told that when Tocher left Yokieshill, the farmer, Mr. Stephen, had the grieve take it back to the blacksmith on a horse cart to be made into a five-tine grubber, to be pulled by a team of three horses.

Tocher was a very modest man and always underplayed the situation. He was second horseman, and the first morning he was at Yokieshill the grieve told the foreman and Tocher to take their ploughs on the horse carts to the smiddy for remoulding. The foreman was struggling with his plough to get it into the cart and Tocher walked over to give him a hand, but the foreman was high-minded and independent and scoffed at Tocher, informing him that everyone loaded his own plough at Yokieshill. So Tocher walked calmly back to his own horse and cart, lifted the plough high over his head like a professional weight-lifter and threw it into the cart, where it went right through the bottom and stuck on the axle. "I dinna need a hand either," said Tocher to the astonished foreman, "I can load my ain ploo as weel as the neist een, but I like tae see the vricht (joiner) gettin' a job as weel as the smith (blacksmith)!"

It was said that as punishment for this prank Yokies (the farmer) sent Tocher by himself to turn a sharn midden on the edge of a field, a task that would have taken three or four men the most of two days to perform. By mid-day however, Tocher was finished with the midden and sitting on the horse troch by the stable door smoking his pipe. "Ye canna be finished already Tocher," Yokies cried, "gyang back and turn't again." So Tocher went back and threw the midden across the ditch into a neighbour's park, and when Yokies came over to see what was happening Tocher said, "That'll surely please ye this time!"

When Yokies went on holiday he ignored the grieve and gave Tocher a long list of jobs; enough to keep him out of mischief for a month he thought. "And what div I dee efter that?" Tocher asked. "Och," says Yokies, jokingly, "ye can tak' the slates aff the barn!"

So Yokies went on holiday, and when he returned with the wife in the gig he was amazed to see Tocher on the roof of the barn throwing off the slates. "Have ye deen a' yer wark?" Yokies asked. "Oh aye," Tocher cried, "I've juist the barn tae finish!"

It was the last time Yokies ever underestimated Tocher's capabilities and he worked for a long time on the farm after that.

LENABO

A History of the Buchan Airship Station

B UCHAN, that bleak, barren, cold shoulder of Britain, scarfed by the grey North Sea, has had its share of those Magnificent Men in their Flying Machines. It began on July 30th, 1914, when a Norwegian aviator, Kommander Trygve Gran, chose to fly from Scotland to Norway, taking off from Cruden Bay, where his Norse forefathers had once fought the Scots under Malcolm Canmore. A model of his flying machine, made by the pupils of Hatton and Port Erroll schools hangs between the flags of Norway and Scotland in the Church of St. Olaf, Cruden Bay, where Trygve Gran returned to commemorate the fiftieth anniversary of his successful pioneering flight across three hundred miles of water.

Unfortunately, less than a week after his flight the Great War was declared and Trygve Gran was temporarily forgotten, but a stone now marks his achievement on the seafront at Port Erroll.

In another Buchan Church, that of St. John's Episcopal in Longside, hangs one of the propellors of an airship lost at sea in action with a German U-boat during the First World War. That airship, C25, came from Lenabo, a stretch of moor and farmland in the parish of Longside; a somewhat dreary valley well chosen for its seclusion and remoteness, and yet not too far distant from the sea, where the airships patrolled in search of the deadly U-boats.

Between the wars we had the air circuses, where the flying machines took off with trippers among the cow dung in some grass field hired from a local farmer, and after looping-the-loop and performing some minor aerobatics came bumping down again among the eager crowds that thronged the dykes and roadways. But all this was foretold by a bard on the borders of Banff and Buchan three-quarters of a century earlier, in the village of Aberchirder, sometimes known as Foggieloan, when in February, 1845, Alexander Harper wrote:

101

A CHIEL AMONG THEM

Bards did presage an iron age;
'T' is come, I've ta'en a notion —
For Luve's saft leam we've gas and steam
Tae put a' things in motion.
And wha can say what projects rare
The sons o' men may form yet?
We'll a be whirlin' i' the air
Like corbies in a storm yet,
Some windy day!

And by the beginning of the present century his wild vision was becoming an experimental reality.

Nowadays, motoring through Lenabo (now the Forest of Deer), from Kinknockie on the A92, on the branch road to Peterhead, it is difficult to see the wood for the trees so to speak; difficult to vizualise the giant ant-hill of human activity that once was here; almost impossible to imagine that during the Kaiser War this was an airship station, peopled with nearly a thousand military personnel, where dirigibles were assembled and inflated with hydrogen gas, in the days before helium had been utilised as the best lighter-than-air gas for balloon buoyancy.

Previously, the sea that washes our doorsteps, and takes away the sewage from our east coast towns and cities had been known as the German Ocean, and if the Battle of Jutland had never been fought, and Lenabo had never been built, the legitimate claim to our maritime oil might have been an occasion for dispute with a still militant Imperial German Government.

Lenabo became operational about the same time as Jutland was fought, but for all its intended use against the German U-boats menacing our merchant shipping, and the upheaval it caused during construction, it came to be regarded as a wasteful and powerless White Elephant.

But the Battle of Jutland and the creation of Lenabo were inevitable exigencies that were concerned with a wider sphere of conflict, and much as these events have been depreciated, it will be seen, after a lapse of some sixty years, and the relatively recent discovery of North Sea oil, that they were important, almost decisive, factors in our heritage. These events took place in the age of steam, when our main

102

sources of energy were derived from coal, with no preconception whatsoever of how important it was for us to re-christen the German Ocean.

The foundation of Lenabo created a far greater furore in our landscape than the Roman camps nearly 2,000 years earlier, and yet, so completely thorough has been the obliteration of Lenabo, that there is less evidence of its existence than there is of Roman habitation. You have to search for the scars (after permission from the Forestry Commission) and all that survive among the trees are acres of solid concrete that were the floors of the giant hangars, and some shattered walls of Cruden Bay brick and plaster work.

The two seventy-foot chimneys were demolished by army engineers as late as 1961, and the huge underground furnaces were filled in with the rubble. These concrete dungeons were nearly twenty feet deep, and before demolition one could walk down the concrete steps and look up through the inside of the chimney stack, where the sky was less in diameter than a halfpence piece. One of the chambers had for years been filled with black frightening water, lapping the top steps and the base of the smoke stack, a death-trap for marauding deer, hares and stray sheep.

Oh yes, there were sheep on Lenabo between the wars. I have herded them there and clipped and dipped them, besides cutting peat in the bogs at the base of Torhendry Hill. There wasn't a tree planted on Lenabo at that time and they have grown to maturity in my own lifetime, though I wouldn't have believed it possible when I lived as a youth in the chaumer on the neighbouring farm of Auchtydore.

At that time Lenabo was an exposed wilderness of uprooted concrete and a shambles of red brick, like a devastated city, and from the hangar floors you could scoop up handfuls of lead and zinc washers that had fallen from the corrugated iron roofs during demolition. One ghostly farm had survived the holocaust, still intact among its native trees, at the foot of Torhendry, and even in those days the ivy from the broken windows was meeting in the middle of the stone floor in the kitchen, while the rusting gantry still hung over the peat fire, and there were broken milk basins on the flagged shelves of the dairy, a sad reminder of departure, a contented family uprooted by the senseless necessities of war.

By the old stone bridge over the stream near Auchtydore farm you

103

can see the outline of the old sewage disposal works from the former metropolis of Lenabo, with the main pipe, dry as a bone, jutting over the ditch. The Athenian twin pillars at the main entrance, most gracefully designed by one Petty Officer Yorke, were demolished with the smoke stacks.

Besides waterworks and reservoir, sewerage, gasworks and fire-station, Lenabo had a barracks, hospital, chapel, theatre, canteens, messes, engineering shops, garages, meteorological office, telephone exchange, wireless station, electrical power-plant, steam generators for the hangars, airship sheds, workshops and a railway to Longside station.

The airship base even had its own magazine, issued monthly, THE BATTLEBAG, but as they had no printing press (about the only amenity they didn't have), it was published from the offices of P. Scroggie Ltd., of Peterhead, where Mr. William Hackett was editor at the time and took a keen interest in the magazine, which was issued with a blue cover and cost fourpence.

A complete folio of THE BATTLEBAG still exists to No. 7 in its third volume, and by the time it folded in January 1919 it ran to twenty seven pages of news of station flights, religious services, sport and recreation, including boxing, soccer and rugby, road-racing and poetry.

One of the resident bards gives us a graphic and amusing picture of Lenabo as it existed while he was in limbo:

> *There is a land, a treeless land,*
> *Where all the bravest go:*
> *It raineth every day and night,*
> *We call it Lenabo!*

> *There everlasting springs abide,*
> *As very well we know;*
> *They flood the wretched countryside,*
> *As well as Lenabo!*

LENABO

The bogs beyond the site are where
The famous rushes grow;
They found poor Moses lying there,
In dear old Lenabo.

The airships are within the shed,
The wind's begun to blow
The poet has a bad fat head,
It's due to Lenabo!

To write that Lenabo was 'where all the bravest go' sounds somewhat vainglorious since it was always believed locally that most of the ground personnel at Lenabo were conscientious objectors in non-combatant roles, though it is hinted that some of them joined up later and lost their lives in combat. Perhaps the boredom of Lenabo drove them to distraction. Those who remained mixed well with the local farming fraternity and romance blossomed between them and the Buchan lasses, some of whom had lost their sweethearts in the Flanders trenches.

Several households are recommended for their hospitality towards the English exiles in Lenabo, and one in particular was that of Dr. and Mrs. Lawrence of Longside, whom the writer eulogises on 'the gracious and warm welcome accorded to all visitors to that hospitable home, presided over by a lady of whom all think with sincere regard and profound respect'.

Another report in THE BATTLEBAG tells us of the record flight of Captain Warneford and his crew in Lenabo airship N.S.II, which remained airborne for one hundred and one hours, breaking a previous record of sixty-one hours — much in the same way as one reads today of capsule-docking and endurance tests in outer space.

But the purr of the 'Lenabo Soos' has long ago faded away over the Buchan farmlands. Nowadays we are more accustomed to the scream of a Phantom jet over from Kinloss, or the vibrant roar of an airliner climbing into the sky from Dyce airport, yet Lenabo in central Buchan was the forerunner of them all, and in some respects even the proto-type.

On the outbreak of the Second World War, while Lenabo was still an ugly and reminiscent scar on the landscape, Longside was again chosen as a strategic fighter station for the R.A.F. All the ejection, upheaval, excavation and chaos of Lenabo was repeated at Tortorston, north-east of the village, at the exact opposite compass point from the former airship station, which enabled our fighter pilots to attack the German bombers from Norway harassing our convoys on the North Sea.

Lady MacRobert's Stirling Bomber, which she gifted to the nation, was serviced at Tortorston, and was frequently seen on the runways. Over in the next parish we had Crimond airfield and the Loch of Strathbeg, which had been used as a seaplane base in the First World War. Throughout the Hitler War the fields of Buchan were 'planted' with wooden poles to prevent an airborne German invasion, and Strathbeg loch was littered with them in case the Germans landed troop-carrying seaplanes.

While a great many forests on Deeside, Donside and Speyside were depleted to defy German airborne invasion, Lenabo itself could now supply a great percentage of that potential on its own. Since the late thirties and early forties, when the Forestry Commission took over, some 2,000 acres of woodland have been planted, mostly with Sitka spruce, which, once established, can withstand the withering blasts of Buchan better than our native Scots pines. Even by 1951, after three years of extensive thinning, 43,000 cubic feet of timber had been extracted as pit-props for the coal mines. Now there is a steady despatch of general purpose timber from the forest of Lenabo.

Until the end of the first decade of the present century Lenabo was farming land, peat-bog and heather on the estates of Ludquharn and Aden, for the freehold of which the Admiralty Commissioners paid Mr. Russell of Aden the princely sum of £5,000 in 1915. The freehold was on condition that Aden's farming tenants vacated their farms on re-imbursement from the Government, and some half-dozen sizeable steadings on the estate and five roadside crofts were demolished to accommodate R.N.A.S. (Royal Naval Air Service) building sites.

Bogend farm was the first to go, tenanted by the Chalmers family, demolished to make way for one of the three enormous workshops, framed in steel and built of concrete, with a corrugated iron roof, the structure embedded deep in cement. Torhendry farm was another casualty, then Lenabo farm, across the Kinmundy road, where the farmhouse was utilised as the station's makeshift post-office — 'which managed to cope with unprecedented custom by service through the window and the installation of an outsize letterbox in the name of H.M. King George V'.

That a whole community was evacuated from Lenabo there is ample evidence. A farming neighbourhood with a nucleus at the shop of the same name at the Lenabo crossroads — a sort of 'Rovers Return' as in Coronation Street — only there was no return for those evicted from their homesteads at Lenabo.

The Emporium was run by Mr. James Rae, the local shoemaker, who was also a tenant of Russell of Aden, his croft on the fringe of the estate, and he narrowly escaped the encroachment by the R.N.A.S. across the Kinmundy road. The general merchant department was run by Mrs. Rae, and later by their daughter, Miss Edith Rae, who survived until the late forties, and it is believed that some of her nephews and nieces may yet be alive.

In Mr.Rae's business ledgers we find the names and addresses of most of the pre 1914-18 War occupants of Lenabo; names like Mr. Kilgour of Torhendry, Mr. Milne of North Torhendry, Mr. Fentie of Bogend, Mr. Warrender of Easterton Lenabo; families bearing the name of Hastie, Kidd, McShea, Smith (the tinsmith), Sangster, Nicholl, Davidson, Duffus, Loggan, Reid, Penny and Robb. The only confusion is that as several families are addressed from the same farm one cannot distinguish between farmer and cottar, master and single servant.

What happened to all these families at the upshot of Lenabo? Throughout the nineteenth century they had lived in splendid isolation on the bleak expanse of Lenabo, their meagre requirements supplied by the 'shoppie' at the crossroads; growing their own crops (perhaps somewhat inadequate from the poorer soil) and digging peat as fuel from the desolate bogs of Torhendry, until their lonely habitat was chosen by the surveyors of the R.N.A.S. as an airship lair and they were uprooted leaf and branch.

Mr. Rae's accounts date from the late 1890's, and by 1916 the familiar farmsteads of Torhendry, Bogend and Backhill are changed to the Tawse Huts, the Auchtydore Huts, Braeside Huts and Lenabo Huts, which gives an idea of makeshift and upheaval, strengthened by pages and pages of accounts for paraffin, lantern glasses, wick lamps and candles, until electrical generators took over on the main site, and the old family names disappear, replaced by a conglomeration of traders from the influx of labour, mechanical and manual, at Lenabo.

Previously these very human transactions reveal that on June 29th, 1910, Mrs. Thomson of Bogend bought 4 lbs. of sugar and one bottle of rennet (to curd the cheese) at one shilling and fivepence, and that during the month of September the same year her husband smoked four ounces of Golden Bar tobacco. On the other hand, Mrs. McKenzie of Torhendry was very fond of herrings, apple jelly and cream of tartar (possibly for baking) and on July 1st, 1911, she bought 2 lbs. of liver but no mention of tobacco.

On shoe repairs we know each member of the family by his or her christian names, the date on which they had their shoes repaired, materials used and the price Mr. Rae charged for services rendered. Thus on October 17th, 1895, Mr. Lawrie of Easterton had his boots 'soed' (sewn) and one heeled, which cost him thruppence-ha'penny; and on October 26th, his daughter Nellie had her boots soled and heeled and tongued, which stung the poor dear half-a-crown. Her sister Maggie, on December 18th, had toecaps and heels fixed on her boots and fifteen protectors for fivepence.

And so on throughout the years, and besides the shoe repairing farmers brought their horse harness to Mr. Rae for stitching: halters, britchens, saddle-girths, bridles and collar facings; mill and reaper belts, whip thongs, gallows-straps (braces), nicky-tams and leggings; and there was a constant demand for bootlaces, buckles and pump washers and leather reins for ponies.

Perhaps the bairns wore down their shoes walking to school, to Shannas or Kinmundy, in either case a distance of two miles, and three miles to Longside. The adults had a choice of three churches: Clola, Ardallie or Longside, in each case a distance of nearly three miles, which would have been hard on their footwear. Kinmundy is a churchless parish, or was until Mr. William Scollie, an ardently religious joiner built a mission hall at Meg's Neuk, at the northern extremity of Lenabo, but by then the community was dead or scattered, except for a handful of foresters, and Mr. Scollie's corrugated hall rusts empty by the roadside.

The importance of Lenabo as an agricultural community must have been considerable, because three market days a year were allotted for the sale of livestock, but the marts were terminated by the roups of the ejected farmers in 1915.

And what was Lenabo like when the R.N.A.S. took over? According to one eye-witness report it was chaos in a peatbog, with all the muck and slurry that wet weather would produce from extensive excavation on the site. 'When we arrived at Longside (station) we found a small advance party ensconced and having a jolly time at the Bruce Arms Hotel, the officer-in-charge, Sub-Lieut. Omaney, being billeted at the Railway Company's Cruden Bay Hotel'. Communications were poor initially, with only one telephone on the site, in the office of the Admiralty Civil Engineer, Mr. W.R. Watson, who apparently remained at Lenabo throughout its active history.

Gradually, under supervision, the station took shape. An army of navvies, Irish and local, laboured under the grey wintry skies of 1915, enlivened at dusk by the flickering light of naphtha flares, those wavering stars that revealed the dying in no-man's land in France; a ghostly reminder to the natives that the devil was at work at Lenabo.

In daylight the mosses were alive with toiling humanity; with all the paraphernalia of mechanical excavation belching smoke and steam. Thousands of tons of dank peat went into wagons for dumping, some of it to heat the boilers of steam scoops, bucket cranes and locomotives, ugly sinister little cockroaches that ran hither and thither on crazy, makeshift rails, across the mossy parks where the crofters had formerly sown their dubious crops, for in one respect the R.N.A.S. were to be complimented, in that they had not chosen the richest of farming land for their Dante's Inferno, apart from some sixty acres of richer soil on the adjoining farm of Auchtydore, where the railway terminus was situated. The rest was peat-earth, gravel, rush and heather.

Huts and cabins were hurriedly erected to house and board the increasing number of labourers, with beer and spirits available at the 'wet' canteen, with military police in attendance.

The transformation of Lenabo was entrusted to Messrs William Tawse and Sons of Aberdeen, an undertaking which must have proved the most exasperating task ever contracted in the long history of the firm. From the very start it was a feverish race with time and the elements; the Government insisting that, come what may, because of the intensified German U-boat menace, the reconnaissance airships must be operational over the North Sea by the autumn of 1915. This meant that the site had to be ready for the building of the dirigibles in the giant hangars by early summer at the latest, and it was a tribute to the firm's organisation and deployment of labour, with the equipment then available, that Messrs Tawse and Sons managed to complete the work on schedule.

Transport was sub-contracted to James Sutherland of Peterhead, with Longside as the nearest railhead, until the Lenabo railway was ready for service. But Mr. Sutherland marshalled all his available resources: horse carts, lorries, wagons and steam engines. From dawn till dusk there was a constant stream of traffic both ways, laden and in tare on the narrow road between Lenabo and Longside railway station. Steel girders, cement, office equipment and furnishings were the initial requirements, while sand, gravel and crete could be had from the local quarries, such as Old Mill and Braeside, while brick and drainage tiles were carted from Cruden Bay. Lenabo was an ultra-modern experiment in building without stone, even though it was available in ample quantities from the local quarries, such as Cairngall and Auchtydore, the latter quarry just across the road, but expediency couldn't wait for stone-dressing and the method of shuttered concrete was adopted, with rapid and durable results. Stone was used in some of the railway structure, especially over the swampy ground at the terminus, and as the bridges were merely culverts over existing ditches the amount was minimal.

Provisions in large quantities had to be carted mostly from Peterhead, about eight miles distant, such as butcher meat, fish, bread, milk and groceries, which might include eggs, potatoes and vegetables, until these could be had nearer to hand from the local farmers. Peterhead benefited from these transactions, and family businesses, hitherto unknown, suddenly became household names in the airship boom. James Booth, Kennie Smith, Tammy Cunningham, John Birnie, John Mackintosh, Robert Buchan, Robert Boggie and Sons, Fife and Duncan, Thomas Heslop, Grant and Black, and even Sir Thomas Lipton got a boost on the side, while McConnochies of Fraserburgh built up a reputation with their supplies of bully-beef, canned soups and vegetables.

With the site prepared, water and drainage installed, roads constructed, foundations laid for the three enormous hangars, ancillary buildings and living quarters, the steel-riggers, spidermen and brick-layers went into action. Most of the brick came from Cruden Bay and

Tipperty, where it could be had in greater quantity, as the local brickworks at Ednie and Downiehills were now defunct. But the quality too was excellent, hard-baked material that would outlast the pyramids of Egypt, for only the best was good enough for Lenabo. The roads were tarred, even though the public roads were still gravel surfaced, and plunging in mire from the heavy traffic converging on the new airship station.

As the work progressed, girder upon girder, pillar by pillar, lintel by lintel, brick by brick, the buildings emerged in neat trim avenues, symetrically perfect, acre upon acre of township and factory, all converging on a main drive to the two entrance pillars, now standing boldly forth in Athenian splendour, each topped with a gigantic ball of concrete, and the spiked steel gates guarded day and night by armed sentries.

The completed metropolis was a credit to the architects and engineers who planned it, a contradiction to the adage that Rome wasn't built in a day, because Lenabo went up in record, stopwatch time to serve an emergency, and it is almost pathetic to ruminate on the transient existence of this monumental achievement. Never was so much accomplished by so many in so short a period to vanish so quickly.

And the cost? — something like £600,000 which in terms of 1980's finance would run into millions, squandered on a peat-bog, and this massive piggy-bank was surrounded by a steel fence embedded in concrete, topped with spikes that would have impaled the roe deer that now roam the Forest of Deer.

One early arrival at Lenabo described it as a primeval swamp in perishing weather, with only timber cabins, lit with oil lamps, and equipped with earth-closets to accommodate the men. He said it took months of unremitting toil by Royal Naval artisans and outside contractors before adequate buildings were erected and services made available to a decent standard of civilised living conditions.

He further informs us that there was no covering building for the first power plant (it was erected later), only massive concrete foundations, and the first oil-engine and direct current dynamo were put in position and connected by temporary cabling on the quagmire surface to the buildings nearing completion. Eventually there were four engines and dynamos and many miles of submerged cable supplying light and power throughout the wide expanse of Lenabo.

The framework for the gasbags was delivered at Lenabo in pre-fabricated sections and assembled in the hangars. This framework was insulated with an overlay of silver-grey rubber fabric to protect the inner balloons when inflated. Gondolas were slung underneath the belly of the airship, with motors of French manufacture, as well as guns, wireless, instrument panels, anchor and ballast. The finished airship was pumped full of hydrogen gas with such an upthrust, that before take-off, and again on landing, a hundred ratings were employed on the guy ropes to hold the ship down, and to garage them, two ships to each of the three main hangars.

Can you imagine those monstrosities hovering over the Buchan fields, their dangling ropes brushing the trees and farmsteads, the purr of their engines frightening cattle in the fields and horses at the plough? To a hitherto rather primitive, rustic, close-living community it must have seemed that the devil himself was flying his kites among the angels, whom they had believed until then were the only inhabitants of the upper air.

Operational distance was limited, and the airships were tricky to handle, a nightmare even in moderate wind, and only heroes could have piloted them over the North Sea in a Buchan gale, never mind searching for lurking U-boats. Yet the patrols were maintained, though few were the U-boats that were ever tracked down, or their movements reported back to Lenabo.

Sometimes an airship got into difficulties with engine failure, like the one over Peterhead in 1917, expelling gas to lose height, when it ripped its belly on the Town House spire and floundered over the Smith Embankment. Spectators ran to clutch the ropes and pulled the ship to safety, while crowds thronged the esplanade, holding on to the trailing ropes until lorry loads of ratings arrived from Lenabo to the rescue.

From the ground these airships looked like a healthy full-grown vegetable marrow, seams and all, and if you can imagine a child's work basket slung underneath to house the propellor screw, engine and crew we are ready for take-off.

Three types of airship were cradled at Lenabo. The earliest was the Submarine Spotter (S.S.) with gas capacity to 70,000 cubic feet, one engine, a speed of 40 miles per hour, and a crew of two; the Coastal (C.) gas capacity 160,000 cubic feet, two engines and crew of five; the still larger and more powerful North Sea (N.S.) gas capacity 360,000 cubic feet, two engines and crew of ten. Some of these airships had petrol engines by Anseldo of Italy, and by the French firms of Clement, Panhard and Renault; later Sunbeam produced eight-cylinder 180 h.p. and 240 h.p. petrol engines, but they also were air-cooled, and frequent overheating caused breakdowns.

It was in April, 1918, that the Royal Naval Air Service and the Royal Flying Corps were merged to become the Royal Air Force, though the R.N.A.S. was later revived as a separate entity.

But the 'Lenabo Soos' were not alone over Buchan, for the German Zeppelins paid a visit to the area on several occasions during 1916. Compared with the Lenabo types these German Zepps were giants, armed with explosive and incendiary bombs and guns and had a much wider range. Over Peterhead they frightened the townsfolk, who were glad to see them further out at sea and clear of the town.

One of the German airships, the L20, on May 3rd, 1916, came to grief on the Norwegian coast, and the following day, her sister ship, L7, which went inland over Rattray and reached the Moray Firth, was destroyed there by a British submarine.

The German L7 was one of the ships which terrorised the English east coast with a night attack in April, 1915, when it was commanded by Captain Pieter Strasser (who planned to bomb New York) Chief of Operations at Nordholz airship base, where L7 and L20 set out on their fatal voyage to Buchan and oblivion in 1916.

Lenabo's first commander was an officer from the Royal Marines, Colonel Robinson, and his operational crews were nearly all pioneer aviators of the Royal Navy. Their task was to patrol the convoy routes in the North Sea as U-boat spotters, but their contribution to U-boat destruction seems to have been negligible, and was never worth the trouble and expense of building Lenabo air station.

But of course Lenabo was not the only airship station in Scotland. There were several on the east coast; one in particular at East Fortune, in the Lothians, and another at Auldbar, near Brechin in Angus, which had limited facilities in support of Lenabo, where airships patrolling south of Aberdeen could be replenished with gas and fuel, and could have running repairs carried out. Hydrogen gas was transported to Auldbar from Lenabo in metal containers and the station took its orders from Lenabo, by wireless and telephone.

A CHIEL AMONG THEM

In 1918, with the formation of the Women's Auxiliary Air Force (the Waafs), a touch of glamour appeared at Lenabo, charming male hearts long in exile, while the love-starved quines of Buchan forsook their farm kitchens for the offices and cooking stoves of Lenabo.

Before me as I write I have a charming photograph of five Lenabo Waafs in early uniform standing around a signpost which indicates 'To Longside 3 miles', and judging by the happy, dimpled smiles on their pretty faces it would seem they are on leave, awaiting transport for the village. Each is dressed in collar and tie, soft peaked cap with badge, winged epaulets, wide fitting belted tunic with brass buttons and sewn-on pannier pockets; long, full skirts, black shoes and stockings, and if any of these girls are alive today they are octogenarians. Three of them are Joey Jaffrey, Chriss Massie and a Miss Findlay.

We are told that from Peterhead to Aberdeen, from Maud to Cruden Bay the girls fraternised with the lads at Lenabo, which isn't surprising when one considers a community stripped of its young men for the war-time trenches, and many bereaved families welcomed the gasbaggers from Lenabo at their lonely firesides.

Although the station had its own facilities for entertainment and recreation, including open-air sports and charity shows at which the local participants and spectators were welcomed, there were also excursions for the ratings to Peterhead. They were conveyed on motor lorries to town with a rendezvous at Robertson's garage in York Street for the return trip. One visitor recalls the delight of Baker Rennie's hot mutton pies at tuppence each, which were devoured with great relish, after a visit to the local club or the Electric Theatre in Hanover Street (later Clarkie's Palace Theatre) which had stage turns and flicks by way of entertainment.

Colonel Robinson was stationed at Kinmundy House, and until 1918 Lenabo was purely a Royal Navy show, geared to battleship routine and discipline, a consistency which prevailed in full sail until the Armistice, when a dispatch rider from Lenabo, namely Percy Codd, conveyed the official information to the Buchan Observer office in Peterhead for a special Armistice publication.

Other names that survive from Lenabo are Petty Officer Bishop, whose 'melliferous' voice we are told charmed the Buchan folk when he led the famous Lenabo pierrot troupe — THE GASBAGS – cavorting at functions on behalf of local and war charities. Others of the troupe were Messrs Brown, Coborn, Hunt, Kelly, Park and Southgate. The

114

HIT THE DECK event of Lenabo theatricals was the revue, HELLO
LONGSIDE! — a real professional job it seems, devised and
furnished with typical R.N. do-it-yourself expertise. Artistes included
the Misses Chrissie and Meg Connon and Bella Summers from
Peterhead, and the fourteen-strong orchestra was conducted in turn by
Messrs George Duncan and John May, also of Peterhead.

Another name which should not be left out of the chronicle is that of
Mr. William L. Morgan, old Oxonian and former Naval Officer at
Lenabo airship station, 1916 to 1920, whose later contributions to the
BUCHAN OBSERVER made the construction of this history pos-
sible, and whose work provided me with much useful material.

In 1919, when the national railway strike suspended many rail
services, Lenabo helped to maintain postal traffic between Peterhead
and Aberdeen, mostly with Crossley motor wagons. In that year the
R.A.F. was established and replaced the R.N.A.S. at Lenabo. But with
the war over there was nothing to do except to continue essential
services and spit and polish. The station served no useful purpose and
was deemed unsuitable for winged aircraft training. Demobilisation reduced its complement to skeleton proportions, and in 1920 the Air
Ministry withdrew and wiped Lenabo from its feet, and the gigantic
extravagance of Lenabo became a White Elephant relegated to the
Disposals Board and the scrap merchants.

Local visionaries regarded the forsaken site as a magnificent,
ready-made industrial town, with factory buildings and living quarters
intact, and even a rail-head, with immense potential development and
sources of employment in central Buchan. One proposal was to use it
for large-scale peat processing, while canned meat and vegetables was
also suggested, but those with procreative imagination received no
official support from the Government and no backing from the banks,
and if Lenabo had been a woe-begone hinterland before, it now became
a God-forsaken wilderness.

The only thing going was the dismantled airship fabric, which was
made into waterproof coats by everyone on the site and the neighbourhood, all of one colour, silver grey.

The County Councillors couldn't see beyond their reading glasses
and Lenabo was sold for a song to the demolition contractors. For a
long time the site lay derelict, with its two forlorn smoke stacks as a
reminder of its former glory and importance, its acres of naked concrete
a symbol of wastefulness, its noble gate pillars the admiration of
artisans yet unborn when they had served their purpose.

The Forestry Commission have restored Lenabo to a sylvan scene of fairyland beauty; but even yet, at certain seasons of the year, a ghostly pall of white mist hangs over the Forest of Deer, especially at dusk on damp winter evenings when frost is settling on the trees, as if all those steam hammers had quietly come to life again in the dark and secret heart of Lenabo.

THE COUNTRY VANMEN

S URELY one of the most dramatic changes in our life style over the last hundred years is to be observed in our shopping habits. Gone are hundreds of the little corner grocery shops and the newsagent down the lane, where one could buy anything from corned-beef and mealy puddings to sherbet bags and Battle-Axe treacola slabs. Now everybody swarms to the supermarkets — by car, bus or on foot for almost everything we require in life, including bedding and furniture, meat, fish and vegetables.

Nowadays even the country people come into the town stores with their motor cars for provisions, once a month or once a fortnight, and what with their refrigerators and deep-freeze storage this is no problem. This has closed a lot of rural shops and taken their vans off the road, especially the grocer vans, though the baker has been hit to some extent but moreso the butcher, except for deep-freeze deliveries. City vans used to be quite common in the country but now there are very few, excepting those supplying goods wholesale to the village shops.

I can remember when country people were almost entirely dependent on their vans for everything they required, including the weekly newspapers, medical supplies and even contraceptives. My first memories are of the horse vans, especially the baker van, when he brought a jeely piece for a hungry loon — a sair-heidie, a curran'-daud, a sugary bap or iced gingerbread. And when the vanman got his dinner the horse ate out of a moo'-bag slung over its ears in the close, and I used to wonder how it managed to chew with a bit in its mouth, though some vanmen removed the bridle. The old vanmen were good gossip carriers, and not above a bit of flirting on the sly, where the women were keen, though nothing serious was ever intended, mostly idle banter.

When the motor vans came, and country people at their mercy so to speak, we were fortunate in those days that there were no transport or drivers' strikes, though we were sometimes taken advantage of where prices were concerned; a penny here and tuppence there, and when you complained to the proprietor he said the driver had to get his tips somewhere. Of course you could change your vanman, only to find he gave you sweated, tasteless cheese, or something that wouldn't sell in the shop, and by the time you got the merchandise it tasted of mothballs. Butcher meat was another complaint, especially if you were at the end of the vanman's round and he was left with nothing but dog-bones and harragles, bordering on offal, but was good enough for a pot of stovies. But he promised to keep a better piece of meat for you the next call and you forgave him for the time being.

One of our grocery vanmen used to call last thing on Saturday night, just before bed time, and being so late of course he got his tea with us. The snag was that the brady or pie he brought in from the van for his own consumption was charged for in my wife's account. We put up with this for years, not because of any embarrassment that a rebuke might bring, but because he brought the weekly newspapers, and we were all so eager to get our hands on them that we didn't say a word. He played the kirk organ on Sundays, travelling in his van, delivering Sunday newspapers all the way; and he wasn't above bringing a sack of poultry food or a gallon of paraffin if you were short, so how could you quarrel with a man like that about a measly brady?

The only strikes we had to fear were inflicted by nature in the form of snowstorms, when all the roads were blocked and we didn't see a van for weeks on end. This was something that taught the country folk a great measure of independence and self-sufficiency in order to survive, and before the days of refrigerators and electric cookers that wasn't so easy. But housewives achieved miracles on a gantry over a peat fire, or with a coal-range oven, in paraffin light, without water on tap and no sinks; baking, cooking, basting, when a hen or a poached hare or rabbit was a delicacy, a pheasant or a brace of grouse if you were in with the laird. But for the cottar there was always meal, milk, tatties and eggs, and making the best of these was the hallmark of a good housewife in those days. Broth, skirlie, stovies, chappit tatties and hard fish and mustard sauce, oatcakes, and maybe a clootie dumplin' — what could ye get better than that?

But people were more content in those days and bairns survived on little, like the cottar loon who joked that he was fourteen and working on a farm before he knew that a hen laid a whole egg, because he had always shared the other half with a member of his family.

Crofters and cottars trudged for miles oxter deep in snow to the nearest emporium, whose proprietor had the foresight to be prepared for such emergencies, and had built up his stocks to meet it, which was a difficult problem during the Hitler War when everybody was on weekly rations. The bigger farmers sent horse-sledges into the towns, returning

118

with pillowslips filled with fresh loaves, meat and provisions (such as could be found) for everyone who was in need, including fags and tobacco.

As a schoolboy, I walked three miles both ways to town every Saturday morning with my 'hurlie' or handcart for the week's groceries, because there wasn't a grocer's van for the district. A great many of the farmers had milk delivery floats and brought home their own provisions, while others went to town with their gigs on Fridays (an old market day) so it wasn't worth while for the grocer to send a van.

I gave the grocer my mother's list and payment in an envelope and he packed the goods into my hurlie. I did this for several years, until I left school, and on one occasion my mother kept me back from the classroom and sent me to town on the Friday. It was February, 1926, when there was a fearful snowstorm on the Friday evening, and by Saturday morning all the roads were blocked and an old man dead in the drifts. The snow was level with the stone dykes and sheep were smothered in the fields. There were no motor snowploughs and the farm men worked for days to clear all the roads with shovels. Country folk had premonitions on the weather and I think my mother sniffed the coming snow.

Most of the cottars lived on credit, paying the vanman at the end of the month when they got their wages. Some fell behind and left in debt at the May Term, or took a moonlight flitting in winter, leaving the van owners to meet their own bills, though some of them called on the eve of the Term to catch the flighty cottars before they left the district. Vanmen who refused tick lost customers and they had to rely on the honest regulars to make ends meet, and fortunately there were enough of these to balance the accounts, though it led to competition among the vanmen in securing them. Maybe the farmers were partly to blame for not paying the men weekly, which would have meant the loss of a month's interest at the bank.

Ah well, I still have my 'hurlie' when we go to the supermarket, though my wife is manager nowadays and she has a much wider range of goods to choose from than my mother had at the old grocery shop. As a loon I would have been delighted with the four-wheeled hurlie I get at Norco House or Asda, and no doubt I would have turned it into a motor lorry in my boyhood imagination, whereas the one I had was simply a wooden box with shafts mounted on an axle and a pair of pram

119

wheels. In only one respect did it equal my modern hurlie, in that it had rubber tyres, nearly sixty years ago. Memory hold the door.

And what about prices? For a real shocker let us go back to 1900, a bit before my time of course, but just for kicks ... The Boer War was in progress and the weekly grocery bill for an average family amounted to seven or eight shillings, or roughly one shilling (5p) a head, excluding meat, fish and sometimes bread, which seems to balance with the working class wage packet of the period. The farthing (¼ of a penny) was at that time in circulation, and in the list of prices given below it is quoted when appropriate.

> 1 oz. black twist tobacco 3¼d.
> 1 lb. sugar — 1¾d.
> ½ stone salt — 2d.
> 1 gallon paraffin — 8d.
> 1 lb. split peas — 1½d.
> 1 lb. whole rice — 1¾d.
> 2 lbs. jam — 5½d.
> (penny extra for jar)
> ¼ stone flour — 5d.
> 1 lb. margarine — 2½d.
> 1 lb. barley — 1½d.
> 1 lb. soap — 3½d.
> 1 lb. semolina — 2½d.
> ½ lb. raisins — 5d.
> 1 lb. syrup (without jar) — 3d.
> 1 lb. cheese — 5d.
> 1 lb. onions — 4d.
> ½ lb. butter — 6d.
> 1 tin cocoa — 8½d.
> 1 loaf of bread — 3d.

Eggs were one penny each and milk at one penny per pint. Biscuits at a farthing each, the 'butter-hardie' became the 'farthing biscuit'.

The 'd' signifies pence in the old currency as compared with the 'p' in decimal coinage. The shilling was indicated thus /- and the £ of course was the same as today. Compared with one hundred pence to our modern one-pound note there were 240 pennies in the old one-pound sterling and it went quite a long way, so that a wage earner taking home £1 or fifteen shillings (75p) on pay day could keep his family reasonably well. The guinea piece (21 shillings) and the golden sovereign (£1) were of course at that time still legal currency.

Two items completely absent from the list are cigarettes and toilet roll. The reason for this was that most working men smoked the pipe. Very few women smoked in those days and if they did it was usually the pipe as well. There were no bathrooms in working class homes (nor in many others) and the weekly newspaper mostly hung in the dry lavatories as bum-fodder. Petrol had not yet become a popular commercial commodity and coffee or tea didn't appear often in the rural shopping list at the turn of the century.

ROUND ABOUT DOUP

LOOKING back over fifty-odd years I can hardly believe that where the R.A.F. station now stands at Boddam I used to drive cattle to the railway yard. I was still at school and I had to get up with my father at five o'clock on a winter's morning, about twice a year, and after we had fed the fat bullocks we loosed them from the stalls and drove them to Boddam Station, nearly three miles from Springhill farm, swinging our paraffin lanterns in the dark. With dozens of other cattle from outlying farms they were loaded on to wagons for the marts in Aberdeen, the train picking up more cattle vans at stations convenient for loading. Then I had to walk home again, and after breakfast, which was mostly brose, I gave my face 'a dicht wi' a cloot' and set off on another three mile walk to Longhaven school, and not a penny did I get for my trouble, neither from my father nor the farmer, seeing I was just the loon.

Motoring north from Longhaven, on the main road, beyond the Roxley Bar at Boddam and the old stone-polishing works on the left, the petrol station on the right, if I have passengers in the car, I am apt to tell them that my wife was born here, right in the middle of the road, just where it begins to climb the Burniebrae. Of course they look a bit shocked and surprised, thinking maybe she was a dyke-sider, until I hasten to explain that the house wherein she was born once stood in the middle of the present road, and that we are now passing over its foundations, where the walls had been used as hard core. It was formerly a bend and the old road went round the house, but the new road now runs where the cradle was rocked for my wife.

Another place where this has happened was at Balmedie, when realigning the road between Eigie farm and the Blackdog shooting range; but in this instance the obstructing house was a habitable farm cottage and had to be rebuilt by the County Council at the side of the new road near Millden farm, where it is still occupied.

But on the Burniebrae there was no such rehabilitation, the old croft house having stood roofless for years, though Willie Durno from Boddam still grew tatties in the garden.

Of all the changes that have taken place on the Buchan farms over the last half century, nowhere is it more evident or more dramatic than on the farm of Sandford Lodge, half-way between Boddam and the outskirts of Peterhead. The fertile fields have been literally rolled up by the bulldozers and earth removing excavators, scooped in a slope from the seashore to the roadside in a landscaping attempt to screen the giant electric power station now taking shape in Sandford Bay. I knew men who worked in these fields who wouldn't recognise them. The contours of the entire farm have been so completely ravaged that transformation is a word too congenial to describe the upheaval. Fortunately the Georgian style farm house is a listed building and has been preserved, as has most of the farm steading and the old cottar houses, utilised as stores or offices for the Hydro-Board.

Towering over all is the mammoth chimney, 570 feet from sea level, dwarfing Buchan Ness lighthouse and higher than the Reform Tower on the Meethill, which used to dominate the landscape. On a clear day the new power house lum can be seen from the Tullos Hill at Nigg in Aberdeen, a long finger pin-pointing Peterhead on the distant shoreline.

It was from Sandford Lodge that the late James Sutherland ran his great transport business in Peterhead.

During his tenancy of the Sandford farm he had a grieve called Sandy Christie, and the foreman's name was Fordyce. At that time, under contract with the local authorities, the slaughterhouse offal at Boddam and most of the village refuse was carted on to the fields at Sandford and Newton of Sandford (Newton was owned by Mr. Sutherland) and when it was the foreman's turn to drive the muck with his horse carts from Boddam the grieve addressed him with the customary salutation: "Haud doon tae Doup for dirt, Fordyce!" Being an order Fordyce had to comply. But if you say it out loud you will savour the rhythm of the couthy Doric tongue, with emphasis on 'for dirt' and 'Fordyce!' — with Doup as the local name for Boddam.

Nowadays, there is a massive underground tunnel from Doup harbour to Sandford Bay, where the sea water will plunge through to cool the giant turbines at the powerhouse, discharging in the bay, heating the ocean on a two mile radius, to the chagrin or otherwise of the local fishermen. Not that this has anything to do with sewage, but one just wonders what Christie and Fordyce would have thought of the project.

Another thing which has vanished from this area is the convict railway, leaving an ugly scar on an otherwise healthy landscape. The railway ran from Salthousehead prison yard to the quarries on Stirling Hill, conveying prisoners to work under armed guard, and the granite they quarried was freighted back to build the Harbour of Refuge, which now forms the bay and safe anchorage at Peterhead. Before it was built the sea stormed Smith's embankment, now occupied by Crosse & Blackwell's canning factory, and over the years had threatened encroachment on the town.

The operation took something like eighty years to complete and hardened criminals spent a life sentence on the task, which ended around 1962. Some of the bridgework on the railway still stands, massive and durable, but over Stirling Hill, when the bridges were built, the Admiralty contractors, who were in charge of construction, wouldn't allow a traction engine to cross them. Crofters awaiting a thrash had to divert the portable mill on a long detour to avoid the bridges, though the traction weighed on average only nine tons. Nowadays these bridges have been taking loads of thirty tons by modern transport lorries without strain, far outlasting the purpose for which they were built, mainly horse traffic, and the narrow weight margin allowed for them by the engineers. These bridges were built of the same Stirling Hill granite as the harbour works, with beautiful arching and corniced parapets, the road approaches rising gently towards the bridgework.

The Dendam is also in disuse, a stretch of water imprisoned on the west flank of Stirling Hill, and conveyed by culvert (under the railway) to the old stone polishing works at Boddam, where a lot of monumental workers were employed, but now defunct. Yachting regattas are held yearly on the Dendam, more so since the original yachting pond, opposite the Lido at Peterhead, was filled in and built over during the post-war housing scramble.

But who said crime doesn't pay? It has paid handsome dividends at Peterhead, because if there hadn't been crime there wouldn't have been a convict prison there, and if there hadn't been convicts, and the problem of finding something for them to do, there wouldn't have been a Harbour of Refuge, and if there hadn't been a Harbour of Refuge it is unlikely that Peterhead would have been chosen as one of the principal shipping depots for supplying the oilrigs in the North Sea, with all the ancillary benefits and employment this has brought to the town.

And Peterhead was sorely in need of the oil boom. In the early sixties even the fishing industry, the town's traditional mainstay was in recession. At that time you could stand on the Lido and look across the bay without a ship in sight. Now the bay is clustered with offshore maintenance craft, oil-rig supply vessels, rig-tenders, tugs and pipeline barges. A busy wharf has been reclaimed from the sea (with sand from St. Fergus) under the shadow of the prison walls, and huge tankers anchor in the lee of the breakwater, discharging fuel oil for the Boddam power plant, which is piped through the derelict village of Burnhaven, where the old pier of the local fishermen can still be seen under the water facing Sandford Bay.

Burnhaven is an old fishing village where all the houses are condemned and nobody pays any rent, only rates, and a village pump still serves the inhabitants. The old cottages are all red-tiled and the occupiers repair them and keep them wind and water-tight at their own expense. All have electric lighting but no plumbing or sanitation. I believe the village was founded for the old fishermen by one of the Keith family of Inverugie, but when the last Earl Marischal turned Jacobite his estates were confiscated and the village sold for a song to the Merchant Maiden Company of Edinburgh. The last factor was Mr. Alfred Taylor of the Anchorage in Mintlaw, but he hasn't collected any rent from the tenants for a long time. The owners seem to have forgotten them. Peterhead Town Council have tarred the road to the village and provided street lamps in return for the rates they still collect from the residents. Some have left for new council homes in Boddam, but about half-a-dozen old-timers still cling to their cottages, perhaps for nostalgic reasons, or because it is cheaper than paying the rent of up-to-date accommodation.

But there are no boats on the sea front where the waves lap the bleaching greens, and the Burn (which gives the village its name) comes purling down the roadside from Glenugie Distillery nearly to the cottage doors, where it tumbles into Sandford Bay, fragrant with the vat bree of Long John whisky. After dark Buchan Ness lighthouse sweeps the little village and the restless waters with a flashing sword of light.

It is a bygone village of the yawl and the baited hook, the fish-hake and the creel, where many a fishwife set out in the morning with her creel on her back to sell her haddock and skate around the country districts, sometimes knitting as she walked the lonely miles. She would return in the evening with a dozen fresh eggs in her creel, or a pat of butter or a small kebbock of home-made cheese, a handful of copper and silver in her small leather purse, forbyes all the gossip of the neighbourhood.

The story is told of the Burnhaven fishwife who strayed beyond her accustomed territory to sell more fish. She took the bus to Slains, encroaching upon the district usually supplied by the fishwives from Whinnyfold and Collieston. The opposition she met however, was not likely to encourage her to try it another time, and it didn't come from the farming folk of Slains, but from a rather unusual source — from one of their rampaging stallions.

When the fishwife returned to Burnhaven, round the village pump in the evening, this was the story she related to her rival fishwives who had come for water:

"As I gaed by the fairm o' Mains o' Brogan,
A big hee horse cam' oot rampagin' —
He'd a trigger on 'im as lang's that I'll wager
(holding out her arm at full length)
And if it hadna been for the fairmer o' Mains o' Brogan,
He wid a been on the tap o' me,
Creel an' a'!"

We will end as we began: round about Doup. Burnhaven was demolished and the distillery shut down in 1981.

THE LAST TOWN CRIER

Author's Note on The Last Town Crier

Writing in the midst of the oil boom in Buchan an author is liable to find his work out of date before it reaches publication in book form. I began this work in 1978 and in the few years since then the landscape around Peterhead has changed to such an extent that a returning stranger finds difficulty in reaching the town centre. Buildings have been demolished and a puzzling network of new roads has transformed all the old familiar landmarks. When it is all finished and signposted it will be easier but in the present upheaval it is all rather bewildering. The camera might have been a better means of preservation but that is not my sphere or media. To rewrite the essays without any reference to the old establishment would eradicate the memories also and no one could picture what it used to be like. The same thing has happened on the outskirts of Aberdeen, where the local historians with camera and typewriter are already at work in preserving the past.

A welcome note, almost as music, on the fields of toil in Buchan was the 'Connies' Horn', the convict prison horn which blew at five o'clock in the afternoon. It meant that in just another hour, though usually the longest one, aching bellies could be filled with saps (bread and hot milk), sago pudding, knotty-tams (milk brose), porridge, milk broth or cabbage brose, whatever the farmwife had prepared for us, with maybe a duck egg boiled or oatbread and cheese and hot tea after a long day at the hoe or hay harvest without any tea breaks.

The prison horn blew at 8 a.m., twelve noon, 1 p.m. and 5 p.m., five days a week, the working week of the convicts on the Harbour of

Refuge Works, with a free weekend in their cells, and but for the fact that they couldn't have their wives with them (or a smoke in those days) they were envied by the farmworkers. The ploughmen had to get up before 5 a.m. to feed their horses, and dairy cattlemen at 4 a.m., three and four hours respectively, before the prison horn went at 8 a.m., and these men were still working a full hour after the prison horn at 5 p.m. It was a six-day week for the farm chiels, with relief work on alternate Sundays.

Before the days of radio the prison horn was also a time-keeper as far inland as Kinmundy and Rora on a quiet day, when the farm billies stopped to check their watches with Admiralty Greenwich Time, and anxious housewives glanced at the grandfather clocks.

But the air-raid sirens of Hitler's War ended the importance of the prison horn, in case of confusion, just as it ended the curfew bell that used to ring at 8 p.m. from the Townhouse belfry in Peterhead, and all the church bells, because they might be mistaken for the bells that were to be rung if the Germans invaded our shores. So all we were left with was the fog horn, and of course 'Lord Haw-Haw' on the radio from Bremen, and however much we hated him he was always punctual.

My first view of the Peterhead skyline was dominated by the Reform Tower on Meethill, the spire of the Muckle Kirk, the tower on the Arbuthnot Museum, the Townhouse steeple, and a marine crane nearly 200 feet high stranded on the rocks at North Head, where it lay derelict for three years until it was salvaged for scrap in 1923. There were a few smoke stacks, like the lum at the Kirkburn 'oo mull, Dickie's sawmill and one at the gut factory, but none of them to compare with the towering lum that now confronts you from the Boddam power station.

Apart from the telephone wires on the main roads, the first inland line I remember, and for a long time the only one, was to Mr. Alexander Birnie's farm at Wellbank — the 'Pearl King', as he was affectionately called. In 1925 he built the footbridge over the mouth of the Ugie to Craigewan Golf Course, where there used to be a ferryboat, and they charged one penny return, children a half-penny, to cross the river. Now at Wellbank, and all over the Buchan countryside, fanning out from the Boddam power plant, we have those giant pylons ranging over the fields to feed the national electricity grid. Where once we had bare hills, like Stirlinghill, Blackhills and Mormond we now have these radar scanners and early warning monstrosities dominating the Buchan skyline.

At Hogmanay they used to fire rockets and squibs from the top of the Meethill Monument, which made it look like a fountain of fire in the darkness, and we all gathered in Broadstreet, in front of the Townhouse to see the New Year in, shaking hands with strangers, singing and shouting, and the drunks swore that on the stroke of twelve Marshall Keith raised his stone scroll and waved it over the populace.

During the war years we had fireworks of a more dangerous propensity. In 1940 I actually saw the first three bombs to hit Peterhead the moment they left the German plane circling over the town. It was a Saturday afternoon in late summer and I waited and listened for the detonation in the quiet sunlight. I had good reason to be concerned because my wife was shopping with hundreds of other housewives in the town. She got such a fright that she forgot half her messages and never waited for the next bus home. She walked the two and a half miles to Hallmoss farm where she had left her bicycle. I watched this spectacle from our farm cottage at Ednie, and I heard the bang when the bombs chipped the rocks on the foreshore at the Ronheads. No other damage was done.

I was on coastal patrol with the Home Guard on the night that Peterhead Academy was blitzed. There were four of us in the squad, with one rifle amongst us, cycling along the sands. A marauding German Heinkel came up behind us and bombed the Loch of Strathbeg. We got such a fright we nearly fell off our bicycles, for we had just had tea there half-an-hour earlier. We were anent the kirkyard on the bents at St. Fergus when we heard the other German bomber. Peterhead was hushed in sleep under the glimmering morning sky. We saw the red flash and heard the crump of the bombs. It was Saturday and in the afternoon I went into town to look at the damage. The place was a shambles, with broken, naked ceilings in mid-air and desks and wall-maps hanging out at blasted windows. Had it happened during the day I dread to think of the casualties. Lord Haw-Haw told us in the evening that the German Luftwaffe had bombed the barracks at Peterhead, but he was at the wrong end of the town.

But the bombing never stopped us from going to the movies, to the Playhouse or the Regal, Peterhead's two classic cinemas. Some of the best films ever produced were shown during the war years: master-pieces like REBECCA, HOW GREEN WAS MY VALLEY, THE WHITE CLIFFS OF DOVER, THE FIRST OF THE FEW, THE WAY TO THE STARS, and the adorable MRS. MINIVER — we just couldn't miss these, despite the bombing. My wife and I were caught on the balcony of the Playhouse on the winter night that James Street was bombed. An air-raid warning was flashed on the screen, advising us to remain in our seats. Most people did and the balcony swayed with the thudding of bombs. Two families suffered severe bereavement with a direct hit on their tenement but those in the shelter survived. Ironically the title of the film was OUR HERITAGE, starring Emlyn Williams.

But you weren't safe in the country either. The Buchan coastline wasn't called 'Hell's Corner' by our merchant seamen without good reason. When the German bombers raided our convoys the red-hot tracer bullets from our own ships were stitched across the night sky and our cottage at Ednie. One dark Sunday evening a German bomber dropped eleven aerial torpedos in one of our fields. Not one of them exploded and not a sheep was killed. When I looked out from our gable the German pilot's cabin was on fire, while he roared out to sea. He had been hit by our flak and was forced to jettison his bomb load. All of them had to be dug up afterwards by the bomb disposal people on the hill of Pizga, overlooking St. Fergus, named after that other Pizga in the Bible where Moses first looked out upon the Promised Land. No wonder our sheep were safe.

My narrowest escape was when I was caught by a hedge-hopping German bomber with a canvas whopper strapped to my shoulders, sowing nitro-chalk on old grass. I couldn't have run if I had wanted to but I could have lain down. But there wasn't time to think in the open field and I just stood erect and motionless in the throb of the great machine as the swastikas passed over me. The twin barrels on the rear-gunner's glass turret twinkled in my direction but he never pressed the button. Minutes later I heard him rattling the stone dykes round the playground at St. Fergus school, where the kids had just gone inside for lessons. The cattleman at Lunderton farm had a narrower margin with death when the bullock next to him was gunned down in an open field by a German rear-gunner. To this day you can still see the pock marks of German bullets on some Buchan farmsteads, and several had direct bomb hits.

THE LAST TOWN CRIER

Conversely, Peterhead's first shot in self-defence against a German bomber, fired from a Bofors gun in the harbour area, went right through the lum of the gut factory, leaving a gaping hole — so you could say that this initial wound was self-inflicted.

Peterhead's greatest loss was the closing of the Buchan railway to Maud junction. Had Dr. Beeching envisaged the present influx in industry now engulfing this virile seaport no doubt he would have stayed the swing of his axe. But at a time when Peterhead survived on a declining fishing harvest and the Euclyd Gear and Cleveland Twist Drill factories, and rail freight depended almost entirely on the products of Messrs. Crosse & Blackwell, it seemed an uneconomic decision to reprieve the railway lifeline. And I scarcely dare to think of the chaos on the roads had the proposed oil by-products and ammonia plant materialised on the outskirts of the town, never mind the gas terminal which has evolved at St. Fergus, especially now that the bulk of the fish trading has found favour in the recently built Peterhead fish market.

Nowadays in Peterhead I can park my car on the exact spot where I used to buy my tackety boots for the sharn rigs, at the Thistle Boot Shop, run by Mrs. Noble, in what used to be Thistle Street. She was one of the town's bootsellers who gave 'tick' to the country customers, and I paid my accounts regularly on the Term Day when I got my wages.

Now the complete triangle of houses comprising Marischal Street, Albion Street and Thistle Street have been flattened, with the historic Drummer's Corner at the apex facing Erroll Street gone forever; besides Wattie Findlay's grain store, Birnie the butcher's corner shop, White the saddlers and Davidson the undertaker's parlour. Ferrari's Cafe where I used to buy my pie and chips has been boarded up, and the name of the Regal cinema changed to the Kingsway and turned into a bingo hall.

Two of Peterhead's high-class bakeries, Nicol's and John Mackintosh next door, have both gone, directly across from the Post Office in Marischal Street, where the delightful early morning smell of freshly baked loaves used to fill the street. J. B. Catto's drapery shop (across from Jack's Ltd.) has become a bookshop, though there is still a tobacconist next door where Mr. Johnston used to serve on his wooden leg, and where I used to buy my gramophone records and tobacco.

131

A CHIEL AMONG THEM

Peterhead is a place where you can pass a driving test without traffic lights, and the same with Fraserburgh, and yet the trainee is supposed to be qualified to drive through our major cities, where most of the traffic is controlled by lights.

The town is also one-way traffic, very confusing for strangers and rather poorly sign-posted, so that even the exiles find it something of a labyrinth.

Where the railway station once stood there is now a monstrosity in red brick used as a recreational and gymnastic centre, though they tell me it is quite beautiful inside and well organised.

I think the greatest changes are to be observed at the harbour, which is crowded with boats, a good sign for the fishermen and the Harbour Board. But the diesel boats have replaced the old steam drifters and all the curing yards have gone. I can remember all the fisher-quines who used to gut the herrings into barrels from the long wooden troughs, their slick fingers wrapped in strips of cloth, their oilskin aprons spotted with blood, their cheery banter and their smiles that ignored the sting of salt in the knife cuts. Then there were the busy coopers and the stacks of barrels full of herrings on the piers awaiting export, the industry that built the princely homes in Queen Street and huddled the town with tenements.

I enjoyed the smell of salted herring and the stale brine in the curing yards; the stench of oily water in the harbour, the scent of fresh paint being slapped on to the boats high and dry on the slipways; the tarry wind that came off the herring nets drying on the pailings, the aroma of drifter smoke, the waft of the fish and chip shops, and best of all, the welcome smell of mother's tea after a long summer's day of discovery.

I can remember when one of the new lifeboats was launched, round about 1921, when we got the afternoon off from the Central School to watch all the ships in the bay, all blowing their steam sirens when the new lifeboat splashed down the slipway. One grey morning shortly afterwards everybody awoke to find a cargo boat wrecked at the south end of the pier on Smith's Embankment, the *Cairnavon* it was called, even within the shelter of the breakwaters, so great was the storm that blew her ashore.

Another event was the unveiling of the war memorial on the links on Armistice Sunday 1921, when almost the entire populace assembled, mostly in black and many of them weeping, to watch the ceremony.

THE LAST TOWN CRIER

Across from the Kirkburn Mills there used to be stables owned by Jamieson the carting contractor. One night the stables caught fire and all the horses were burned. Next morning was Saturday and I went with another boy and we saw nearly a dozen horses still lying where their stalls had been, all toasted like kippers and their poor heads against the stone walls. The burnt smell of roasted horse flesh was still strong in the air and it stuck in our nostrils for several days afterwards.

Over the years in my former essays on Peterhead I have always omitted to mention the old-established firm of James Simpson & Son Ltd., the cartwrights in Prince Street, near the centre of the town. They later performed as garage proprietors in Erroll Street and York Street, but I understand the firm is now completely out of business. The original premises in Prince Street have recently been demolished, where they had the biggest oil combustion engine I ever saw in my life. It was here in the old days that Simpson's earned themselves a reputation for building the finest and sturdiest horse carts in Scotland. Farmers prided themselves in being the owners of those seasoned two-wheeled carts that had been bought by their grandfathers and were still in use when the tractors came in. The local blacksmiths fitted them with rubber-tyred wheels from old motor lorries and a welded drawbar for the tractors and the old carts enjoyed a further lease of service.

A Simpson cart, lip-full of unriddled potatoes, was the cottar's measure for a year, and the farmers couped it in your backyard where you could make it into an earth pit against the winter frost. It was also pretty near your ration of coal for a six-month and they toppled a load at your shed door from the railway station. Those perquisites were like a godsend for the old-time cottar families and most of them had good reason to remember the capacity of a Simpson horse-cart. The 'Toon' or Council cart, mostly from Aberdeen, were just that wee bit clumsier when loaded with turnips in the muddy fields, a sore drag to the gates in rutted wheel tracks, the horse beasts plunging in glaur and their drivers beside them splashed with mud. The Toon carts were meant for the causey stones and were never as popular with the Buchan farmers as the strong but lightweight Simpson cart of Peterhead.

Here I must also mention Flukie Williamson's Cheapside Stores at the corner of Ellis Street and Longate. In my day it was Harper's Cheapside Stores and the huge monogram was stencilled in wrought iron on the roof of what is now a tenement building. But nicknames last longer than life in Buchan and the townsfolk still referred to the store as 'Flukie Williamson's' throughout Harper's tenancy, thus honouring the founder from Queen Victoria's day. Flukie traded in bedding, drapery and haberdashery and was famous for his seasonal bargain sales, where a woman could buy a felt hat for a shilling (5 pence), and a summer frock for seven shillings and sixpence (37½ pence), a traditional concession to public needs that was carried on by Harper's management. They also advertised in the Buchan Observer and the country deems and cottar wives could send for a hat by post.

The byname has an intriguing reference to the fluke or skate of the harbour area, just down the brae, and one wonders if Flukie earned his nom-de-plume as a fish merchant. In Scots the word 'fluke' can mean a freak or failure; but it can also imply an unexpected success or the prongs of an anchor and perhaps this is where it applied to our Flukie Williamson, who sold needles but not the proverbial anchor.

Another Peterhead drapery arcade, namely Jack's Ltd. of Erroll Street (now MacKay's) used to be known as 'The Little Wonder' and one wonders just where that one came from.

I can remember Peterhead's last Town Crier. He went round the streets ringing a bell and crying out the latest happenings concerning the town, or the next public event. He was James Chalmers, a native of New Deer, who had served in India with the Gordon Highlanders, and after his discharge from the army he made his home in the town. When a vacancy occurred for the post of Town Crier, Chalmers applied and got the job, being, as he said 'newly come over', from India. But when the local boys got word of it they made it his nickname, crying after him as he went his rounds.

He was an energetic official and conducted himself in military style, and to show their appreciation the town council provided him with a dazzling red-striped uniform and peaked cap to match. He strutted the pavements with back erect, a conspicuous figure, clanging his bell and crying forth to the populace, and strangers thought he was a Royal Hussar. The boys followed him everywhere, crying after him: "Newly come over! Newly come over!' But he ignored them with an official dignity that overawed their intimidation. When Chalmers died the post of Town Crier was never filled again.

Past visitors to Peterhead include General Wolfe, a few years before he died on the Heights of Abraham, when he spent a fortnight in the town, declaring that he found the climate as cold in July as it was in Kent in November. Sir Arthur Conan Doyle was at one time a medical officer on a Peterhead whaler. Later, he fought a legal battle for the release from Peterhead convict prison of Oscar Slater, who had served eighteen years of a sentence for a murder he never committed — no doubt listening every day for the welcome blast of the Connies' Horn.

THE PITFOUR CANAL

LET me take you on the tortuous road from Peterhead to Fraserburgh (A952 shortly due for realignment) beyond the mammoth new Waterside Inn and the Balmoor Bridge crossing the River Ugie. On the first turning to the left, at the farm of Hallmoss, and about another quarter of a mile along this byroad, just beyond the old smithy and joinery shop and Hallmoss croft, the road rises gently over what looks like an old humpbridge, exactly at the old three-mile stone from Peterhead, but there are no sign of arches, if they were ever built. From this point you can just see the ruined turrets of Ravenscraig Castle, and what looks like an old railway track, with trees growing in it, running in that direction, fenced round the curve of a field. What you are looking at is one of the best preserved stretches you will ever see of Buchan's one and only canal. Its position here is so intriguing, so tantalisingly present-century, that the mind yearns for further quest, especially when one observes from the old mile stone that this early nineteenth century waterway, when we face north, is heading straight for the British Gas terminal at St. Fergus.

I find it absolutely fascinating to trace man's former habitation by observing the scars and rubble he has left behind, whereby we can build up a picture of social and material change over the centuries. Even our canal at this spot lies in the shadow of a former antiquity, the notorious Hangman's Hill, surmounted by a huge bass or mound where the gallows stood, and here in medieval times the criminals from Peterhead and the prisoners from the ancient castles of nearby Inverugie and Ravenscraig paid the fatal price. Between the two castles, on the banks of the River Ugie, there used to be three flourishing meal-mills, grinding corn for the local lairds and farmers, driven by water power from the river. One reason for the existence of our canal was to collect grain and deliver oatmeal throughout the lands of Buchan, from Pitfour to St. Fergus, before the days of railways or road transport.

But why was the canal directed towards the gas terminal which arose nearly two hundred years after its initial planning? What was it that James Ferguson, the Laird of Pitfour wanted so eagerly from St. Fergus that he saw fit to build a canal to obtain it? Surely not maritime

136

gas in an age which was mostly ignorant even of coal gas. And as Peterhead was the seaport, why direct the canal to the sand bents at St. Fergus where no ships could call?

From Hallmoss our canal runs almost parallel with the main road to St. Fergus, through the farm of Lunderton, and crosses at a sharp bend in the road at Inverquinzie, within sight of the village. The embankments here are in splendid condition, but still heading for the gas terminal the canal gets lost here on the farm of North Kirton, on fields relcaimed from former bent and rushes, where the building of lock gates were necessitated by a sudden drop in the land, but were abandoned by the engineers as impracticable.

Inland from Hallmoss the canal swings westward from the meal-mills and follows the course of the River Ugie, past the farm of Ednie, where the embankments still exist, having been utilised by a later brickworks as a means of water-power. And thus along the haughs to Rora, where it was intended to flood the canal from the river, near the junction of the North and South Ugie Rivers — 'Down in the Haughs o' Rora where all men are asleep' as the old rhyme says — and sure enough the Pitfour Canal peters out here and never reached the laird's estate as was intended. For financial reasons the laird abandoned the canal at this point and it was never completed; a decision almost coinciding with the first appearance of George Stevenson's Rocket on the Darlington Railway.

Had the canal continued towards Longside the barges could have called to collect linseed oil and deliver flax at the old lint mill at Auchlee, which was probably the intention, besides wool from the mills at Aden.

But sand was the answer. It was sand that the laird and his tenants wanted; sand as fertiliser and poultry grit, shell sand obtainable at St. Fergus as nowhere else, though I leave it to the geologists to determine why. Even without the canal, for the next hundred years the farmers came with their scores of horse carts for the sand that made eggshells, from as far afield as Kinmundy and Ardallie, and I myself have joined the cart queue at Scotston, waiting my turn to load. But coastal defence precautions in the Hitler War ended the sand bonanza.

ST. FERGUS TO THE BROCH

I N 1763, when St. Fergus parish kirk was being rebuilt, a monolith stone was discovered in the foundations. On it was inscribed:

> *As lang's this stane stands on this croft,*
> *The name of Keith shall be aloft;*
> *But when this stane begins to fa'*
> *The name o' Keith shall wear awa'.*

A prophesy which was fulfilled, for by that date the Keiths had been seventeen years in exile.

A mile beyond St. Fergus, on the Blackwater estates, the marine gas terminal sprawls over the land where for centuries the crofters had struggled to grow crops on a hotbed of couch and knotgrass weed, where it spread unhindered on the sandy soil, encouraged by shallow ploughing and primitive cultivation which failed to smother its roots, merely cutting them into smaller pieces to grow in wider profusion. In the tractor age of deeper ploughing and suitable weedkiller sprays, just when the local farmers were learning to cope scientifically with the couch or string-grass menace, British Gas and Total Marine decided they wanted the land for redevelopment, since they had been denied a site at the Loch of Strathbeg, some five miles further up the coast, which has since been declared a nature conservancy.

The only notable changes in Crimond parish are the enlargement of the Keyhead Inn, the expansion of the village, the Sunday roaring of racing cars on the disused aerodrome, and the fact that the parish kirk has been given a facelift, where the old Haddo clock ticks out sixty-one minutes to the hour, giving the folk of Crimond a twelve-minute longer day than other less fortunate mortals, and a similar extension of their snoring time in this quiet sleepy corner of the Buchan coastline.

Nearing Lonmay, the only obvious change is one of neglect, where the once beautiful Lake of Cortes is now a shallow bog of weeds and rubbish, and the surrounding woods desecrated. The Ban-Car Hotel is still with us, with a luncheon and reception hall extension, but Sammy Fraser's shoppie at the Cortes road junction no longer exists. I can

138

remember when Forrest's horse-brakes used to run from the Post Office and Territorial soldiers drilled in the old wooden dance hall. The Chapel of St. Columba has been turned into a garage for combine-harvesters and my old school at Blackhills has been converted as a drying kiln for farmers' barley. The Deer on Mormond hill has seen it all, though his vision nowadays is somewhat blinded by the encroachment of nature and the engineering of man.

The oil boom has by-passed Fraserburgh, where lack of visible change leaves it as a town where memories of fifty years ago are more easily recalled. It is the only Buchan town with trees in its graceful streets, and its old-world buildings still smile pleasantly on returning exiles. But the railway now has gone and the old familiar station somewhat dishevelled, the branch line to St. Combs a dead scar on the bents.

The handsome buildings of the Consolidated Pneumatic Tool-works Company still adorn the town approaches, and also the ornamented war memorial at the corner of the slip road to Strichen. But the Brochers have knocked down the old gut factory lum at the back of Broadsea, and they have built council houses on the Banff road nearly to Watermill. Worst of all they have closed the two picture houses, the shrines of my youth, where I worshipped the Queens of Celluloid, except the one in Mid Street, still open for Bingo, which in my young day would have been a flagrant sin.

A CHIEL AMONG THEM

THE LAIRD O' UDNY'S FOOL — JAMIE FLEEMAN

L ONGSIDE is Jamie Fleeman country, and hundreds of people visit his grave in the local kirkyard, near the parish church. His real name was James Fleming, and although we don't know the exact date of his birth we do know that he was baptised at Longside on the 7th of April, 1713, and we may assume that he was born just a few weeks previous to his baptism.

Was his mother disappointed in Jamie when adolescence revealed that her son's behaviour was somewhat abnormal — and that his features and mannerisms might one day label him as a sort of parish idiot? Was that why she later drowned herself in what is still remembered as 'The Fleeman Pot', a deep pool in the burn near the bridge of Ludquharn?

What is also little known is that Mrs. Fleming had another son, who was killed in the navy, on board H.M.S. *Serapis,* although we don't know when. If we could ascertain the date of her suicide we might be able to judge which of these misfortunes unbalanced her mind, or whether it was an inherent trait which manifested itself in the simple genius her surviving son displayed.

Her daughter Martha was also mentally afflicted, though very slightly, and her eccentricity turned itself upon religion, and since she was able to read she harangued her associates and neighbours with rich bible quotations. When her daughter was found in disgrace with a lad on the evening of a Longside feeing market, Martha ran from house to house proclaiming: 'Rejoice not against me, Oh mine enemy: when I fall, I shall arise; when I sit in darkness, the Lord shall be a light unto me.'

Martha was twice married and had children. She lived nearly thirty years after the death of her famous brother, dying at Nether Kinmundy, within sight of the Fleeman cottage where she was born.

The cottage was situated at the entrance to an old quarry on the road from Longside to Lenabo (now the Forest of Deer) on the farm of

Braeside, marked by a cluster of old trees, all that remains of Martha's garden.

I remember the Fleeman cottage when the walls and chimneys were still intact, and a few red tiles on the roof; but all that now remains is the foundation stones, buried in grass. The cottage was by then two-hundred years old, originally a croft house with a thatched roof when Jamie Fleeman was born. Nobody so far has sought to mark the site of Fleeman's birth, and it is not on the map. I have pointed it out to several people in a position to keep the legend alive, and by that means it may not be entirely forgotten. What I don't know (and alas no one now alive can tell me) is the site of the cottage where Fleeman and Martha died, about half-a-mile distant across the fields at Nether Kinmundy.

I spent my young life in the Jamie Fleeman neighbourhood, stooked corn sheaves around the cottage where he was born, and I have hoed turnips in summer and plucked them in winter in the fields where he played as a boy. He was brought up in the house of Sir Alexander Guthrie, commonly known as the 'Knight of Ludquharn', on the home farm of that name on the estate of Ludquharn; a rather squat mansion with longish chimneys, almost Georgian in appearance, and said to be haunted by a green lady in days gone by. The fields on the home farm were sheltered by tall beech trees, as they still are, known as the belts of Ludquharn, where a cottar's daughter drowned her illegitimate baby, within a stone's throw of the Fleeman Pot, to hide her disgrace from her parents. Unfortunately for the girl the farm men discovered the baby when they were cleaning out the ditch and she went to prison for her crime.

Even as a boy, or what we would call a loon, we are told that Jamie Fleeman, because of his bluntness of manner and shrewd remarks, attracted the attention of his associates, and more especially of his betters, who, because of his peculiarities, indulged his humour and per-mitted him a sense of freedom and liberties which would have been sternly denied to any normal child. At an early age he provided amusement for Ludquharn's visitors and found great favour in their company, a precociousness of his role as the court jester, which was to manifest his character with such distinction in later life. And when he left Ludquharn he soon found an open door and a ready welcome at almost every gentleman's mansion in the neighbourhood.

Fleeman went bare-headed and bare-footed, at least in summer, and until the Laird of Udny provided him with footwear, which Jamie wore on the occasions that suited him, though he seems to have shown a slight aversion to having his feet covered. His hair stood on end most of the time and his eyes were lively and sometimes fixed in a stare, while his face twitched perpetually in nervous mobility. A sackcloth doublet served for covering his upper body, which he wore like a tunic, and he chose a petticoat, rather like a kilt or skirt, mostly in blue, instead of trousers.

His voice we are told was hollow, yet loud, almost sepulchral, echoed from a bone-strewn mortuary, completely at variance with his impish good humour; and he spoke through his nose, slowly, with a slyness and roguery which attracted immediate attention, and was usually accompanied by his singular remarks and sarcastic witticisms. And apparently he spoke what he thought, as if his mind was untrained to do otherwise, sparing nobody in his flashes of wit and criticism, and if oratory was wanting from his vocabulary it was substituted with a richness of observation which astounded his listeners, especially in one so conspicuously rustic and completely uneducated, for there is no mention anywhere of Jamie going to school.

His feelings were the extremes of affection and loyalty to that of hate and aversion, and when his opinion on a fellow mortal had been defined he was fixed and unwavering; either loving and faithful, or forgiving and forgetting nothing throughout his life. Once a friend of Fleeman you were always a friend; once an enemy you were doomed to his ill-will for ever more.

The time came eventually when he had to leave the family home at Ludquharn, and it was a sad Jamie when one of the ladies of the family told him they could no longer afford a servant of any sort, not even for board and lodgings, except for those who were indispensable. Jamie listened with downcast look and heavy heart; and having some indistinct notion that the worthy ladies were under the necessity of curtailing their comforts on account of limited means, he offered his services for nothing. To him, he said, worldly considerations were of no value compared to the regard he had for his benefactors. In a faltering tone, quivering with emotion, Jamie stammered: "Ye hae been kind, kind tae me, an' I canna leave ye in your strait. I'm gaen wi' ye, should ye gang to the ill pairt". To hell, Jamie meant, whither he would follow those he loved.

A CHIEL AMONG THEM

It was then that poor Jamie found favour with the Laird of Udny, who had often been a visitor to Ludquharn, and was well aware of Jamie's whimsical characteristics as an entertainer for his numerous guests; and for many years Fleeman was at his service, giving birth to a legend which has survived two centuries in an ever changing society.

Many are the stories told of Jamie Fleeman, sharp and sly in wit, pregnant with unexpected wisdom, and enlivened with the humour of a wise fool. No doubt some of the stories have been exaggerated by oral repetition over two centuries, but even in essence the Fleeman genre is preserved uniquely as his own.

He lived during the Jacobite risings. In fact he was only two years old when the Old Pretender landed in Peterhead in 1715, and a man of thirty-three in the year of Culloden. After their defeat, Fleeman was sometimes employed as a trusted messenger between members of the Jacobite faction, concerning each other's safety and whereabouts in hiding from the searching Redcoats of Butcher Cumberland's army. On one occasion Jamie was entrusted by the Countess of Erroll to convey a letter to Lord Pitsligo, then in seclusion at Auchiries House, in the parish of Rathen.

On the way Jamie encountered one of the local lairds, who was a staunch Hanoverian, and who was determined to question Fleeman in a manner which might induce him to divulge information concerning his benefactors.

"Where are ye going, Jamie?" the laird asked.

"I'm gaun tae hell, sir," Fleeman replied, seemingly in a great hurry, and gave the laird no chance of further conversation.

But the laird wasn't satisfied, and he awaited Jamie's return in the evening, when he might subject Udny's fool to further questioning.

"What are they doing in hell, Jamie?" the laird demanded, while Jamie paused in the warmth of the evening, his features mobile, his body in the usual state of mild convulsion, never standing still a moment. "Juist what they're deein' here sir," Fleeman answered, "lattin' in the rich fouk and keepin' oot the peer".

"And what said the devil to you, Jamie?" the laird probed, trying to waylay him.

"Ou," Fleeman replied, "the devil said na muckle tae me, sir, but he was speerin' sair aboot you!" which left the laird scratching his head in the middle of the road.

THE LAIR O' UDNY'S FOOL

Jamie was never on very good terms with the Laird of Waterton, who farmed on the banks of the Ythan near Ellon. Jamie was lolling in the sun one day on the river bank when he observed Waterton on horseback across the water, asking where was the best place to cross. Fleeman knew the shallows, but he directed the laird to the deepest pool in the river. The laird plunged in, his horse to the neck in water, himself soaked and chilled, and when they clambered out at Jamie's side he riled at Fleeman for trying to drown him, shaking his fist in anger.

"Gosh be here, laird!" said Fleeman, "I've seen the geese and the dyeuks hunners o' times crossin' there, an' I thocht your horse had langer legs than them!"

Another day at Waterton Jamie met a man who tried to take the size of him, something not uncommon in Jamie's lot. "Ou Jamie," says he, "have ye heard the news?"

"Na faith I", quoth Fleeman, "fat news, man?"

"Ou Jamie, that seven miles of the sea are burnt at the Newburgh this mornin'!"

"Od, little ferlie," Jamie retorted, "for I saw a flock o' skate aboot breakfast time flyin' past Waterton to the woods o' Tolquhon, maybe to big their nests there!"

On another occasion, while loitering along the road, Jamie Fleeman picked up a horse-shoe. Shortly after he met the Rev. Craigie, then minister of St. Fergus, and held up the shoe. "Mister," says he, "can ye tell me what that is?"

"That?" said the minister, "You fool, that's a horse-shoe!"

"Oh!" Jamie sighed, smiling gleefully in the minister's face. "Ae! sic a blessin' as it is to be weel learned! I couldna tell whether it was a horse's shoe or a mare's ane!"

But the Rev. Craigie, it is noted, delighted much in a joke himself, and used to recite this encounter with Fleeman in great glee, remarking that wise men ought never to meddle with fools — least of all with the Laird of Udny's fool.

Another local minister, one who upbraided Fleeman with a remark on his vagrancy, was rebuked by Jamie's biting retort: "Ah weel, Reverend, but I dinna hae tae misca' the deevil tae mak' a livin'!" Which we may assume put the minister in his place, and maybe gave him a new slant on religion.

A CHIEL AMONG THEM

There cannot be many people in Buchan who have not seen, or heard, of the Rock of Skerry, that clump of stone sticking out of the sea about three miles offshore at Peterhead. In fact it seems nearer Boddam than the Blue Toon, and some folk think the lighthouse should have been built on Skerry, rather than at Buchan Ness. Be that as it may — but not so many Buchan folk know the story of Jamie Fleeman and the Skerry Rock.

One fine day the Laird o' Udny's fool was standing on the pier at Peterhead, just about where the old Russian cannon used to be, captured by the British at Sebastopol, in the Crimean War — or for shorter memories — not far from the present lifeboat shed. Jamie Fleeman was ambling about there among a puckle other folk that were having a news on the pier. One of the menfolk Jamie knew from old acquaintance, a man who was peering through a spyglass very intently at something out at sea. He gazed fixedly for such a long time that he aroused Fleeman's curiosity, and since Jamie couldn't see any ships in sight he went up to the gentleman and enquired what he was looking at.

Merely glancing at Udny's fool, and without lowering his glass the man said: "Oh Jamie, I am looking at a pair of crabs with so little to do they are trying a race on the Skerry Rock."

Jamie stared for quite a while at the Skerry Rock, and as his friend never offered him the spyglass, he cocked his head to one side and seemed to be listening with an open hand behind is ear. "Man", said Fleeman, "I canna just say that I see onything particular, but I can hear the stamp o' their feet!" Jamie had the laugh on his side from the bystanders who heard their remarks.

On another occasion, returning in the gloamin' from Aberdeen, Fleeman was confronted with the devil blocking his path on a narrow bridge at Udny. Jamie went down on his knees and begged Satan to let him pass.

"Oh gweed deevil, let me past!" he begged. "I'm naething but Udny's feel! Oh gweed deevil, let me past!"

But the devil was inexorable, and which ever way Fleeman dodged to get past, this way and that, the devil leapt in front of him. "Ah weel," cried Jamie, gathering up a handful of stones, "Be ye gweed deevil; be ye ill deevil, I'se try ye wi' a lea arnot!" And he proceeded to pelt his horned tormentor.

The devil fled ingloriously, scratching where it wasn't itchy, and in

146

flight he dropped his cowhide, tail and horns, while he scuttled to the safety of the trees. Jamie gathered up the gear, and entering Udny Castle he threw the trophies on the floor at the feet of the servants, one of whose number in hiding had tried to frighten him. "Ye need never fear the deevil now lads," he cried in ecstacy, "for there is his skin!"

But Fleeman had his tantrums too, when he wouldn't do the laird's bidding except on his own terms, and ways and means had to be found to humour him and make him comply. There was the time that Udny wanted him to go an errand some three miles distant from the castle and Jamie refused to go except on horseback. But it was a bit like giving a schoolboy a motor car and the laird shrank from the responsibility of letting his prize fool scamper off on a lively gelding.

Then one of the stable boys had a brainwave, and he handed Fleeman the small branch of a tree. "Here, Jamie," he cajoled, "here's a horse for ye, get mounted!" So the Laird o' Udny's fool, with characteristic simplicity and great delight, instantly bestrode the proffered stick, and arming his right hand with a stout switch, gave his wooden steed a few stinging blows and went louping down the castle drive.

His errand accomplished, Fleeman went darting back to the castle, and meeting the laird with some gentlemen he cried: "He's a very rough rider yon beast! Heigh sirs, gin it hadna been for the honour o' the thing, I micht as weel hae been on Shank's mare!"

The laird and a tenant were discussing the poor qualities of a certain field, wondering what they could plant in it that would grow. Fleeman was capering behind them, muttering to himself, and when the laird overheard him and asked what he meant, Jamie replied: "Plant it wi' factors laird, they thrive wherever ye plant them!" The embarrassing thing about it was that the tenant was Udny's factor.

One Sunday, in the kirk at Udny, the whole congregation was nodding, while Jamie Fleeman, in his usual habit, was wide awake and all attention. The minister, observing this, thought it necessary to admonish his flock with some severity. "My brethren," he apostulated, "You should take an example from that poor fool there. Fool though he be, *he* keeps awake, while you — think shame of yourselves — are nodding and sleeping!"

"Aye aye, minister," cried Jamie, "but gin I had nae been a feel I'd hae been asleep tee!"

But for all his wit and flashes of humour Jamie Fleeman could neither read nor write. Nor was he sufficiently aware of his eccentric greatness to have any desire or wish for immortality. Indeed he was so very much unconscious of his legendary importance in the community that he shied away from having his likeness painted. Several efforts were made to capture Jamie in oils but he foiled every attempt, refusing to sit still long enough for any artist to concentrate on his irascible and mischievously mobile features.

Indeed we are fortunate in having a portrait of any sort of Jamie Fleeman, and but for the persistent efforts of a vagrant artist named Collie, who happened to be in Longside, we would never have had a contemporary likeness. Collie was so struck with Fleeman's unusually rustic appearance, that above all else he wanted to sketch him; yet there was in Jamie's nature a certain waywardness which gave him great delight in frustrating anyone who sought to meddle with him, a sort of impish annoyance which made the artist's task doubly difficult.

Tobacco and ale was the bait, an inducement Jamie couldn't resist, and having got him into the inn at Sandhole, near Kininmonth, word was sent by the conspirators to the artist that now was his chance. But Collie was not at hand, and when he eventually arrived at Sandhole he was without his materials. Determined however, not to lose the only opportunity he was ever likely to get, he cut a square of white pasteboard and burnt the end of a stick in the fire, and concealing himself in a corner of the inn, where he had a full view of Fleeman, who was unaware of the ruse, Collie produced with his rude instruments a most striking charcoal resemblance of Udny's famous fool.

Two portraits of Fleeman survive; the other portrays him with a furrowed brow and his hair standing on end, which it did perpetually, as if he were in a state of continual fright, but the one I refer to conveys Fleeman in his wide-fitting toorie bonnet, and a pleasant grin on his jocund features, just as Collie caught him over his jug of ale.

Collie gave the picture to the Rev. John Skinner of Linshart, the author of TULLOCHGORAM, and here we should bear in mind the ironic coincidence, that it was on the boundary of one of the Linshart farms that Jamie's mother drowned herself.

Miss Boyd of Ludquharn, across the ditch from Linshart (later Mrs. Gordon of Insch) begged the picture from the Rev. Skinner, who made a present of it to her. Lady Mary Hay of Erroll, having seen the picture, pressed Miss Boyd so much to give it up that she consented, and

THE LAIRD O' UDNY'S FOOL

Fleeman's portrait graced the drawing room of Slains Castle, where its live original was so often seen in the kitchen.

The picture was lost for over a century, but eventually turned up at Arnage Castle, when it was copied by the printers for the Rev. John B. Pratt's biography of Fleeman.

I have written about it elsewhere, but for the benefit of those who don't know the story of Fleeman's escapade at Knockhall Castle I will repeat it here. Knockhall Castle is a ragged but picturesque ruin on a green knoll overlooking Newburgh village and the Ythan estuary. It was built in 1565 and destroyed by fire in 1734. In its latter days the castle was the property of the Lairds of Udny, and Jamie Fleeman, the Laird of Udny's fool was sent to Knockhall to assist the resident house-keeper in running the castle. But she treated Jamie rather harshly, kept him scant of food, and her continual cry was: "Peats Fleeman!" "Sticks Fleeman!" "Water Fleeman!" with the threat of eternal damnation, hell-fire and brimstone in after-life if he disobeyed her, until the poor man was nearly demented. Jamie slept with his dog on a pallet of straw in the attic, and it is said that on the night the castle caught fire the dog licked his face and awoke him. Fleeman roused the household (all except the housekeeper) and then broke into the strong-room, where he rescued the charter-chest or deed-kist by throwing it out from an upstairs window, a feat which would have required the efforts of two men of normal strength.

Back on the ground, while he mingled with those who had come to put out the fire, someone noticed the absence of the housekeeper and asked Jamie if he had wakened her. "Na na," said he, "she was aye on aboot the Devil, so she'll get hell at hame the nicht!"

But eventually, and only just in time, even when the flames and smoke were at her bedroom door, Fleeman was prevailed upon to rescue his mistress. So he scrambled up the smoke filled stairs and woke her before she suffocated. "Come awa' ye jaad," he cried, "or ye'll get twa het hurdies!" Some say she was yelling at the window and that Fleeman climbed a ladder to save her, but in either case the outcome was the same.

Around 1968 it was rumoured that Fleeman's ghost or that of his housekeeper had returned to haunt the ruins of Knockhall Castle. The story was so prevalent that a photograph of the castle and a story of the ghost appeared in the local press. Nothing was seen but just after nightfall a strange sepulchral sighing was heard in the ruins by the local villagers and farming folk. I went down to investigate and a rather frightened little girl pointed out the niche high up in the walls where the sighing came from, quite near Fleeman's sleeping quarters. I didn't wait until nightfall but several weeks later it was discovered that the sighing came from an asthmatic owl that had taken up residence at Knockhall.

The deed-kist of Knockha', 'Fleeman's kist', as it is sometimes referred to, was at one time supposed to be still at Udny castle, but later reports affirm it can now be seen at Castle Fraser, between Dunecht and Kemnay.

Most people regard the mention of Jamie Fleeman as an occasion for fun. Others regard him as a tragi-comic figure of folklore, puzzling and humorous, but once they have heard some of his witticisms their interest is aroused and they are most anxious to learn more of the creature. We have now reached a stage when a great many of our younger people have never heard of Jamie Fleeman; even library assistants who are working every day with books.

Yet his life has been dramatised on the local concert platforms, comparing favourably with MILL O' TIFTY'S ANNIE as Buchan's most poignant tear-jerker, and in humour and pathos a popular rival for Gavin Greig's MAINS' WOOIN'.

A stone was erected by subscription on Fleeman's grave at Longside eight years before Jamie's principal biographer, the Rev. John B. Pratt, died; and as he mentions the stone in the biography we must assume it was written sometime between 1861 and 1869, which at the latest means the book is well over one hundred years old, some of it based on an earlier record of 1832, which even then was fifty years after Fleeman's death.

Towards the end of his life Fleeman was just as much neglected in reality as he was later in print. As Pratt tells us, so long as he was able to amuse people and make them laugh he was always welcome in their homes; even encouraged to stay longer than he intended, for a bite or sup, though he usually betook himself to an outhouse to bed down. But when Udny's fool reached old age and lost something of his physical strength and faculty of wit, he was no longer an entertainer, or even a figure of fun, and he was cast out upon his own to wander the roads at will.

The poorhouse of Fleeman's day was a most forbidding institution, in the nature of 'All ye who enter here abandon hope' variety; a dire refuge for the utterly destitute, and while his sister was alive it is unlikely that Jamie would have considered entering their loathsome portals. It is also likely that he still subsisted on his sixpence a week and peck of meal from Udny's laird as the reward for saving his Lordship's deed-kist from the fire at Knockhall Castle, though the laird was sometimes forgetful of his fool's clothing and of shoes for his feet.

Even so, and assuming that Jamie Fleeman, being unmarried, received nothing from the church funds or parish relief, and being quite incapable of consistent manual employment, if such were to be found for him, after the age of sixty-five he was little better than, and as little respected as, the average parish tramp or village idiot; the butt of every idle joke and the victim of every conceivable prank that could be played on him. Previously he had the strength of several men and nobody with sense would have dared to meddle with him.

And as human nature was just as thankless then as it still is (generally speaking) the Buchan weather was just as cruel. In the spring of 1778, wandering the cart tracks of Cruden, and if not actually begging from door to door, yet nevertheless presenting himself for food, Fleeman was subjected to a season of persistent rain which afforded him little opportunity of keeping his bodily garments dry. And nobody offered him a stitch from a drying line, nor an invitation to sit at the fire and dry out what he wore.

Jamie developed a seated cold, then jaundice and fever, and no doubt showed symptoms of what we now regard as pneumonia, while he tottered from the straw of one barn to the next, until he reached the farm of Little Ardiffery in Cruden, where he took shelter in the barn.

But the door didn't bar on the inside, and to keep out the draught and seeping rain, Jamie struggled with a heavy slab of wood, probably a ship's beam, and set it against the door.

Next morning, when Ardiffery's lads came in to flail corn they burst in the door, toppling the plank that fell on Jamie and severely gashed his head. Blood streamed down his face, and like a wounded animal, Jamie crawled into a corner and hid himself with corn sheaves. He was now sick with pain and fever and a burning thirst.

The farm chiels paid little attention to the old tink, for as such they now regarded him, though no doubt they knew a little of his reputation. They beat their flails upon the threshing floor like the hammers of hell to the bewildered Fleeman, now more in need of quiet than he had ever been in his life, his mind on the verge of delirium.

Nor could the lads see very well with their cruzie lanterns, a mere gloom prevailing upon their labours and the growing heap of corn, while they wisped the straw into bundles as cattle feed. When daylight came, and they went into breakfast, the foreman told Mrs. Johnston, the farmer's wife, that feel Fleeman was in the barn and that he looked the worse of drink.

But kindly Mrs. Johnston knew that poor old Fleeman was no drunkard, and she roused her daughters and sent them to fetch Jamie from the barn. Weakened further from his loss of blood, Jamie staggered from the barn, and supported by the lassies he reached the kitchen, where they bathed his wound and tended him with food and warmth. But all to little purpose, for the cold hand of death was upon Jamie's shoulder, and he had little appetite for food. Had he met these people sooner it might have fared better with him.

Before dressing the cut on his skull, one of the daughters cut off some locks of Jamie's hair, when he faintly cried "Aliss!" — an expression of pain.

Then he said to Mr. Johnston: "When I am gane, ye winna lay me at Cruden, but tak' me tae Langside, and bury me amang my friends!"

The sympathetic farmer, unaware that Jamie's end was near, replied: "Na, na, Jamie, we'll try ye here first, and if ye winna lie, we shall then be forced to carry ye across the hill by Cairn Catta."

Tears welled in Jamie's eyes and Mr. Johnston realised that the time for jesting with Udny's feel was long gone by. Fleeman, without a word, and in spite of every remonstrance, prepared for his last journey to Longside. They begged him to stay but he wouldn't listen. He thanked them all and departed, the great strength of his youth now ebbing fast, scarcely able for the task he now had to perform.

And whether Jamie scrambled over by Hatton and the moss of Kinmundy, or whether he crawled by Aldie and Savoch, the distance was seven or eight miles, it took him the whole day, resting frequently by the roadside. The crows were winging to roost in the woods of Ludquharn by the time he reached his sister's cottage.

Martha made a bed for him and he died two days later. While standing round his deathbed one said to another: "I wonder if he has any sense of another world, or a future reckoning?"

"Oh no, he is a fool!" replied the other; "what can he know of such things?"

Jamie heard them and opened his eyes, and looking at this man in the face he said: "I never heard that God seeks where he did not give."

He lay quiet for a time, and when again he opened his eyes, he looked at one who stood nearby, one he respected and trusted, and said in a firm tone: "I am a Christian, dinna bury me like a beast."

These were his last words, and a few minutes later he died without a gurgle. Jamie's executor, presumably Mr. Kilgour of Kinmundy, sent all his wool-combers and weavers to assist in carrying Fleeman's body to Longside churchyard, and he generously treated all those who attended the funeral with cakes and porter, so that the poor creature who died almost friendless, had a decent burial.

A CHIEL AMONG THEM

SHIFT FIVE

MISS HENDERSON

WRITING about Buchan, the land of my birth, one of my best memories concerns my last surviving schoolteacher, Miss Agnes Henderson of Rosehearty. I hadn't seen her for fifty-three years, not since 1925 until the summer of 1978, and when she opened her cottage door for me I scarcely recognised her. My boyhood picture of Miss Henderson vanished at first glance. Gone was the auburn haired young woman with the dairymaid complexion and gold-rimmed spectacles, buckled shoes and Gordon tartan skirt with matching cardigan, and in her place a still good-looking matronly woman of eighty-one winters that had whitened her hair, though her eyes still shone like sunlight on blue waters.

But she recognised me immediately, her mind alert as an instant camera, even to the short breeks and bare knees as she remembered me from two years in her primary class at Coldwells School, Longhaven. She had written to me when my novel BLOWN SEED came out, and said she had lain awake a whole night wondering who this loon might be whom the reviewers said had walked three miles to school. From dozens of schoolboy photographs she had whittled it down to the boy who had lived furthest from school, and my real name came to her in a flash before she fell asleep.

I told her I had gone on pilgrimage to my old school, where the cart road over the moor was now overgrown with grass, and most of the crofts in ruins where my schoolmates lived. She gave me a life history of most of my contemporaries at school, boys and girls alive and dead over the years, and I was amazed at how she had kept in touch with some of them right up to date — some of them I had forgotten completely.

Her letters to me speak of many changes, written in a tidy compact hand without her glasses, though she has worn them throughout her life for longer vision. She writes of the days when she cycled from Boddam, where she was in digs, to teach at Longhaven, and stanced her bicycle all day in the school porch. In those days it was a three-mile stretch of empty road, though a hard climb over Stirling Hill and the Last Shift, as they called it, where now she wouldn't be safe to cycle in the murderous

155

flow of modern traffic.

Last Christmas Miss Henderson sent me a greetings card and one of her colourful notelets reflecting on the lavishness of gifts for the modern bairns compared with the old days. In her own words I quote: 'Well I hope you had a nice time over the festive season which is made so much of these days. I think we were more content when we just had an apple and orange in our stocking. I once had the poker up the sleeve of my frock ha! ha!'

I could have told her about the time I had my stocking filled with cinders and soap-powder, which, at the age of eight disillusioned me for all time on the fantasy world of a benignly generous Father Christmas, especially when I had beseeched Santa almost in prayer for a clockwork train set.

Back at the cottage in Rosehearty, where Miss Henderson still tends her bounteous garden, she conveniently lapsed from the English she had taught me and resorted to a softened version of our native Doric. "Speak aboot changes," she hied me, "I had this hoose biggit in 1939, and it took every penny I had saved, but compared wi' modern buildin' costs it was a flee-bite. Just recently I had this porch built on in front and it cost as much as the hoose itsel' had done afore the war. I could never afford it nooadays! It was juist afore the war, and then Hitler's bombers cam' owre and I thocht they would have it knocked doon aboot my lugs, like some ithers in the village".

It is indeed quite a large and handsome villa by modern suburban standards.

Miss Henderson was almost a fanatic on history lessons, especially Scottish history, with Wallace and Bruce and the Stuart Kings as her special heroes, suggesting a pro-Jacobite tendency. Nowadays she would have been labelled a fervent Scottish Nationalist, though her views have mellowed over the years in favour of the all-British monarchy.

But throughout my adult life I have never forgotten her teaching. While standing on the field of Bannockburn, or at Stirling Castle, Falkland Palace or Linlithgow, climbing the Wallace Monument or on holiday in Glentrool, Miss Henderson has been my inspiring angel, urging me on with the pen where once the sword of our national heroes had flourished in victory.

We talked of the day in 1925 when a kilted battalion of Gordon Highlanders in full kit marched past Coldwells School from Aberdeen to Peterhead and the north. A message came through to Miss

MISS HENDERSON

Henderson from the headmaster, Mr. William Craighead, to let her pupils out and we all ran outside to watch the soldiers.

We could see them approach from Longhaven House, where they filled the road to Turnylieve smiddy and Mr. Matthew's joinery shop. We were not allowed on to the road, so we leaned over the stone dyke around the playground, and on each other's shoulders, so great was the crush to watch the soldiers. It was a sight I have never forgotten: all these soldiers marching four abreast, in silence because there was no pipe band, only the crunch of their feet on the gravelled road, and some of them smiled to us or gave us a nod in passing, each one with a rifle on his shoulder, something you could never witness nowadays with motorised transport.

It was a field day for Miss Henderson and we got a thundering history lesson in the afternoon on the relief of Lucknow and the siege of Mafeking, glorifying the achievements of the British army. How they got the tip-offs I never knew, unless it was from Pratt's Post Office and grocery shop at the end of the village, but if anything unusual was on the road the school bairns were allowed outside to see it.

Our next entertainment was the legless man who was 'walking' all the way from Land's End to John O' Groats, and taking the east coast route our teachers had been alerted of his approach.

He was a mere speck on the road from Longhaven House, but by the time we were outside he was coming nearer, bouncing on his buttocks, on a sort of bellows or spring-loaded cushion that lifted him forward, while he propelled himself with his leather-gloved hands on the road, about the speed of average walking pace, or perhaps two and a half miles per hour.

He was like a sort of octopus with only two tentacles and a human head, but he never looked at us watching him from the dyke. I saw him one day later in Peterhead and people who spoke to him said he snubbed them and scorned their sympathy, and they thought he was a victim of war wounds with a very independent attitude to life, bitter and defiant of its cruelties.

Apart from the occasional horse cart, a traction engine or a puffing-billy there was very little traffic on the roads, though Sutherland's red buses had begun a daily service from Peterhead to Aberdeen. The only motor lorry in the village was a small Ford, I think, with solid rubber tyres and it belonged to Tosh Gray the carrier. Tarmacadam surfacing was in progress and we watched that also, with a huge tar kettle on wheels boiling the tar, pulled along by a steam-roller. We got sticky

157

hands on the hot tar while the men were working near the school and most of us liked the smell of it. Women in the towns used to take their babies to sniff the reek of the tar kettle when they had the 'kink-hoast', better known as whooping cough, and it sometimes eased their coughing or 'back dracht' as they called it, when the bairn could hardly get its breath back in a fit of coughing.

The roadside stone-breaker was another worthy of those days, before the mechanical stone crusher, when he sat by his cairn, chipping stones, first splitting the granite boulders with a heavy hammer, where the traction wagons had toppled them into his recess. All day long he hammered, his 'piece bag' on his bicycle by the wire fence, and at the end of the week he measured the length of his 'bing' of stone chips, for he was paid by the length of it, so much per yard. When it rained he sat with an oilskin jacket over his head or went home, for there was no pay for wet weather working.

The bairns bought all their sweeties at Pratt's shoppie, though some of us cottar bairns seldom had a penny to spend. We took our boots for repair to Willie Mackie, who had a timmer shoppie at the end of the road to Blackhill quarry, after he moved up from Turnylieve. Sometimes in the summer months we went home barfit to save our boots, which were tied by the pints (laces) over our shoulders, with our socks inside.

Miss Henderson even remembered my playground fight with Wullie Grey from the Bullers. We had fought for nearly an hour at dinner time and only ended when the whistle blew. We were about fit for each other but neither of us would give in. The real difference was that I was unmarked and Wullie was covered in blood. The girls took his side however, and told Miss Henderson in the porch. But perhaps she thought that I had absorbed some of her battle-cry history lessons and he got little of her sympathy. "Ah well," she told the girls, referring to Wullie Grey, "He's just come off second best!"

I remember but few of my classmates at Coldwells School: Mary Pittendreich (who sat beside me), Willie and Jean Durno, Willie Sangster from Greenhill, Jean and William Scrogie, James and John Cordiner from Quarryknapps, Nattie Davidson, David and John Sim, Eddie and Nellie Milne, Sandy Gall, Ronald and Rene Steven, Jean and Sandy Warrander, Robbie Middleton, Alec Beagrie, Doddie Marr, and of course Wullie Grey, while Brosie Buchan, Shoddy Davidson and Winkie Cruickshank are nicknames I'll never forget. But Miss Henderson remembers them all.

MISS HENDERSON

I went to five different schools by the time I was fourteen and met so many different scholars that a great many of them have faded from my memory.

JIMMIE SUTHERLAND

IF Jimmie Sutherland had known there was oil in the North Sea he would have been there first with a fleet of lorries for pipe installation and rig supply, and with helicopters for transporting their crews. That was the sort of man he was, and although our younger generation have no recollection of his enterprising and pioneering spirit, if indeed they have ever heard of him, yet the older of us who remember him will agree about his commercial genius and alert business promptitude. Hard-headed industrialist he may have been, but he had a soft centre for deserving causes and a sympathetic attitude towards his employees, some of whom spent their entire lives in his service, ending up as executives from a yard-sweeping apprenticeship, an important branch of the transport business in the days of draught horses.

James Sutherland was born in 1863 at Newfield, about three miles south of Peterhead, where his mother, Babee McRae, was a tenant farmer. He had one sister, Barbara, but no brothers, and there is no mention of his father, so the young Jimmie seems to have taken control very early in life and never looked back. He was greatly influenced by his mother's grieve, James Connon, who first encouraged his interest in horses, and Jimmie's first triumph was the purchase of a Cleveland gelding at Aikey Fair. Later he was known to have thirty horses gathered overnight in one field for sale at the fair, and if one was missing he could identify it by some odd marking or colour.

During the First World War he had forty-eight horses and four traction engines working at Lenabo, the airship station near Longside. Sutherland's engine drivers with their threshing mills were household names among the Buchan farming folk: William Fenty, Joe Wyness, George Kidd, Joe Buyers and Andrew McConnochie, and their depot was an old herring curing yard in St. Peter Street, Peterhead, later known as Victoria Stables, where they kept over a hundred horses. Peter Magee, one of the stablemen, had one of his arms cut off in a hay-cutting machine supplying all these animals. Jimmie Sutherland's first employee was Peter Aiken and his first lorry driver was James Chalmers, later yard gaffer at Victoria Stables.

To those who thought they knew Jimmie Sutherland in his day the greatest surprise would have been to learn that he was very fond of the theatre and that he was an exquisite dancer. His public image was that of the lonely old man who lived in the big dark mansion among the trees overlooking the pinky braes at Sandford Bay, a man you were afraid to speak to, and if you asked him for a job all you could get out of him was "Ca' Herrin'," and then you were entrusted with a heavy workhorse and lorry and sent down to the harbour with a load of empty barrels.

To the man in the street he was always the gruff, workaday, almost unapproachable, stoutish figure in tatty cap standing with his hands behind his back against the wall of the office block at Victoria Stables, watching the traffic entering and leaving his busy premises in Peterhead's St. Peter Street.

It would have seemed incredulous to imagine this stolid, business obsessed, individually isolated figure in a white, lace-fronted shirt, with black tie and tails on a polished dance floor, bowing gracefully to the Edwardian-gowned ladies of Bon-Accord after a whirl to the beat of the dance band at the Athenaeum in Aberdeen's Castlegate. After a show at His Majesty's Theatre, Mr. Sutherland would rendezvous at the Athenaeum with some of his friends for a sumptuous meal and a spot of dancing, where Mr. Hay organised the social programmes. The transformation was so ridiculous you would have thought that Mr. Sutherland had poured himself out of Dr. Jekyll's bottle into a new Hyde.

He was popular with the ladies, three in particular he fancied, or who fancied him (or his position) but when they visited at Sandford Lodge they were mostly under the chaperonage of an older female.

Sometimes thirty guests were entertained on the lawn at Sandford, where James Whyte, the resident gardener kept it in good trim. On these occasional Sundays, the housekeeper and her maid had to make ice cream in a big wooden churn, and tea and home bakes were also provided. Business associates were cordially entertained and his visitors included Provost and Mrs. Dickie of Peterhead; Mr. James Milne of Port Henry Coal Stores; Mr. and Mrs. Kenneth Smith of Meethill; Mr. and Mrs. Noble of Peterhead; Mr. John Mackintosh and his wife from the bakery in Marischal Street; Mr. and Mrs. Sellar from Boddam and Mr. William Wisely, the haulage contractor from Aberdeen, the only one of his business rivals who shared and enjoyed Mr. Sutherland's hospitality.

Croquet was played on the lawn in summer months, another ploy you could scarcely imagine Jimmie Sutherland getting involved in. Evenings in winter were spent at card games, with a big fire in the drawing-room grate and Mr. Sutherland always the genial host, jokes and laughter abounding.

Sometimes the Birnie Andersons were there, and Mr. McIntosh, Sutherland's general manager, who was later shot by Birnie Anderson

161

during a board meeting after Sutherland's death. Mr. McIntosh recovered and ran the farming side of the business until it was disbursed after the war, when he then managed the transport division until he died on the farm of Middleton of Rora, which was bequeathed to him by Mr. Sutherland. Birnie Anderson was imprisoned and after serving his sentence he farmed Damhead, of which he had a lifetime tenancy from Mr. Sutherland.

Mr. Sutherland enjoyed his morning cup of tea in bed, which was conveyed to him by his housekeeper. The only time he was denied this luxury was the one morning during her entire service that the housekeeper overslept. She went straight to the byre milking, over which she presided personally, informing her master in passing his door that there would be no tea that morning because she was half-an-hour late. When she reached the byre it was empty and no cows in the stalls. The cattleman had absent-mindedly returned them to pasture, assuming that they had been milked at the usual time — or perhaps for devilment.

The housekeeper had to take the cows inside again and chain them up, while her maid was lighting the fire in the kitchen range. Mr. Sutherland observed this ongo from his bedroom window, and the housekeeper was busy milking when he entered the byre, asking why she had to gather the cows herself when it was the cattleman's job. After breakfast he went up to the 'stem mull' at Newton of Sandford, which he owned and farmed, and in irate fettle he reprimanded the cattleman in full hearing of his workmates for being so damned unobservant that he didn't know if a cow was milked or no. But what really annoyed him was the absence of his morning cuppa, which really started the day for him; without it he was on his beam-end.

He was not fastidious about his food but liked his tattie-soup with the potatoes boiled in the stock, which the housekeeper didn't like, preferring to boil the potatoes separately and strain them off before mixing them with the beef bree. But he compromised and suggested she sup his type of tattie-soup one week and he would sup hers the next, and something of the same principle was agreed upon with pea and lentil soup.

There were a few occasions when her master indulged in a much stronger stimulant than morning tea, especially after a successful business transaction or a remunerative cattle sale, when the housekeeper would have to struggle up the stairs supporting him, and would topple him into bed in a stupor, removing his shoes and covering him with the blankets, his pockets bulging and pound notes sticking out of him everywhere. But he relied on her implicitly on these outbursts, and apart from his housekeeper and his trusted chauffeurs nobody else knew of this occasional indulgence. His only other luxury was a pipe, but he wasn't a heavy smoker and seldom seen with it in business hours. He always ran a bright red motor car, his favourite colour, and his private chauffeurs over the years were George Leich, Billy Watson, Ernest Reid, Billy Hutcheon and Doddie Allan.

Two notable absentees from Sutherland's dinner table were Bailie James Booth of Downiehills (otherwise Tartan Jim) and Alexander Birnie of Wellbank (the Pearl King), probably because, like himself, they were self-made men who had started out with nothing and ended up with everything they could have wished for — excepting each other's closer friendship, for which you would have thought they had a common bond.

Being a bachelor Jimmie Sutherland was obliged to confide in his housekeeper about his business affairs, and especially concerning his rivals, and how he would take them down to size. Strangers called her 'Miss Sutherland', thinking she was his daughter, and one of them offered her his chair at table, asking her to sit down, that he would serve during the remainder of the meal, remarking that she had done enough for them already. On this occasion Mr. Sutherland, at the head of the table, informed his chivalrous guest that the lady in question was not his daughter, adding, in his usual gruff monotone, "But I wish to God she was!"

She had replaced his sister Barbara, who had married Mr. Hugh Reid, a whisky salesman with Irish connections. Barbara died after a prolonged illness and left the young housekeeper in full charge of her brother's household.

The domestic budget was balanced with the produce of the byre, garden and hen run; eggs, cheese, butter, milk and vegetables were sold to selected shops in Peterhead to pay for other necessities. As chief accountant, Mr. McIntosh had to examine the housekeeper's grocery bill, and on one embarassing occasion he caught her two shillings and ninepence short. She found the discrepancy on the back of a page in her grocery book, where she hadn't space for it on the front list, and Mr. McIntosh hadn't seen it — the price of a scrubbing brush she had bought at the last moment.

Sutherland's marathon enterprise was built on such accountancy. Mr.Sutherland got his pay packet at the week end with his workers and it contained exactly one pound, which didn't always last him through the week, when he would borrow from his housekeeper, who had to go to Mr.McIntosh to get her money back. But he treated her with such kindness that she could never find it in her heart to refuse him.

If a rival's steam wagon was on the road to Boddam he would take his housekeeper to the window to watch it. "Listen," he would murmur, "the beat isn't right; the thing isn't running right, he would need one of my lads to look at it. It won't be long on the road, you mark my words!"

On another occasion Sutherland found himself in the marts at Aberdeen, talking to a farmer from the Peterhead area.

"Weel Jimmie," said the farmer, "I'll hae till awa' and catch ma bus, she leaves Mealmarket Street at three o'clock ye see!"

"But," says Jimmie Sutherland, "I hinna a bus leavin' the toon at three o'clock on a sale day."

"Aye but man," says the farmer, "I didna come in wi' your bus. I cam' in wi' Whyties bus, and I'm gaun hame wi' Whyties bus. It's cheaper than your bus Jimmie!"

Jimmie Sutherland went straight home and told his housekeeper. Up till then he had been charging five shillings return fare between Peterhead and Aberdeen, but he told his housekeeper he would reduce this to three shillings and ninepence return fare, and that he would put a notice in the Buchan Observer the next week declaring it. "And," he added, musingly, "if onybody can run it cheaper than that I'll stop the bus at the New Inn at Ellon and gie abody a dram that's on it!"

This wasn't necessary of course and he eventually monopolised the Buchan bus services. This low priced fare remained for many years, until the Road Transport Commissioners came into being and dictated to Sutherland that he must bring his fares into line with other operators.

My own recollections of Jimmie Sutherland are herring guts and town muck couped in parks by the wagon load, hand worked baling machines, traction engines and puffin' billies, mill men that smoked Stonehaven pipes, a run to Aikey Fair on a 'char-a-banc', a sulky-like, clean-shaven, red-faced man in the back seat of a bright red motor car, and a cow suckling a foal on Damhead farm, where it's mother had died giving it birth. A loon remembers these things. When I was about seventeen he personally took my order for a motor-lorry to flit my parents. So I did a business deal with Mr. Sutherland and I remember him as a kind and obliging gentleman.

JIMMIE SUTHERLAND

He died at the age of seventy in 1933 and was buried in Landale Road Cemetery, Peterhead.

JOHNNY IRONSIDE

WE usually associate New Deer with the late Gavin Greig, the great folk-song and ballad collector, and with George Bruce Thomson, who gave us such marvellous 'cornkisters' as McFARLANE O' THE SPROTS O'BURNIEBOOZIE and THE WEDDIN' O' McGINNIS TO HIS CROSS-EYED PET — but nobody ever mentions Johnny Ironside, the blacksmith's son who learned shorthand at his father's anvil, who became one of Buchan's leading journalists, and later a great athlete, winning prizes at most of the Buchan sporting events.

Johnny Ironside was born at Brucehill, about two miles from New Deer village, son of Peter Ironside, the local blacksmith, and it is to be noted that young Johnny was born on the camping site of Sir Edward Bruce, brother of the Scottish King, before he engaged the remnants of the army of the Comyns on Aikey Brae in 1308, after their flight from Barra.

It was a stormy winter of the 1890's and Johnny had just left school, but being the possessor of a bursary it wouldn't have been difficult to persuade him to go back and finish his studies. He had not yet decided what he should do, though his brother George had suggested he should try his hand at the 'smithying', and had emphasised the fact that standing at the cosy smithy fire was preferable to tramping to school daily over miles of snowdrifts or slushy roads, most likely with wet feet, and never a chance to warm your hands at the smithy forge. Winter at New Deer has always been severe, where the snow lies longer in the higher altitude of central Buchan than it does on the coastal plains; sometimes it is late in spring before the thaw comes, sogging the ground and filling the streams with fresh clear water. And it was worse in Johnny Ironside's day, before the motor snowplough had been invented. In view of all this, and considering his brother's advice, Johnny decided to follow in his father's footsteps, so he tied on his leather apron and became an apprentice of Vulcan.

For the first few weeks Johnny's duties consisted of heating and beating out old horseshoes and wielding the fore-hammer for his father, flexing his soft young muscles for the harder tasks to come. Johnny considered it was a fine healthy occupation and a pleasant change from pondering over deductions in Euclid and translating passages from Latin and French.

Farm servants used to gather round the smithy fire, and while their plough irons were being repaired — a plough-sock laid or a coulter sharpened, they related their funniest stories. An occasional farmer came in by for a 'pucklie nails', not that he was in desperate need of them, but it was an excuse to have a news with Johnny's father, Old Peter, as they called him, and he was reputed to have a great lore of humorous stories, and some others that were of a different colour ...

Son of Vulcan

Having gained some experience in the Vulcanic art Johnny was allowed to have a bash at shoeing horses on his own. He was a big hardy loon for his age and his physique was already showing signs of the broad shouldered athlete he was to be in manhood. All he needed was a bit of work to toughen his young sinews. The horses were mostly Clydesdales; heavy, cumbersome brutes with sharp teeth, and some of them didn't think twice about biting our Johnny on the hip when he bent down under their bellies, trying to lift a hairy, stubborn hoof, struggling to get it up onto his knees. The mares, especially, were particularly vicious when Johnny's back was turned. With a great hind foot in his oxter, or between his knees when he was bent double, and the mare would withdraw the foot and give him a kick that sent him head first out at the smiddy door. In contrast to this Johnny sometimes got a great big easy-ozie, greasy-leggit brute that wouldn't lift a foot, rug and tug how he may, and then when he had her fetlock between his legs she leaned all her great weight on his body, nearly breaking his back.

Now Johnny was a bit quick tempered in his youth, or maybe he just didn't have a way with horses, and one day a most meticulous farmer with breeches and a red fusker brought his mare to be shod — a big, clean legged animal with a white, wild eye. Johnny's father was busy at the forge and never took his hand from the bellows' handle, pumping away with easy strokes and spitting tobacco juice into the spurting flames. White hot irons were glowing in the fire and the hot sparks were streaming up inside the wide chimney. He had to use the anvil while the

167

iron was hot, so he glanced at Johnny over his shoulder and jerked his thumb towards the waiting mare.

Johnny got his box of tools with the leather strap and started to rive off the mare's old worn shoes. But she objected to the use of the turkis on her overgrown hoofs, and with a smart kick she sent the young blacksmith sprawling on a heap of muck in a corner of the smiddy. Johnny scrambled up from the dung heap and shook the hoof parings out of his hair. But now the blood of youth was up in a passion; farmer or no farmer he would teach the old bitch a lesson, so he grabbed a 'stracht edge' or pattle from the smiddy floor and laid on the mare till she fairly danced with pain and fright and rage.

This outburst of temper fair nettled the farmer and he tore off his jacket and challenged Johnny to fight. He said he would give the fiery young apprentice as much as he had given the mare, and maybe 'gaur him claw whar it wasna yokie!' Johnny was a bit taken aback but he threw down the pattle and squared up in front of the ruffled farmer with knotted fists, ready to duck the first swipe aimed at him. Of course Johnny should have known better than to lose his temper, because this sort of display was going to give the smiddy at Brucehill a bad name. Johnny's father realised this and in a twinkling he dropped his hammer and sprang between the contestants. He apologised to the farmer and reprimanded his son severely, ordering him to shake hands with the offended customer, who twitched his red fusker and put on his jacket again but wouldn't shake hands. He clapped and petted his mare and held her by the bridle while Johnny got hold of his turkis again. He had to subdue his temper, there was nothing else for it but to make friends with the mare, until she gave her foot again. He had to learn to be patient and to use a little kindness with the dumb brutes, though sometimes he wondered if they were as dumb as they looked.

Roasted Cheese

Johnny prised off the old shoes as cannily as he could, and with the farmer at her head she was better behaved. He dressed her feet with the rasp, scraped out the frog with the paring knife and fitted the red-hot shoes on her smoking hoofs, using his knees as a vice on each foot. The

168

blue acrid smoke smarted Johnny's eyes and the burning hoof smelled like newly roasted cheese, pungent and strong. Each time Johnny applied the fiery shoe the melting hoof spluttered like eggs in a frying pan, until he had a perfect fit. He ran between the mare and the blazing forge, between the forge and the anvil, hammering the shoes into shape, then back to the mare to try the fit, the sweat from his brow dropping on the backs of his hands. He dipped the sizzling shoes, one at a time as he required them in the cooling tub under the bellows, holding them with a spike through a nail hole, then hammered them on the mare's hoofs, cut the nail ends with a twist of the pliars, smoothing them down with the rasp, level with the hoof, then painted it with linseed oil till it shone like varnish, completing each foot in rotation. But when the farmer left the smiddy with his cantankerous mare Johnny Ironside knew that he would never be a blacksmith. He had discovered that smithying wasn't the congenial sort of work he had imagined it would be; nor was it the rosy picture his brother had painted, so he made up his mind to try some other occupation.

Deaf Davie

Now about this time a well known worthy called 'Deaf Davie' went around the Buchan district posing as a 'smoke doctor'. Davie was an intelligent, widely read individual, and when chimneys refused to carry off the smoke properly he usually managed to cure the fault. Chimney sweeping wasn't exactly in Davie's line, but if this had been tried without success he fitted a vane or revolving 'granny' on the chimney can which drew the reek up the lum, much to the relief of many a 'kippered' housewife, who rewarded him well for his pains.

Deaf Davie was a frequent visitor at the Brucehill smiddy, mainly for getting sheet iron for his experiments, and while Johnny hammered and shaped out the iron to Davie's specifications the old man yammered on about the events of the passing day. Because of his deafness, and partly to aid his memory, Davie used to scribble things down on odd scraps of paper, which he quickly crumpled up and crammed into his pocket. If he didn't catch your meaning the first time Davie had to shout out 'Eh, what's that?' with his hand cupped over his lug; but once he got your instructions, if they were important, he wrote them down. But Davie was mighty quick about it and he had your words on record almost before you could blink, and just as quickly translated.

So one day Johnny had a look at what Davie had written down, because he felt sure it was only a pretence at writing, like what a bairn would do before he went to school. Nobody could write that fast Johnny thought, and it was just what he suspected, a lot of squirmy creepy scrawls that he couldn't make head nor tail of. Yet Davie could read it and he repeated exactly what Johnny had said to him a few moments earlier. The old man still held the piece of paper in his grimy hand, and he seemed to sense the scorn in Johnny's smile while he looked at it. Then Davie said something that opened a new door in Johnny's life, the door he had been looking for since he left school. He told Johnny that this was Pitman's shorthand, and that with these 'whirligigs' a body could write as fast as a man could speak.

Davie and his 'whigmaleerums' fair startled the young blacksmith and he could hardly believe that the old man was in earnest. There was only one way of finding out and that was to master Davie's shorthand to see if it made sense.

Johnny got hold of the necessary books and by hard work and enthusiasm he wasn't long in mastering Pitman's system without a teacher. He spent every spare minute over meals in forming the stenographic characters, using a slate when he could. In the smiddy his anvil and every piece of iron he could lay his hands on were chalked with what his father described as 'hen's toes'. Little did he think that these chalky squiggles were to be the switch to run his son's life onto new rails, and that one day he would be destined to be a shorthand writer to the Sheriff.

Burning Daylight Oil

Except from Deaf Davie the young vulcan got scant encouragement to persist in his studies. But when working in the neighbourhood Davie always stayed overnight at Brucehill. In the dark winter evenings he read aloud from newspapers and books and Johnny took down the passages in shorthand. After the evening practice he and Davie would

170

enter into some sort of discussion on current topics. And many a scolding did they get from Elsie, Johnny's sister, the thrifty house-keeper for 'wasteful burning of precious paraffin'. Davie, however, was a slow, dull reader and Johnny soon got abreast of his rate of delivery. Having attained a speed of about eighty words a minute Johnny was determined to have a go at taking down a public speaker.

Sunday after Sunday for many weeks the young blacksmith dressed himself in his best Sabbath suit and took a corner seat in the gallery of New Deer Congregational Church, where the Rev. James Rae was the preacher. And while the minister gave his lesson Johnny slipped a note-book from his inside pocket and slogged away at the sermon. While heads nodded and people coughed to keep themselves awake the student of shorthand worked on in silence, practically unnoticed, for every word was important to him.

But by and by the Rev. James Rae spotted the young man diligently pegging away at his sermon in that secluded corner of the balcony. Of course his suspicions were immediately aroused and he asked one of his elders to find out what young Ironside was up to. But you can imagine his surprise, and perhaps not a little pleasure, when he was told that the young man was taking down his sermon in shorthand.

But Johnny was equally surprised when the minister put in an appearance at the smiddy one day and asked to see him. He also spoke to Mr. Ironside Snr. and said he wanted to take Johnny to the house for shorthand exercises, where he really tested his abilities as a copyist. Seated in the kitchen he rattled off part of a sermon he had delivered the previous Sunday, while Johnny battered it down for all he was worth. He translated that sermon to the complete satisfaction of the minister, who advised him on the spot that he should go in for journalism.

But Johnny's anvil still clanged and the sparks still flew while he patiently awaited opportunity. And so the long nights of winter passed away and the days blossomed into spring — when a door was opened for him. One day early in the year of 1898 Johnny opened the BUCHAN OBSERVER and saw their advertisement for a juvenile reporter. On the afternoon of that same day he was on his way hot foot for Peterhead. In his pocket, from the Rev. James Rae of New Deer, he carried a certificate testifying to his qualifications as a stenographer. He was admitted to the editor's sanctum, and after an interview with the late Mr. Scrogie, the proprietor, and with Mr. Watt, the editor, he got the appointment.

There was some shaking of heads when Johnny returned to Brucehill in the evening, after he had informed the household that he had got the post. The smiddy was busy at this time and his brother George pleaded with him to remain at home. But Johnny had made up his mind to be a journalist, and on a bleak Monday morning towards the end of March, 1898, he was on his way to the Buchan capital.

But he wasn't long in finding out that shorthand was much in the same category to a journalist as a pick and shovel to a navvy — you had to work at it but it still didn't make you a journalist. You could be a first-class shorthand writer and yet hopelessly at sea when called upon to write a descriptive report. You could take down a political speech verbatim, yet find yourself inadequate when asked to condense the report to a quarter column, retaining all the essential points.

In Johnny Ironside's day the tendency in daily newspaper offices had been for one man to take charge of a special department, but the general all-round man of intelligence and wide experience was still required. But our young apprentice mastered all these contingencies, and from fifty years of experience as a reporter and journalist in the Buchan area, his impressions of men and affairs are unique of the period.

Towards the end of his long life Johnny Ironside wrote: *But often as I tap out an editorial on the typewriter my mind goes back to the old smithy at Brucehill; to the gallery in the old kirk at New Deer, to my father and his 'hen's toes', to my brother George and my sister Elsie; and above all to old 'Deaf Davie', but for whose whirligigs on odd scraps of paper I should still be hammering on the anvil and shoeing wild horses.*

Nothing now remains of the smiddy at Brucehill, nothing but the circular stone with the hole in the middle on which old Peter Ironside used to put iron rings on farmers' cartwheels. The stone has been built into the end of the dyke enclosing the clothes green where the smiddy stood. The croft house is still occupied and the small byre is now used as an outhouse. George Ironside, Johnny's elder brother, got into financial difficulties after his father died and had to sell the six acre smiddy croft. George and Elsie were both celibate and moved to Turriff and died there. The croft is now farmed by Mr. William Fowlie of Brucehill. Actually the croft is not on the summit of the Brucehill, but in a dip in the road between New Deer and Cuminestown.

Johnny Ironside never achieved the world-wide fame of Berty Forbes, 'the baggy-breeked son of the local tailor Robbie Forbes', as Jack Webster tells us in his book, A GRAIN OF TRUTH. Bertie Forbes became a magazine mogul in America, who was on first name terms with men like John D. Rockefeller, Frank Woolworth and William Randolph Hearst. Both Bertie Forbes and Johnny Ironside came from New Deer and from similar humble backgrounds and one can't help making comparisons.

Johnny Ironside was a journalist for fifty-one years. He died at Balmoor House, Peterhead, on July 20th, 1949, aged 76, survived by his wife.

BOB BOOTHBY

O N page eighteen of his book I FIGHT TO LIVE, Sir Robert Boothby informs us that in the early stages of his political career, when he was in a spot of bother with his Conservative partners he asked the advice of Lord Birkenhead. Boothby says his Lordship's reply was characteristic: "You will always be in and out of trouble. But so long as you stick to your constituency, and they stick to you, no one will ever be able to break you. The first essential in politics is a territorial base".

Boothby found his territorial base in Buchan, in East Aberdeenshire, and the Buchan folk stuck to him through thick and thin and proved Lord Birkenhead absolutely right. But there was more to it than blind faith, for not only were the voters brought to the polls blindfold, but some of them were literally handcuffed.

Lord Boothby was our Conservative member of Parliament for thirty-four years, from 1924 to 1958, without a break, and sustained as such for so long, he proudly asserts, by the friendship and loyalty of his constituents, the people of Buchan, some of whose ancestors two hundred years earlier were likewise faithful to the rebel Prince Charlie. In his latest book A REBEL REMEMBERS, Bob Boothby declares himself a rebel, and we, the Buchan folk, may have an affinity, or an affection, or even a sympathy for a rebel without a cause, which was how some of the folk referred to Old Bob.

Personally, I would say that Lord Boothby was kept in office for such a long time by the farmers and their cottar folk, not because the cottars favoured him, but because their masters took them to the polls in their own private cars, throwing hints that they would have to vote Tory, seeing that they were getting a hurl for nothing, or a free ride, and the more compromising or simple-minded amongst them complied with this request. And when you consider the great amount of farm workers in Buchan in Boothby's heyday, married and single, and the kitchiedeems of legitimate age, who also got a hurl in the boss's car with the farm mistress, the majority far outnumbered any feasible opposition. This was before the so-called agricultural revolution and the drift to the towns, when the rural population was much larger than it is nowadays and the towns were much smaller, still within their original urban boundaries. Peterhead and Fraserburgh, Buchan's two main towns were mostly fisher folk, who also supported Boothby, so with the farmers and fishermen on his side there wasn't much opposition.

The only time I ever gave Baron Boothby a vote was when I was being herded to the polling booths in my employer's car, and I felt it was almost under duress or obligation — an expression of thanks for the convenience after a tiring day in the fields and byres, glad to get it over with, as were thousands of others in the same position. It was a method of canvassing that should never have been allowed, because the Unionists monopolised car ownership, thus enabling the pro-Conservative farming hierarchy to exploit the polling results.

Most of the farm workers disliked Boothby, because they considered him a farmer's man who favoured the moneyed classes and did nothing for the workers. In theory of course, it would seem that a man who was doing his best for their masters was bound to be helping their servants indirectly. But Boothby's hands were tied, for how could he help the workers independently without taking sides against their employers — his strongest supporters, and he was too clever by far to land himself in such a predicament. Insistent clamour by the farm workers' union brought about the establishment of the Agricultural Wages Board, which impelled the farmers to share profits with their workers, however reluctantly, and it allowed Boothby to shirk the responsibility.

Boothby gained his seat in East Aberdeenshire two years before Gene Tunney took the World Heavyweight Boxing Championship title from Jack Dempsey, and fifty-four years later (from 1924) Boothby issued his latest book A REBEL REMEMBERS, almost in the month that Tunney died, November 1978. Tunney was eighty-two and Boothby seventy eight, and like Tunney he retired undefeated, unmarked, a professional gentleman — the chief difference being that Tunney reached the top of his profession, world class, and Boothby didn't, because he never became our Prime Minister, which I believe was what the Buchan folk expected of him, and in this respect they felt that he had let them down.

Baron Boothby retired from active politics in 1958, stepping down in favour of a much younger man, Patrick Wolrige Gordon, the kilted grandson of the late Dame Flora MacLeod of Dunvegan in Skye, who kept the Tory candle flickering for a few more decadent years in the Buchan Howes, until it was snuffed out completely by the up and

175

coming S.N.P. But things are different now in Buchan, where the cottar families have their own motor cars and their numbers have diminished by seventy-five per cent, and I'm doubtful if Robert John Graham Boothby K.B.E. (from 1953) could have survived this emancipated climate.

In 1945 he contested his seat with the Labour candidate John R. Allan, the noted author and farmer, but in spite of petrol rationing and a national swing of the political pendulum in favour of Socialism under Clement Attlee, Boothby carried the local Tory flag to fervent victory, sweeping his opponent to oblivion in the political arena, though not as a writer and patriot still beloved by his countrymen. By then however, Boothby had become a cult figure in Buchan, his name a political institution; and to vote otherwise was almost a betrayal of the common faith.

Lord Boothby has been with me and our family all our lives. I can remember him from my schooldays as the young Unionist candidate opposing the local Liberal, a blind man, Fred Martin from Mintlaw, just before Ramsay McDonald had given the Labour Party a constitutional footing on the ladder to Westminster. Fred Martin was swept from his seat by public enthusiasm for the young Boothby. It was the first election I took much notice of, local or general, when I was about eleven years old, and I still remember the photographs of the contestants and reading all the printed circulars that were distributed round the parish by the postman before polling day, when my parents got their first (and only) hurl in the farmer's Chevrolet car.

Boothby was promoted by Bailie James Booth of Downiehills farm, in the verdant Howe o' Buchan, known locally as Tartan Jim, because he always wore a conspicuous suit of black and white squares; a 'barfit loon' out of Peterhead who rose from droving cattle for the local butchers to become himself a Baron butcher-farmer of the Buchan farmlands, and a judge of pedigree cattle in South America. Bailie Booth 'discovered' the young Boothby when he lost the election in the Shetland Islands, where Booth had gone to buy cattle, and presenting the novice to his fellow councillors in Peterhead he said: "He doesna ken onything aboot fishin' or fairmin', but we'll teach 'im, and when he gets up tae speak he's like an alarm clock gaun aff in the mornin'!"

And they taught Boothby farming, at least on paper, those shrewd, hardy chiels of Buchan, and the fishermen lectured him on the life history of the herring and its wiles in foreign markets. To be quite fair to Lord Boothby he really did stand up for them in Parliament for a long time, especially during the economic slump of the thirties. They thought that he was losing interest in their affairs during the war, and they began to cool on him after that, especially during the post-war Tory revival when Sir Anthony Eden succeeded Churchill as Prime Minister, when they thought it should have been Boothby.

In 1967 he married Miss Wanda Sanna, a thirty-four year old private secretary from Sardinia. Boothby was then sixty-seven. He is now an octogenarian and living in quiet retirement. God bless the man and long may he continue, though he has made it plain to us where his last resting place should be. He wants to come back to Buchan, though not where he originally intended. At first he expressed a desire to be buried beside the old ivy-covered Chapel of Rattray, dated from the twelfth century, near the Loch of Strathbeg, about halfway on the coast between Peterhead and Fraserburgh. It is a sylvan countryside of lush meadows and hawthorn scented hedgerows, rich in the balladry of LOGIE O' BUCHAN and SIR JAMES THE ROSE, ancient seat of the Cumines, Earls of Buchan, where horn and hoof are plentiful.

But then there was talk of bringing the North Sea gas ashore here from the Frigg Field and our Bob changed his mind, which perhaps is a pity, because the loch area is now a protected nature reserve and the gas terminal (officially opened by the Queen and Prince Philip in May 1978) has been sited some four miles further south at St. Fergus. Now Lord Boothby has decided he will be cremated and his ashes are to be scattered at high tide from the top of Rattray Head Lighthouse, which was engineered by the grandfather of Robert Louis Stevenson.

Now the gas complex at St. Fergus is a sprawling giant of space-age turrets and piping installation where all petrol-driven vehicles are banned from the inner perimeter fence, and where even diesel-powered butane tankers are only allowed in restricted numbers, where smoking is strictly forbidden, and security guards are at every corner lest the slightest spark from fag or carburettor should ignite an explosion unprecendented on the Buchan coastline.

British Gas and Total Marine are so much concerned about this danger that they have protested about the naval radio station recently installed at their formerly proposed site at Strathbeg, lest sparks emitted from the aerial masts should fuse an explosion in the air above the St. Fergus gas terminal, over Boothby's head so to speak, for the lighthouse at Rattray Head is bang in the middle between the spark emitting aerials at Strathbeg and the highly inflammable gas plant at St. Fergus. He will be between two fires, and the irony lies in observing the Doric connotation that Boothby will go out as he had reigned — that 'ye canna win!'

But with all due respect, let me add that our Bob couldn't have chosen a better spot for his interment, almost within sight of Crimond Kirk (at least from the top of the lighthouse), birthplace of the famous hymn tune for the twenty-third Psalm, composed there last century by Miss Jessie Irvine, a daughter of the manse. It is a vale as peaceful and serene as the land of cool Siloam's shady rill, where his Lordship may wander at will by the still waters and the green pastures of the farmer chiels he heckled for at Westminster all those lugubrious years.

Now I salute him. Long live Boothby!

SHIFT SIX

THE PEAT STACK BIBLE

I came across the Peat Stack Bible quite unexpectedly in St. Andrew's Cathedral in Aberdeen. I had never known of its existence and the sight of it took me back fifty years or so, to the days of my youth when I chauved in the peat mosses of Savoch, Kinmundy, Torhendry and Rora, all around the village of Longside. These reflections were brightened by the sight of the Rev. John Skinner's walking cane, under the same glass with the Peat Stack Bible. Why it came to be known as such, and how it came to be lying in St. Andrew's Cathedral, is a story I shall relate in my own roundabout sort of way, so that no peat shall be left unturned in the telling.

The Rev. John Skinner, poet author of TULLOCHGORUM, was minister of Tiffery Chapel, on the outskirts of Longside, two hundred years before my own time around the village. He was ordained as Episcopal minister at Longside in 1742, having changed his cloth from the Presbyterian diety he formerly served at Monymusk. Four years later, in 1746, Tiffery Chapel was burned by the Redcoats, when for three months that year Scotland was under Martial Law. Hanoverian soldiers were pillaging the countryside, burning and destroying everything connected with the Episcopalian Church, which was considered an enemy of the state, and the Chapel of Linshart was one of their prime targets.

In the twilight of a summer evening, when the minister and his family had just gone to bed, a company of Cumberland's Campbell Highlanders, with bayonets fixed on their muskets, burst into the farmhouse manse at Linshart and ransacked the house, scarcely leaving them with a change of clothing, but mercifully sparing their lives.

Next day the soldiers put bundles of straw around the heather thatched church and set it on fire. While the church was blazing, a lady with Royalist or Protestant sympathies rode horseback around the inferno urging the soldiers to throw in the prayer books. The Episcopal Church at New Deer was also in flames, so the lady of rank rode to the

179

Hill of Coynach, about six miles distant, where she could see both the churches blazing, and clapping her hands gleefully she cried out: "The wark o' guid gangs bonnily on!" But as you can see the Culsh monument at New Deer quite clearly from Braeside of Ludquharn, about a mile from Linshart, she could have saved herself such a long ride.

Skinner later lampooned the lady in verse, comparing her to Jezebel, and in revenge she reported him for holding religious services in his farmhouse, which could also have been burned down. He was jailed for six months in Old Aberdeen, narrowly escaping transportation for life in the penal colonies.

This was during the penal laws, when it was illegal for more than five persons at one time to gather for religious worship. This did not include the minister's family but the number allowed was later reduced to four persons.

Skinner had defied the authorities in this and had been addressing a congregation of villagers and crofters from an open window in his farmhouse, while they gathered in the close around a giant beech tree. Two hundred years later I stood in the farm kitchen and looked from the window at the famous 'Linshart Tree', for thus it had become legendary, surviving all these years, but was blown down in the great gale of January 31st, 1953.

When I worked on the farms of Nether Kinmundy and Cairngall, one on each side of the farm of Linshart, I never realised at the time that I was hay-making and tattie-lifting on hallowed ground. With my head in the clouds looking for impossible stars it never occurred to me that the real diamonds were under my feet. It wasn't until I had moved away from Longside, and had read a great deal more of local history that I reflected on the true metal. It was 1946, the bicentenary of Skinner's most vital year at Linshart, yet I was quite unaware that I was standing within yards of the spot where he had composed some of his sermons and his poetry. To atone for my ignorance I returned to pay homage at his gravestone in the old churchyard at Longside, quite near to that of Jamie Fleeman, his old contemporary.

The Rev. John Skinner survived the persecution of his church and served a further fifty-eight years as minister of Linshart, a total of sixty-two years in the parish. His son, also John Skinner, was born at Linshart on May 19th, 1744, two years before the fire. He became

THE PEAT STACK BIBLE

Bishop of Aberdeen and served the congregation as pastor of St. Andrew's for forty years, dying on July 13th, 1816. John Skinner Snr. died in the home of his son in Aberdeen at the age of eighty-five in 1807. And this perhaps explains in part why the Peat Stack Bible came to be exhibited in St. Andrew's Cathedral in King Street.

But there are no signs of burning on the Peat Stack Bible; no charred leaves, so it wasn't thrown in the flames with the prayer books at Longside. Certainly it is stained with wet peat, where rain had probably penetrated the stack where it was hidden until the Redcoats dispersed, when it was considered safe by the person who hid it to bring it forth to the light again. It is a fairly large bible or prayer book and lies open at the Communion pages and the Ten Commandments, printed in an era when the letter 's' was represented very like an 'f', and the type so badly stained with peat in parts to be almost illegible.

I had visions of a grand story here of how the Peat Stack Bible had been rescued by Jamie Fleeman from the blazing chapel at Tiffery, because he wanted it for his sister Martha, who was very keen on reciting scripture, but that he had to hide it in the peat stack at Tiffery until the Redcoats disappeared. Tiffery is something less than a mile from Fleeman's cottage at Ludquharn. He was bound to have seen the blaze and I'm certain he must have been there, dancing around among the spectators, until somebody dared him to rescue one of the prayer books. It was the sort of thing he would have done, for Jamie liked 'a good bleeze' like the one at Knockhall Castle when he saved the housekeeper.

But the Rev. John Skinner's walking cane was a red herring in the case and I had to make further investigations to unravel the mystery of the Peat Stack Bible — how it had escaped the flames, and where.

Even before the Jacobite uprisings the Episcopal Church in Scotland had been considered as alien to the Hanoverian Government. After the '45 Rebellion the ministers of George II declared that Eipscopasy in Scotland had to be destroyed, rooted out and annihilated. Peterhead had long been recognised as a trouble spot and the Chapel of St. Peter (Patron Saint of the town) just off Broad Street, to the left of the present Royal Hotel, was marked down for immediate destruction.

On May 6th, 1746, nine days after Culloden, a company of dragoons entered the town. They were commanded by Lieutenant-Colonel Ancrum, who was resolved to burn the chapel, but was prevailed upon by the town bailies and the churchmen to spare it from the flames. They argued that because of its central position in such a conglomeration of wooden houses it would set the whole town alight. So Lieutenant-Colonel Ancrum had his men demolish the chapel stone by stone, which took two and a half days, to a heap of rubble, during which time someone rescued the minister's bible, perhaps during the night, and hid it in a peat stack until the Redcoats had left the town. Someone must have taken it to the Rev. Skinner of Linshart, who eventually left it with his son when he became pastor of St. Andrew's Cathedral, which is the proper resting place for a bible rescued from an Episcopal Chapel in Buchan.

But all this persecution and anarchy didn't deter the spread of Episcopasy in Scotland, and despite the penal laws people still assembled for worship, in secret places and in small numbers, so as not to attract the attention of the military. For proof of this we move to another Buchan chapel, St. Drostan's in Old Deer, where there is a memorial tablet to Graham of Claverhouse (Bonnie Dundee), Champion of the Episcopal Church establishment in Scotland.

To consecrate Claverhouse in any church whatsoever seems as blasphemous as allowing an effigy of the Wolf of Badenoch to lie in state in Dunkeld Cathedral. But so it is in our hypocritical world, and the deeds of wicked men are sanctified in our churches, so that we may regard them as heroes. Just think of the Covenanters martyred by Bonnie Dundee — or the cathedrals ravaged by the Wolf of Badenoch, and just because he repented he was given a church burial. Viscount Dundee was supposed to have a charmed life, until one of General Mackay's soldiers fashioned a silver bullet from the buttons of his tunic and shot Dundee at the Battle of Killiecrankie in 1689.

There is a mistaken belief in some quarters that John Graham of Claverhouse (Bonnie Dundee) was actually buried at Old Deer, perhaps because of the plaque in the church. But he lies in the old church at Blair Atholl, whither he was carried after winning the Battle of Killiecrankie.

LITERARY ASSOCIATIONS OF
THE NORTH-EAST OF SCOTLAND.

L ITERARY events in North-east Scotland and in Aberdeenshire in particular, have been like the proverbial pebble thrown in a deep pool of water, setting up a circle of ripples on the surface that widened with the sinking of the stone. The trouble is that when the pebble has lodged at the bottom, and the ripples have disappeared, nobody remembers where the pebble was dropped in the pool, or who threw it in the first place.

Cruden for instance is one of the best-known place-names in Aberdeenshire and is rich in literary association. The name is derived from *Crojie Dane*, meaning Kill the Dane, originating from the famous battle between King Malcolm II of Scotland and Canute, son of Sueno, King of Denmark, in 1014. Euphonically, one might assume that Cruden derives from the Doric 'Crood-in', or 'Crowding in', implying that the warlike Danes did in fact 'Crude-in' on this sandy bay, 'Cruden Bay', and as the battle raged inland, so great was the slaughter on both sides that the neighbouring parish became known as Slains.

The best known literary coincidence of Cruden of course is the emergence of DRACULA, the vampire whose blood-sucking antics are now known worldwide, since the author, Bram Stoker, began to write the book at Cruden Bay in the early years of our present century. It is generally believed that the interiors of Count Dracula's castle are an exact reproduction of the wainscoted walls of nearby Slains Castle, which the author had observed on a visit to the Hays of Erroll, before the building was demolished.

Numerous vampire horror films have been based on the book, the earliest of which, in 1930, starred Bela Lugosi. Fifty years on DRACULA is still popular horror fiction on television, and yet, when we watched the original Dracula movie locally, very few people knew of its local setting, probably because the author had transplanted Dracula's castle to its mythical origin in a fictional Ruritania in eastern Europe, thus widening the ripples, though he had first cast the stone in Buchan waters.

With DRACULA the ripples are still in motion where the pebble was dropped, and people know about it. But with another literary reference to the name of Cruden they are less familiar — that of

Alexander Cruden, compiler of the first complete CONCORDANCE OF THE BIBLE in English, now widely used by theologians and university students on scriptural research.

Alexander (Sandy) Cruden was born just off Broad Street, Aberdeen, round the corner from Byron's birthplace, in 1699 and he died at Camden Passage, Islington, London, in 1770. He was intended for the Presbyterian ministry, but ill-health, which for a time affected his mind, led him to take up teaching at the age of twenty-one.

Previous to redevelopment in Aberdeen there was a plaque on the wall of the former Press & Journal offices indicating the site of Alexander Cruden's birthplace, at the entrance to Cruden's Court, no doubt named after him, and since demolished to make room for the new extension to the Town House, opened on November 17th, 1975 by Lord Provost Robert S. Lennox — an event commemorated by another plaque at the front of the new building, a few paces from where the Cruden plaque was formerly inset on the wall. The Cruden plaque has been reset behind the new building, out of the public view admittedly, but actually nearer the spot where he first drew breath. If you go into Concert Court and mount the flight of steps on your left you will find the Cruden tablet set into the dyke on your right-hand side.

Alexander Cruden had to wait nearly two hundred years for his nameplate in Broad Street, when it was unveiled by Sir John Betjeman, the Poet Laureate, in 1968. It was taken down three years later and we are grateful to Aberdeen Corporation for resetting the plaque, otherwise it might have landed in the builder's skip.

But our lexicographer has wider fame, with another plaque in his honour in Islington, London. The one in Aberdeen states briefly: *Alexander Cruden (1699 — 1770), Master of Arts, Marischal College, compiler of the Concordance of the Bible, was born in a house in Cruden's Court, near this spot.*

The London plaque is more explanatory: *Alexander Cruden (1699 — 1770). Humanist, scholar and intellectual. Born Aberdeen. Educated Marischal College. Came to London, 1719. Tutor. Appointed bookseller to Queen Caroline in 1737. Compiled the Concordance of the Bible. Lived for many years in Campden Passage where he died on November 1st, 1770.*

The boy Cruden was a delicate, white-faced, pimpled urchin who remained outside the playground circle, but was good at his lessons, and you can imagine him trudging round to the old Grammar School in Schoolhill, a cold and cheerless place we are told, with one main room and a draughty loft overhead. The boy spent long days at the curriculum, with debates on Saturdays and Sunday afternoons on sermon exercises, with twelve days holiday a year and Christmas almost ignored, though none of it cooled the lad's intense and abiding love of Holy Scripture.

At thirteen Cruden went to Marischal College and took his arts degree. While a student there, he met and fell in love with a girl who eventually rejected him, an experience which so affected his nerves and mental outlook that he was detained for a fortnight in the old Tolbooth at the far end of Cruden's Court, only yards from his home. After his release he awoke one morning with a firm resolution in his mind, a decision which was to direct the course of his future life. He walked down to the harbour and boarded the *Phoenix*, sailing for London, and he wasn't to see his native city again for forty-eight years.

What we owe that girl for giving young Cruden the cold shoulder she shall never know, but the result conditioned him to a life of celibacy and the task of compiling the CONCORDANCE, a devotional exercise which wouldn't have borne the stress of matrimony and a family life. He turned his back on women, and was ever afterwards embarrassed in the presence of ladies, except towards the end of his life, when he formed an attachment for a woman of the streets, whom he rescued from the gutter and despair, and for compassionate reasons he made her his maid servant. Their relationship was strictly platonic however, and it was this reformed creature who found the old man dead one morning clutching his beloved bible.

At the age of nineteen, when Cruden went to London, he served for a time as a teacher, then as a private tutor. In 1732 he opened his own bookseller's shop, and five years later he was appointed Royal Purveyor of Books to Queen Caroline, ill-starred wife of George IV, and despite his aversion to women he worked ardently in the sunshine of her regal smile.

These were the years on which he laboured on his great work, five exacting years of research and devotion, tabulating and indexing in alphabetical order every single word used in the Bible and giving its source in context. I think it is a greater achievement than Dr. Johnson's Dictionary, and since they were contemporaneous, Cruden's work may have inspired Johnson, whose compendium was published in 1775, some thirty-eight years later.

The latest volume of the CONCORDANCE, published in 1973 by the Lutterworth Press, runs to 774 three-column pages in small print; (783 with the appendix) and contains 225,000 references, which must have been a mammoth task for Cruden while earning his living as a bookseller. It was first published in 1737, and for all his bible-peering, thumb-leafing, quill-dipping, editing, proof-reading, eye-rubbing and intricate research in candle light, Cruden was paid the niggardly sum of twenty-five pounds.

But hold your breath, for maybe it wasn't bad going when you consider that seventy years earlier John Milton was paid five pounds for the first printing of PARADISE LOST. But the CONCORDANCE was so highly esteemed by the colleges of Oxford and Cambridge that a quarter of a century later the publishers paid Cruden five hundred pounds for a second edition, and a year before the poor man died they advanced a further three hundred pounds for another revival. Since then the CONCORDANCE must have reached three-figure editions, with many rivals, but theologians and divinity students everywhere still reach for their 'Cruden' in defining the sources of Holy Scripture.

But fame was the spur for Aberdeen's Sandy Cruden, and he didn't care all that much for money, nor for the sparkle of love in a woman's eyes, though he enjoyed the radiance of a Queen's smile. He rather preferred to imagine himself as the John Knox of his day, preaching and catechising the nation to sublime obedience, all with such vehemence and ardour as brought him into conflict with the authorities, leading to imprisonment, sometimes unjustly sentenced. But despite his rhetoric and public rantings, Cruden was a kind and gentle man, a champion of the poor and the prisoners' friend at Newgate, where he strove to save several criminals from the gallows. He campaigned vigorously for the abolition of capital punishment. "If I had a thousand votes," he protested, "I'd use every one of them to vote against execution." This was after eleven of his friends had been condemned to die on the scaffold.

Towards the end of his life this John Bunyan of Bon-Accord still sighed for another sight of Aberdeen's Castlegate. By then he was an old man, famous but poor in health, and when he returned he lectured the Aberdonians on Sunday observance and reprimanded their laxity in moral behaviour, handing out tracts to emphasise his preaching. Then he returned abruptly to London.

Before he died Cruden had expressed a desire to be buried in Aberdeen, near his native university. But it was in the days of stagecoaches and slow sailing ships and his wishes were not carried out. It seems an unfair paradox therefore, that despite his life-long exhortation for abstemiousness and self-denial he was buried at Southwark, London, on ground which later became the property of a famous firm of brewers.

But though his grave be lost, the name of Cruden lives in his CONCORDANCE and with the bursary he provided as a prize for students of Aberdeen University, pebbles that have gone very deep in the scriptural pool, and the ripples have widened considerably in the ecclesiastical affairs of men.

His other works were A SCRIPTURE DICTIONARY and THE HISTORY AND EXCELLENCY OF THE SCRIPTURES.

It is also interesting to remember that other classic, recently reprinted, PRATT'S HISTORY OF BUCHAN, was written in St. James the Less Episcopal Church manse in the parish of Cruden, which overlooks the den of Ardendraught, where King Malcolm II routed the forces of Canute.

About twelve miles from Cruden Bay, as the vampire flies, lies the village of Maud, more noted for its cattle marts and old-time feeing markets than a venue for fiction of worldwide renown. But Mabel Cowie was born here, daughter of a Maud minister, the late Rev. William Cowie, in 1899. Miss Cowie graduated from Aberdeen University, and with the tremendous success of her stage plays she changed her name to Lesley Storm. It is a name befitting central Buchan and its wintry bleakness, its lonely isolation, its drabness and its bitter climate.

It is indeed marvellous to think that such stunning London West End stage successes as BLACK CHIFFON and ROAR LIKE A DOVE, came from the pen of a daughter of the manse in this tiny market town. ROAR LIKE A DOVE took over £45,000 by the time it ended its London run in March, 1960, and ran for over one thousand performances. Above this Miss Storm sold the film rights for £90,000. Her first play was TONY DRAWS A HORSE. Others were THE DAY'S MISCHIEF, TIME AND YELLOW ROSES, THEY RIDE ON BROOMSTICKS, and her last, LOOK, NO HANDS!

187

was staged in London's West End in 1971. Dame Flora Robson starred in BLACK CHIFFON.

Miss Storm's film scripts included THE FALLEN IDOL, THE HEART OF THE MATTER, and THE SPANISH GARDENER, all of which the villagers of Maud can now see on television.

THE SPANISH GARDENER was one of Dirk Bogard's most successful starring roles in 1957. When I saw the film in Ellon I had no idea that A.J. Cronin's novel had been adapted for the screen by someone almost in the next parish. Speak about a small world — this was Miss Storm in a tea-cup. I had gone to see it because it also featured a boyish Jon Whiteley, son of the schoolmaster at Kemnay, also in Aberdeenshire, and world screening was revolving on this tiny hub of regional talent.

Miss Storm was the wife of Dr. James Clark, a Harley Street mental specialist, and the mother of four children. Until her death in 1975, at the age of seventy-six, she had often visited her native village.

Two railway stations from Maud, on the old Fraserburgh line, the sylvan village of Strichen nestles at the foot of the heathery slopes of Mormond Hill. Here was born, on June 16th, 1886, in North Street, Lorna Moon, who also gained international repute as a film script writer in Hollywood, USA. This is a long way from Strichen, in Aberdeenshire, but Miss Moon made it there and wrote the screen play for MR.WU, a silent film starring Lon Chaney in 1928, which was a popular success on both sides of the Atlantic. But when we watched MR.WU in the Broch or Peterhead, none of us guessed that the film had been scripted for us by a very lovely girl from Strichen who had never had the opportunity of university training.

Her real name was Helen Nora Wilson Low, daughter of a plasterer, William Low, and his wife, Margaret Benzie. Lorna Moon also left us two remarkable books, DOORWAYS IN DRUMORTY and DARK STAR, both best-sellers in this country and in America. In her obituary notice we read that: 'These character sketches were charming both in their humour and in their pathos, and were undoubtedly based on people known to hundreds of parishioners of Strichen'.

She died at the age of forty-four in New Mexico, on May 1st, 1930. A month later, on June 3rd of that year, Miss Moon's ashes were scattered on the Hill of Mormond, overlooking her birthplace.

LITERARY ASSOCIATIONS

Now who would even dream of tracing Frankenstein's monster to the Braes o' Gight? I know it's a bit weird but it's more of a reality than you might think. There is a tremendous gulch there in a wide bend of the Ythan River, gorged out at the end of the last ice-age, where glacial movement in past aeons is still evident on the rocks, and it might have been a lair of dinosaurs. High up on the braes and overlooking the gorge stands the ivy-covered ruins of Gight Castle, old stronghold of the Mad Gordon of Gight, father of Lord Byron the poet. Byron was born in London, but until his mother had been forced by her squandering husband to quit the castle, she had lived at Gight. In CHILDE HAROLD'S PILGRIMAGE Byron refers to his ancestral home — 'where superstition once had made her den'.

> *Deserted is my own good hall,*
> *Its hearth is desolate;*
> *Wild weeds are gathering on the wall;*
> *My dog howls at the gate.*

Frankenstein was written by Mary Wollstonecraft Godwin, second wife of Shelley the poet, who married her three weeks after his first wife, Harriet Westbrook, had been found dead in a ditch in an advanced stage of pregnancy. Mary Godwin and Shelley had been living together for two years before this happened, on the shores of Lake Geneva, in Switzerland, next door to a villa occupied by Lord Byron, close friend of Shelley.

Mary Godwin's own child by Shelley had been born prematurely and died within weeks of birth. Post-natal hallucinations concerning the loss of her baby daughter had driven her to distraction, and in Shelley's absence she confided the state of her mind to Byron. Over the fireside in Byron's villa she told him she had a nightmare the previous night in which she had a vivid recollection of nursing her child on her lap by the fire when she accidentally dropped it into the flames in their own grate. She was almost in hysteria from recurrent nightmares over the death of her child, and while she wept bitterly by the fire Byron did his best to console her. He advised her to write something to occupy her mind; to divert her thoughts from the tragedy, to get it out of her system. Why not create another child in her writing, Byron suggested, and maybe the exercise would relieve her distress.

189

A CHIEL AMONG THEM

Because of the traumatic state of her mind, Mary Shelley became so engrossed in her novel that her thoughts went haywire. Her fictional child was created beyond the bounds of reason, not at all what Byron had in mind for her; but the diversion had so much improved her mentality that he encouraged it and gave her full scope in the venture.

Several are the reasons put forward by the pundits for the state of Mary Shelley's mind when she began writing the first ever science fiction novel, even before the name of scientist had been coined in our dictionaries. Some say it was because Mary Shelley's mother, also Mary Wollstonecraft, had died of puerperal fever ten days after Mary herself was born; also that she had been ostracized by her widowed father, William Godwin, after her mother's death, and neglected and ignored by her step-mother when he remarried, which is admittedly a built-in feature in the attitude and behaviour of Frankenstein's child-chasing monster.

Another critic has argued that the monster represents two sides of Shelley in relationship with his wife. Still another that the strength and pathos of the monster, and its terrible sense of having been wronged, derive directly from Mary's own orphaned feelings. Still a third asserts that Mary is herself the monster, and behind the monster's eloquence is Mary's grief. But it is a brooding grief, far more potent than the loss of her mother, or her father's negligence, and much more likely to be the result of her own maternal loss, which is never mentioned by the inquisitors.

Did Mary Shelley suspect that her husband was the father of Harriet Westbrook's unborn child? Or that she and his estranged wife were both with child to him at the same time? Perhaps Mary Shelley was so distraught that she sought to create life by other means than natural conception. Another depressing factor was that Shelley was deprived of the custody of his two children by his first wife three months after her death. Nothing further can be proved with certainty in Shelley's matrimonial affairs, but there seems little doubt that his behaviour drove his second wife to the creation of her volatile monster, thanks to the suggestion of Lord Byron.

Wollstonecraft has a phonetic resemblance to Wolfstonecroft, which is easily associated with the moon-struck, bat-infested, owl-shrieking atmosphere that enshrouds the ivy-covered ruins of Gight Castle; moreso in a lightning storm and a cloud-riven sky, perhaps the environment that Mary Shelley had in mind for the creation of her galvanic monstrosity.

In her introduction to FRANKENSTEIN Mary Shelley informs her readers that as a young girl she lived for a number of years in Scotland:

> On the blank and dreary northern shores of the Tay, near Dundee. Blank and dreary in retrospection I call them; but they were not so to me then. They were the aerie of freedom and the pleasant region where unheeded I could commune with the creatures of my fancy. I wrote them, but in a commonplace style. It was beneath the trees of the grounds belonging to our house, or on the bleak sides of the woodless mountains near, that my true compositions, the airy flights of my imagination, were born and fostered.

And if we want to bring Mary Shelley nearer to Buchan, or at least to the Highlands of Scotland, even to the environs of Gight Castle, we have it almost in her own words, when, after referring to her stay in Scotland, she adds: 'I made occasional visits to the more picturesque parts.'

Her own excuse for writing the novel was an arrangement between herself and Shelley and Byron to pass the time during a rainy season in Switzerland in 1816. The trio first contrived to write ghost stories, but the two poets tired of writing prose, and that when the weather cleared they left her and went to explore the Alps, and she was the only one to continue writing. Obstetric observation is avoided, or in Mrs. Shelley's case its post-natal effects on her subconsciousness and emotional behaviour after the death of her child, but she does admit that, 'Everything must have a beginning ... and that beginning must be linked to something that went before'.

She listened to prolonged conversations between her husband and Lord Byron. These discussions were varied and philosophical and sometimes explored the mystery and origin of life, debating whether there was any probability of its ever being discovered and communicated. Darwin's experiments were a favourite topic, of how he had preserved a piece of vermicelli in a glass case until by some extraordinary means it began to move with voluntary motion. 'Not thus, after all, would life be given,' she says, but 'perhaps a corpse would be reanimated; galvanism had given token of such things: perhaps the component parts of a creature might be manufactured, brought together, and endued with vital warmth'.

No other conceivable circumstances could be more conducive to these thoughts of reanimation in a woman's mind than the distress and emotion of miscarriage, or of losing an infant child. Reading between the lines there is a hint of the truth breaking through; almost an admission of her loss and a final outcry of grief and pain when she wrote:

And now, once again, I bid my hideous progeny go forth and prosper. I have an affection for it, for it was the offspring of happy days, when death and grief were but words which found no true echo in my heart. Its several pages speak of many a walk, many a drive, and many a conversation, when I was not alone; and my companion was one who, in this world, I shall never see more. But this is for myself; my readers have nothing to do with these associations.

This was nine years after Shelley's death, but the memory of his lost child still haunted her.

Before closing the trap-door on the horror subject I would like to remind my readers of that other Scottish terror Hollywood saw fit to film. I refer to DR. JEKYLL AND MR. HYDE which also has a North-east connection. R. L. Stevenson, the author of this concoction resided for a time in Braemar, where he actually began writing Treasure Island. Perhaps even by then he had the potion bottled up for us.

Our last pebble thrown in the literary pool once more concerns, or at least begins with the River Ythan in Aberdeenshire, though the ripples in this instance became waves which engulfed the entire field of Scottish historical literature.

I refer to Grace Aguilar's THE DAYS OF BRUCE, which, by 1884 had reached its 26th edition and was widely read in the Victorian age. Why did this frail young Jewish girl living in England involve herself so profoundly in the adventures of our fourteenth century hero? Did she find some comparison between the beleagured Scots and the persecution of the Jews? Or did she find the supreme in womanhood embodied in the personality of Isabella of Buchan? Whatever her motives, the result is an historical romance which would have brought a twinge of envy to Sir Walter Scott himself, and quite overshadows that other Scottish saga, THE WOLF OF BADENOCH, by Sir Thomas Dick Lauder.

Her research must have been elaborate and exhausting, and for her, with little knowledge of the Doric, Barbour's BRUS must have been unintelligible; yet she immersed herself in the archives of Scottish history covering that period in our national development. Her novel is so very intricate and authentic to the last detail that very few faults may be found in her narrative. True, she sites Old Slains Castle (The Tower of Buchan) on the banks of the River Ythan, when in fact at its nearest point it is three miles from the estuary; and she feeds the moat at Kildrummy Castle from the River Don, 'which at that point ever rushed darkly and stormily along', and as we know this is not the case, for the moat was flooded by rain water, or supplied by a subterranean passage from the burn in the Den of Kildrummy. But apart from these minor geographical misplacements, Grace Aguilar's history is worthy of its heroes.

Her description of Buchan in a storm is almost brutal in severity, comparable to what Dr. Johnson had envisaged from the ramparts of the newer Slains Castle further up the coast:

'The wind howled round the ancient Tower of Buchan, in alternate gusts of wailing and fury, so mingled with the deep, heavy roll of the lashing waves, that it was impossible to distinguish the roar of the one element from the howl of the other. Neither tree, hill, nor wood intercepted the rushing gale, to change the dull monotony of its gloomy tone. The Ythan, indeed, darted by, swollen and turbid from continued storms, threatening to overflow the barren plain it watered, but its voice was undistinguishable amidst the louder wail of wind and ocean. Pine trees, dark, ragged, and stunted, and scattered so widely apart that each one seemed monarch of some thirty acres, were the only traces of vegetation for miles around. Nor were human habitations more abundant; indeed, few dwellings, save those of such solid masonry as the Tower of Buchan, could hope to stand scathless amidst the storms that in winter ever swept along the moor'.

A CHIEL AMONG THEM

Apart from Barbour's epic poem and the delightful modern translation by Archibald A. H. Douglas, a direct descendant of the good Sir James Douglas, chief lieutenant of King Robert; and the work of Nigel Tranter in this field, and perhaps some acquaintance with Dr. Ewan M. Barron's THE SCOTTISH WAR OF INDEPENDENCE. very few of our modern generation of students have ever heard of Miss Aguilar's DAYS OF BRUCE.

Grace Aguilar was born at Hackney, London, in June, 1816, in the reign of George III. Her parents were Jewish and of Spanish descent. She was always a delicate child, which inclined her to literary pursuits, especially of an historical aspect, and an attack of rheumatic fever at fourteen affected the remaining years of her short but active life.

She travelled widely in her youth, visiting most of the chief towns of England, but there is no record of her ever coming to Scotland. She resided mostly in Devonshire, whither her family removed in 1828. By the age of twelve she was deeply emerged in literary composition, comprising a dramatic play GUSTAVUS VASA, and a volume of poems, which were published in 1835. Soon afterwards, on the death of her father, she was obliged to earn a bigger proportion of her living from her pen. At first she devoted her interests to Jewish subjects, and several of her works survive from this period: THE SPIRIT OF JUDAISM and THE WOMEN OF ISRAEL. She then turned her attention to novel writing, which included HOME INFLUENCE, A MOTHER'S RECOMPENSE and A WOMAN'S FRIENDSHIP. HOME INFLUENCE was the only novel published in her lifetime; the others, including the two historical novels, THE DAYS OF BRUCE and THE VALE OF CEDARS, were published after her death under her mother's editorship.

In the month of June, 1847, Grace Aguilar's health, owing mainly to her literary exertions, was clearly breaking down, and she made up her mind to leave England on a visit to her brother who was studying music in Frankfurt. Before her departure the Jewish Ladies' Association of London presented her with a testimonial and an address, 'as the first woman who had stood forth as the public advocate of the faith of Israel'.

Grace Aguilar became seriously ill in Frankfurt and died there on September 16th, 1847. She was buried at the age of thirty-one in the Jewish cemetery in Frankfurt. Two of her works, A MOTHER'S

RECOMPENSE and THE VALE OF CEDARS were translated into German. This last book is a story of the Jews in Spain under Ferdinand and Isabella, and one wonders if poor Anne Frank ever read it before she wrote her diary of persecution under the Nazis in occupied Holland.

In the preface to THE DAYS OF BRUCE (1852), Grace's mother, Sarah Anguilar, writes:

'As these pages have passed through the press, mingled feelings of pain and pleasure have actuated my heart. Who shall speak the regret that she, to whom its composition was a work of love, cannot participate in the joy which its publication would have occasioned — who shall tell of that anxious pleasure which I feel in witnessing the success of each and all the efforts of her pen?

THE DAYS OF BRUCE must be considered as an endeavour to place before the reader an interesting narrative of a period of history, in itself a romance, and one perhaps as delightful as could well have been selected. In combination with the story of Scotland's brave deliverer, it must be viewed as an illustration of female character, and descriptive of much that its author considered excellent in woman. In the high-minded Isabella of Buchan is traced the resignation of a heart wounded in its best affections, yet trustful midst accumulated misery.

How far the merits of this work may be perceived becomes not me to judge; I only know and feel that on me has been devolved the endearing task of publishing the writings of my lamented child, that I am fulfilling the desire of her life.'

Sarah Aguilar. May. 1852.

For those who find the BRUS of Barbour of Old Rayne unreadable, this book is a revelation. Grace Aguilar traces the genealogy of the Bruce from the days of David I, and shows how slender a threat it was on which the destiny of our country depended. The story of the lineage of the Lords of Brus or Bris is related by Old Dermid, the seer of Kildrummy (the Merlin of the legend) to Sir Nigel Bruce, younger brother of the king and commander of the castle. Alas he never lived to relate the story to Bruce after the siege.

The chapters dealing with King Edward I of England are master-pieces of characterisation. Here we see 'Longshanks' reclining on his gouty couch and receiving his despatches of how things are going in the thraldom of Scotland. Even his own daughter or his highest nobles are not above reproach and sarcasm when they exhibit any leniency towards the traitorous Scots. Every grimace, every sneer, each flash of the eye or curl of the lip is registered, and we get a life-size picture of the Hammer of the Scots.

According to Grace Aguilar, Bruce commissioned the building of the Brig o' Balgownie to make it easier for his followers to assist in the harrying of Buchan. We are informed that the spring of that year was particularly dry and free of snow, so that the woods and homesteads on the Comyns' estates blazed like tinder, with the inhabitants put to the sword or forced to flee to the hills, which was Bruce's attempt to exterminate the Comyns and to erase the name from the annals of Scottish history.

Actually the old Brig o' Balgownie wasn't built until 1318, four years after Bannockburn, and was set about by Bishop Cheyne of Aberdeen, with some financial assistance from King Robert.

For Buchan readers the most vital pages in the book are pages 173 to 268, concerning the siege of Kildrummy Castle, spelled with an *ie*, written nearly a century before Dr. Douglas Simpson examined the site, and makes one wonder where Miss Aguilar got her information, which is not far from the truth, except that she exaggerated a bit by stating that the mound on which the castle stands was 'full two miles in circumference', whereas it occupied an area of about four acres. Nor is there any mention of the Snow Tower, which would have been the most prominent feature of the castle, and the triple Gothic windows of the chapel are also evaded, but perhaps these were an embellishment of later building, after the siege of 1306.

Kildrummie was a strong fortress situated on a circular mount, overhanging the River Don, which at that point ever rushed darkly and stormily along; the mount, though not steep, was full two miles in circumference, from base to brow occupied by the castle, which was erected in that massive yet irregular form peculiar to the architecture of the middle ages. A deep, broad moat or fosse, constantly supplied by the river, defended the castle wall, which

*ran round the mound, irregular indeed, for there were indenta-
tions and sharp angles, occasioned by the uneven ground, each of
which was guarded by a strong turret or tower, rising from the
wall. The wall itself was some four-and-twenty feet in height, and
nine in thickness, consequently the spaces between the turrets on
the top of the wall formed broad level platforms, which in case of a
siege were generally kept strongly guarded.*

*Facing the east, and commanding a view of the river and
adjacent country, stood the barbican gate and drawbridge, which
latter was further defended by strong oaken doors and an iron
portcullis, forming the great gate of the castle wall, and the
principal entrance into the fortress. Two towers of immense
strength, united by a narrow, dimly lit passage, guarded this gate,
and on these depended the grate or portcullis, which was lowered
or raised by internal machinery.*

*Within the castle wall was the outer ballium or court, con-
taining some small, low-roofed dwellings, the residence of many
feudal retainers of the baron. A rude church or chapel was also
within this court, holding a communication with the keep or
principal part of the castle by means of a passage in the third wall,
which divided the ballium from the inner court. The keep itself was
a massive tower, covering but a small square, and four or five
storeys high. . .*

The interior of the castle is also elaborately described:

*. . . but to modern taste the Norman luxury was little better than
rudeness; and certainly though the cushions were soft and richly
embroidered, the arras in some of the apartments, splendid speci-
mens of needlework, and the beautifully carved and often inlaid
oaken walls of others, gave evidence of both taste and talent, yet
the dim light seemed to shed a gloom and heaviness over the whole
range of rooms and passages, which no skill of workmanship or
richness of material could remove.*

But there is no reference to Osborne the blacksmith of Kildrummy,
the traitor who threw a burning plough-coulter into the forage store in
the castle, where the hay was soon ablaze and the grain a smouldering

mass, which meant starvation and surrender for the gallant defenders against the forces of King Edward of England.

For this act of felony the English had promised Osborne as much gold as he could carry away with him, but after the capitulation of the castle garrison they seized Osborne and poured the molten gold down his throat. Grace Aguilar has confused this incident with the treachery of one Ewan Roy, but the outcome is the same eventually.

THE DAYS OF BRUCE is the throbbing pulse of a nation at war for its survival. The turmoil of battle is prevalent, but the intimate emotion of its people pervades the action, embracing the spirit of Scottish patriotism against several odds. What Tolstoy did for the Russian literary reputation with WAR AND PEACE, and what Margaret Mitchell accomplished for the American scene with GONE WITH THE WIND, Grace Aguilar has done for Scotland with THE DAYS OF BRUCE. True, it was written in an age when women were still the wallflowers of society, and the dialogue may be somewhat refined and sugar-pill for modern taste, but if we accept this in the spirit for which it was intended, then we have a novel of unparalleled merit on the adventures of our nation. Alas, it is sadly out of print, but may yet be obtained at some of our College Libraries.

BRAIN SCAR — AUTOBIOGRAPHICAL STUDY

IT was in August, 1929, while I was working with my parents on the farm of Nether Kinmundy, in the parish of Longside, in Aberdeenshire, that I was seized by an attack of epilepsy. I was sixteen at the time and I had been working with my father in the moss, wheeling out peat to his casting, when a young hare jumped down on us from the heather bank. My father killed it with his cutting spade and next day we had hare soup when my mother cooked it for dinner. It was a meal I shall never forget, because I was just half through my plateful when my lower jaw suddenly slipped to one side and I fell from my chair unconscious. I was told later that I went into convulsion and kept thudding the stone floor with my head and my right foot. My mother thought I had choked on a small bone from the hare. She thrust her fingers into my mouth and I bit her to the bone, my teeth snapping shut like a gin-trap. But her timely action kept my jaws apart and probably saved my life. I say this because one of my cousins had a similar attack shortly afterwards and died of lock-jaw. It was fortunate for me I lodged with my parents at the time, because strangers in a farm kitchen may not have shown such concern for my welfare. There is also a danger of swallowing the tongue in a seizure and the patient may die of asphyxia.

I was out for the better part of half-an-hour, and when I regained consciousness I was lying above the blankets in the kitchen bed, Dr. Wood of Longside bending over me, and I was aware of a sharp neuralgic pain in my lower jaw, which was still slightly twisted. It was haytime and some of my workmates enquired for me at the door, believing I had sun-stroke from the heat. But the doctor diagnosed epilepsy, though he could give no explanation for its occurrence, merely stating that for the next six months or a year I must never be left on my own, or if I was, and being a pipe smoker I was to keep my pipe in my mouth, in case I should have a seizure, as apparently it was important to keep my jaws apart. Mother said I had an attack when I was four years old and that the foreman on the place had kept my jaws apart with an egg-spoon.

A CHIEL AMONG THEM

All the same she wasn't satisfied and wanted a second opinion, and she took me to Dr. Yule in Peterhead, who was said to be an extremely clever man, in spite of his occasional drinking bouts. He immediately ran his fingers through my hair and discovered a scar over my left temple, which he said had been caused at birth and had healed inwardly, a scar wound that was touching the brain, probably by a change in bone structure as I approached manhood. By the time I was twenty-one I would have grown out of it Dr. Yule said, and in the meantime he would prescribe a mixture I was to take for several months and which he hoped would dissolve the brain scar.

For six months before the attack I had been severely depressed and subject to momentary lapses of consciousness, which I never told to anyone, until my mother found me one day in tears, and even then I couldn't properly describe my condition of melancholia. However, it culminated in this attack of epilepsy and I had to live in apprehension of another seizure. Strangely enough my depression left me, perhaps because my affliction was now out in the open and was shared with others who cared for me. I suppose also that pubescence had something to do with my condition, signified by a growth of downy hairs on my cheeks and an awakening interest in girls, which brightened my prospects considerably, although my enforced isolation was going to restrict my association with the female sex. All the same it wasn't going to be easy, nor did I think it very fair that I should be insulated at home in the flush of adolescence and eagerness for life, thwarting a gregarious desire to meet others of my own age group, both male and female. Unlike most other country chiels I had no desire for dance halls, but I had an all consuming passion for the movies, and my mother was terribly worried about what might happen to me if I had a fit in a darkened cinema crowded with strangers. Fortunately for me however, the only other single man on the staff was also a cinema fan, and he assured my mother he would take me to the pictures and look after me and that she had nothing to worry about. He would know what to do in an emergency he said, and he would sit beside me and see that I had my pipe in my mouth most of the time, unlit of course, but between my teeth as a precaution.

So Bill Kidd took me to the pictures every Saturday night after we had finished work in the byres and stables. We cycled the double journey of twelve miles, mostly in the dark with gas lamps and without mishap. It was still the era of silent movies and we saw some wonderful pictures, especially WINGS, that aviation spectacular which the talkies have never equalled, not even with HELLS' ANGELS, and we followed the TARZAN serials of Frank Miller, long before Johnny Weissmuller started swinging on the tree vines. Poor Bill Kidd, he left the farm at the November Term; in fact we attended the Ellon feeing market together, when he was engaged to Mains of Waterton as third horseman, while I had to stay on with my parents at Nether Kinmundy. But Bill and I had formed a friendship which went beyond this association, well into adult life when we both got married and went our separate ways. But while I was content to remain a cottar Bill became a farmer in his own right, alas to die in the prime of life, while I have survived these twenty years since his death to write this gratuitous epitaph to keep him in fond remembrance.

When Bill Kidd left us I felt confident enough to go to the movies alone, though I knew my mother worried excessively all the time I was away, and sometimes stayed up from bed until she saw me safely home. But I wouldn't be deterred and was determined to manage on my own, still taking my mixture and so far I hadn't taken another fit. Indeed it seemed that Dr. Yule had performed a miracle.

It was about this time that I met Happy Harry. Harry Mitchell was his real name and I don't know how he got his nickname. Perhaps it was because of his breezy disposition and ready smile, which was merely a disguise for his salesman patter. Harry had initially hailed from New Deer, and after an adventurous youth and war service he ended up with a weak heart in the business of home photography. He had at one time been a cinema projectionist and manager in England, but either poor management or ill health or both had driven him from the lucrative sphere of moving pictures to still photography, which he practised in a darkened room wherever he happened to be living. When I first heard of him he was living at Grange, on the outskirts of Peterhead; then he moved to Invernettie, at Burnhaven, and eventually to a cottage at Stockbridge, in the parish of Longside, which is still standing, but alas sadly dilapidated.

In the early thirties however, there wasn't much scope for family photography, so Harry went round the cottar houses on his bicycle and persuaded the women to have their existing photos enlarged and framed, especially studio portraits of their ancestors or families, which were of better quality generally than the average black and white snapshot, though these could also be tackled and blown up to life size if business was slack. Thus a great many Victorian and Edwardian grandads and grandmas got a new lease of immortality in the homes of succeeding generations, where they graced the papered walls in new frames furnished by Harry Mitchell at around seventeen shillings and sixpence, including enlargement, and depending on their size.

To give Harry his due he did a grand job of rejuvenating these family portraits, and the occasional pair of favourite work horses, some of them still surviving in their carved frames, now a bit aerated with woodworm holes, the texture of the plates a bit faded, and perhaps to be had at farm roups, because Harry included the farm wives in his push for trade. Even the most unlikely uncle or maiden aunt was liable to be resurrected from some drawer or old trunk and hung on the wall, especially after several years in Harry's itinerary, when he had exhausted the family favourites and the cottar wives had yielded further to his persistence in reviewing their photo albums.

My mother was a perfect foil for Happy Harry's persuasion and some of our relations eventually found a nail on the wall where we could spit on them or clobber them with chappit tatties. But even I fell under Harry's spell, especially when PICTURE SHOW issued coloured supplements of my favourite film stars, like Marion Davies, Estelle Brody, Colleen More and Gary Cooper, and thus he discovered I was what is now known as a film buff. I suppose at the time I was the only farm worker in Aberdeenshire who had the FILM WEEKLY delivered regularly by the grocer's vanman, and Harry wasn't slow to catch on. He talked me round to coming to see his private film show, performed on an old discarded cinematograph machine he had got for next to nothing from a cinema which had gone over to talkies, or even earlier, because it had a cranking handle and was lit by acetylene gas, before the days of electric motors and carbon lighting. It was a standard 32 millimetre machine of German make and stood over six feet to the top spoolbox and weighed nearly two hundredweights. Of course I was fascinated and it must have been plain to Harry that I would be daft enough to give a six months' wage for this cumbersome contraption that made the pictures move. In no time at all he had me threading the machine and splicing broken film and he lectured me on the workings of the Maltese Cross and the Geneva Movement, change-over signals, lens adjustment, rewinding and spooling of film; everything in fact concerned with film projection, and by the end of the evening I had made up my mind that all this was my life's desire.

I had cycled down to Invernettie and I was introduced to Harry's wife, a slim and cultured woman who was very nice to me, and I was taken into the darkened room where Harry processed his photographic plates. Looking back on this scene it is all so reminiscent of William Friese-Greene and the London Bobby whom he had invited to his laboratory to see his first ever picture show, though at the time I knew nothing of the Bristol inventor and his experiments to give us moving pictures, but now at least I understood the miracle that made it possible, thanks to Harry Mitchell.

Harry lit the acetylene lantern and set the machine in motion, flashing the pictures on to a white sheet draped on a blackboard stand. In the days before television and 8 millimetre home movies it was just marvellous: Mutt and Jeff and Felix the Cat jumping all over the place; Cowboys and Indians and even a travel film in equisite colour, all the things I had seen and marvelled at in the local picture houses and here it was at the fireside of Harry's home. Harry gave me the cranking handle and I was running the show myself. To say that I was impressed was putting it mildly: I was infatuated; completely hooked, as they say nowadays and determined to have Harry's cinematograph.

Harry said the price was ten pounds, plus two pounds for the films, which I agreed to pay, and his wife gave me a cup of tea to seal the bargain. My fee for the six months term was seventeen pounds ten shillings, which left me with only five pounds ten shillings in hand, and thirty shillings of that went to my mother for washing my clothes throughout the period, which left me with only four pounds for the next half-year term, and as we were leaving the farm, and with little prospect of a job for me because of my epilepsy I would be in the dog-house. But the prospect of being the proud owner of this gigantic magic lantern blinded me to all the pecuniary consequences of my behaviour.

It was the year of the roup, when the old farmer was selling everything off, and we would get our wages a week before the Term, which enabled me to pay Harry for the cinematograph before we flitted, for my father had got a fee at another farm at Udny, twenty-three miles distant, and we would be moving at the end of May. It was also the first year of the great depression and most people were trying to save money, not spending it. Bankruptcies and suicides were rife in America, but a youngster of sixteen takes little heed of such emergencies.

In the meantime the farmer loaned us the pony and float and one evening after supper I set off with my father to get the cinematograph. I paid Harry the money before we carried the machine, now dismantled, piece by piece, down the stone stair at the front of his house. The parts were heavy and it took two of us to carry them and my father must have thought I was daft; at least movie daft, though he didn't say anything and went along with me all the way. This was a big advance from my shoebox theatre and my silhouette puppets, perhaps my first step towards becoming a film producer or cinema owner, a Sam Goldwyn or an Alfred Hitchcock, names that meant nothing to my father, though for me at the time they shone brighter than the stars of heaven.

Back home we unloaded the cinematograph at the cottar house and stabled the shelt at the farm. It was after ten o'clock but my father gave me a hand and we carried the machine upstairs to the loft, where I hastily assembled it for a late picture show. Mother hung up a white bedsheet on the gable and darkened the skylight, while I threaded the film into the machine and lit the acetylene lamp in the lantern behind the lens. It was playing with fire really, highly inflamable celloloid exposed to a naked flame, and the friction of the film on the sprockets, the lantern oven hot, and a gasometer under the stand. It was a wonder my mother allowed it, especially up in the tinder dry loft, and downstairs she had packing boxes stacked everywhere for the flitting. Even a chimney fire was enough to make her frantic, but in the circumstances I think she put up with me in the hope that this new contraption that showed pictures would keep me at home with my epilepsy. But Harry had warned me about the risk of fire, and he had taught me how to control the acetylene lamp and how to spool the film, not to let it tangle on the floor.

However, there was no fire scare, and my parents carried their chairs up from the kitchen to watch the picture show. My sister Flora was in bed by this time and she would have to wait for the next performance to see Mutt and Jeff. The show lasted for just over an hour, with two changes of spools, while the small apartment got warmer from the heat of the machine, and I sweated at the handle cranking through the films. But it was quite delightful, especially the Western, TWO-STRAW BILL — who married the local schoolteacher — and perhaps my parents thought it had been worth all the trouble and expense, though they didn't say as much.

It was another week before the Term, and I ran a show every evening, when most of the neighbouring cottars came to see it, and my sister invited her school friends. It was one of Buchan's greatest ferlies: moving pictures in a cottar house, in the days when television had never been heard of, and radio very occasionally. Talking pictures were on the way, but so far very few people had seen them.

Then came the Term and the flitting, when we had to dismantle the cinematograph and carry it down the stair again, on to the lorry-trailer which had been left overnight for loading, while the driver and fireman went elsewhere with their steam-wagon for another load of furniture, returning in the morning to hitch up with the trailer we had loaded in the early hours, assisted by Tammie Beagrie from the shoppie at the Creashy Raw.

My mother and sister travelled in the cab with the driver and fireman, while I rode with my father on the back of the steam-wagon, under a tarpaulin cover, facing the trailer, which was also covered, and we were soon black with soot from the funnel, the smoke streaming back over the covered load and hitting the trailer, where it swirled and eddied between the two vehicles, burning our faces with hot sparks and almost stifling us for lack of fresh air, while the solid tyred wagons tore along the dusty roads at an average speed of twenty-five miles per hour.

My father had instructed the drivers to stop at the New Inn at Ellon, where he intended to buy them a beer, and while he went into the bar with them I remained on the trailer, being under age for drinking, though I had a burning thirst and my face still stinging from flying cinders. I was soon diverted however, for they had left the steaming wagon where I could see the hoardings advertising the current week's films for the mobile cinema show in the Victoria Hall. They advertised the silent film WINGS, which I had seen the year before at Peterhead, and it seemed like a greeting from old friends in a strange land, while I peered at the coloured posters of Clara Bow and Charles Buddy Rogers. We were parked near the spot where the monument commemorating the Mormaers of Buchan was erected some fifty years later, in 1977, by which time I had become interested in such things, including Saint Mary's Chapel on the Rock; but at seventeen the cinema was the only history and religion I knew, and to say otherwise

205

would be like washing my face with my glasses on, and that I couldn't see the mirror for the froth.

There was only one bridge over the Ythan at Ellon in 1930, a very narrow structure which can still be seen outside the new bridge erected in 1940. The steam-wagon and trailer just managed to scrape through between the parapets, and it was one-way traffic when buses and motor lorries were converging on the bridge, though there were no traffic lights, each driver awaiting his turn to cross, including the odd horse cart and motor car. Cyclists managed to squeeze through with the pedestrians, but there was no real congestion as traffic was thin in those days. It was over this three-arch bridge in 1933 that John Ramensky, the famous safe-cracker made his first escape from Peterhead convict prison. He crossed the bridge in darkness, under the helmets of the local bobbies, and he did it on his fingertips, clinging to the stone parapet, his legs dangling over the river some twenty feet below.

Our 'puffing-billy' belched out more black smoke as it struggled up the Craighall brae, where it forked sharp right at the old Coaching Inn, now demolished and replaced by the modern Mercury Hotel. Ellon was a small place then and there were no houses on the Fortrie Road, only the railway viaduct spanning the Ythan in the valley at Meiklemill, and we headed up the steep gradient surmounted by the ruined castle of Esslemont, a former stronghold of the Cheynes of Buchan.

We were heading for Chapelhall farm, worked in those days by Mr. Henderson, who later moved to Little Ythsie of Tarves. It was a dairy farm with hand milking, and my father got the job as second cattleman with dry stock because my mother could milk in the dairy byre. She was paid sixpence for each milking, which at twice a day was seven shillings a week, and my father's wage was around one pound a week, plus house and the usual benefits. He got the job through the papers and cycled the odd forty-six miles double journey for an interview with Mr. Henderson. It was getting fairly near the Term and he was fortunate in getting the work when there were so many applicants.

On the top of Esslemont Hill, the farm of Chapelhall came into view, the farm house and steading in the middle distance, with the ark-roofed cottar houses above it on the brae, cottages with their chimneys in the centre of the roof, with overhanging eaves on the stone gables, typical of the Esslemont estates. Not that I could see or classify all this in my early teens, moreso from the back of a steam-wagon, my eyes filled with whirling coal smoke, but writing in retrospect I have the benefit of later analysis to enhance the description. But indeed it was always exciting for a cottar loon to get a first glimpse of his new home, and to ponder what thrills and surprises awaited him there — maybe even girls next door to flirt with, new trees to climb, new roads to explore, and for the younger, new school friends ...

Our driver wasn't sure of the farm and my father shouted to him from the wagon when he went past the road end, and he had to reverse the trailer about a hundred yards to the entrance. Chapelton farm is first encountered, then Chapelhall farm in the valley, with names that give the impression that the district had once been closely associated with religion, especially with two neighbouring farms bearing the address of Monkshill and Cloisterseat, however, that may be.

It wasn't easy for the driver to take his fire-breathing, rubber-shod monster up the steep narrow cartroad to the cottar houses, where there was scarcely space to turn a horse cart, never mind a steam-wagon, but he managed it and uncoupled our trailer, informing us he would be back for it when we had unloaded the furniture, sometime in the afternoon. And off he set with the steam-wagon and its load for another farm in the area, the contractor killing two birds with one stone so to speak, *that* was Jamie Sutherland of Peterhead.

Next day, being the Term-day holiday, and all the lino down and the furniture placed I persuaded my anxious parents to forget their troubles and spend the afternoon in Aberdeen. So we all rigged ourselves in our best clothes, which were nothing very grand, but about the cheapest readymades you could buy — locked the door and walked up the footpath on to the road for Logierieve railway station. There were four cottages on the brae, with two new cottar families besides ourselves, still busy with their odds and ends, and they spoke to us in passing on our way to the station. We learned later that the grieve and the head cattleman had stayed on from last year and that the newcomers were the Smarts and the Adams families. Mr. Smart was in his thirties and had seen the worst of trench warfare, while Mr. Adams was an older man nearing retirement.

We had a wonderful afternoon in the city, where I managed to get my parents and my small sister in to see one of the new talkies, Hal Skelly and Nancy Carroll in THE DANCE OF LIFE which was done to the tune of Swanee River at the old La Scala in Union Street, later the Majestic cinema but demolished in the mid-seventies. Perhaps it was too much to expect my parents to share my enthusiasm for the new media, but I think they enjoyed it from association with my cinematograph, and they partly understood what was going on in the projection room at our backs, and we could see the projectionists peering from the small windows in the gallery walls, while the light beam played on the screen out in front, over our heads in what was once a highly orientated cinema, with some of the lush symbolism of the mysterious east in its design.

But I can't say that my poor father was completely involved. Always apprehensive of change, even as a nomadic cottar, the next day he would have to begin work on a new farm with strange workmates and I think he brooded on the thought of it. For the last year I had worked by his side, but as there wasn't a job for me at Chapelhall he would be on his own among strangers, and with a new master, for better or for worse. In the meantime my parents had decided they couldn't risk letting me take a fee away from home. I might have another seizure, and it was difficult for my father to find a job for himself, never mind an epileptic son on the same farm, where I would be at risk with horses and livestock, so I was left out in the cold, my first and only experience of unemployment, and strictly speaking I should have been on sickness benefit.

After the Term, when we had settled in, my father at work, my mother at her twice daily milking, and my sister at Esslemont primary school, I set to work planting potatoes in the garden. It was a bit late planting them in June but the place had been too far away for us to do it in the spring, especially in those days when we had only bicycles to get about with, and no half-holidays on Saturdays. Another job I did for the old man was to shovel the load of coal he got as a perquisite into the coalshed, solaced the while by smoking my pipe and with erotic visions of Clara Bow and Joan Crawford, who were the (pipe) dream girls of the late twenties and early thirties, and who would nowadays be designated as sex symbols, and my day-dreaming as sexual fantasies, yet without the dreaming, life would be a colourless existence. My ego was encouraged in this by the current fan weeklies, and by the trade magazines I got from the cinema managers, all of which was grist for my journalistic turn of mind and glamourised imagination. I even had film posters on my mother's newly papered walls, and this was thirty years before the pin-ups among teenagers were accepted in their bedrooms as commonplace.

It wasn't long before I had transformed our shabby wooden panelled kitchen into a cinema vestibule, with my cinematograph stanced upstairs, where the skylight was easily darkened, and I had built a plywood projection box around the machine, mostly from packing cases, with the necessary peepholes for the lens and myself, so that my audiences could see nothing of what was happening except on the white screen over the fireplace. By the end of the second week I was giving nightly shows to the families from the nearby farms, playing to packed houses with TWO-STRAW BILL, Mutt and Jeff, my fashion show, travelogue and ageing newsreel. Some of the kids had never seen a film show before and they were mystified; some of them were even frightened and crying and had to be carried downstairs by their distracted mothers, who were otherwise anxious to enjoy the picture show. Some of the cottar wives gave me a sixpence or a three-penny bit for my pains, but mostly I was out of pocket for acetylene gas and adhesive to splice broken film, which became more commonplace as the films became more brittle from heat exposure and sprocket friction over a period of constant use.

In two weeks I had exhausted my local audiences and I was left on my own with my film shows. It was rather like the song of the period IF I HAD A TALKING PICTURE OF YOU, which was being popularised by Janet Gaynor in her first talkie, SUNNY SIDE UP, and my case was particularly synonymous with the lines which read:

> *I would sit there in the gloom*
> *Of my lonely little room*
> *And applaud the moment you came in view —*
> *We would talk the whole thing over, we two,*
> *If I had a talking picture of you.*

Only I had no Janet Gaynor in my repertoire, though I did manage to buy a recording of her song, which I played on our old horned gramophone while changing a reel of film.

And while my audiences dwindled the condition of my films deteriorated, until breakdowns became a nightmare, three or four times in a single spool, with only minutes between them, and tension mounted wondering when the next break would come. I had run the films through so many times that Amelia Earhart's ATLANTIC CROSSING had become a shuttle service, and in TWO-STRAW BILL film scratch had turned the confetti into a shower of snowflakes.

I made enquiries about leasing the local hall for public showings, which would have enabled me to hire new films, but as this was denied me, because of entertainment tax, and I couldn't afford to rent films privately, my days as a film exhibitor were short lived. But my film shows in the cottar houses were something of an inovation, and I sometimes wonder if any of the children who saw my movies remember anything about it, now that they would be nearing sixty and gathered round their television sets.

Since I was out of a job my frustration turned to boredom, relieved to some extent by my kindling interest in literature. But this too was handicapped by a scarcity of reading material. Books were unobtainable; school libraries scarcely existed and public libraries were confined to the towns, and my knowledge of books was so restricted I wouldn't have known what to read to my best advantage in any case. However, I became friendly with Mrs. Smart, the foreman's wife next door, whose reading diet was the RED STAR WEEKLY, which she loaned to me every week, and we shared the adventures of Red Headed Kitty in weekly instalments. From there I took off and wrote one of my first short stories in red ink and sent it off to an editor. When it came back I was soured of literature and didn't put pen to paper for a long time.

I became so depressed that mother sometimes found me in tears. After about five weeks in idleness I wanted to go back to the farms, but considering my epileptic condition my parents thought this to be unwise and dangerous. I argued that it was nearing a year since I had my last attack, and I had become so very confident of complete recovery that I had even stopped taking my mixture. It was also rumoured for a time that the farmer, my father's employer, would give me a job painting all the doors and windows about the steading, but it never materialised and I got tired of waiting.

In the second week of July I became desperate. Unemployment didn't suit my chemistry and the days dragged like a heavy chain loaded with weights. I wanted to get back to my pals in the chaumers of Buchan; back to the picture houses in Peterhead, but my mother wouldn't let me go, terrified that I might have another fit, with no one aside who knew about putting something in my mouth to prevent lock-jaw, which nowadays would be known medically as a form of tetanus. I argued that my pipe would save me but my parents couldn't be convinced. I would have to take the risk myself and defy them. There was nothing for me at home now that the cinematograph had been a failure, and with my writing refused I was completely flummoxed and dejected.

I was a stranger in the Udny district, and without a job and isolated at home, I made no contact with youngsters of my own age group. I was homesick for my native Buchan and its chaumer chiels who were my pals. I missed the companionship of youth and I was eating my heart out in loneliness. It was the first time in my seventeen years I had been out of a job and I discovered I hated idleness. I envied the lads at work in the fields; something that now seemed an oasis in my wilderness of sloth. I was tired of being on my own and there was a gregariousness in my nature I had never before suspected; a hankering to belong, to identify with something, and the farming fraternity was the only society I knew. I felt like a stirk on a tether that had eaten everything within his reach, and I had to break free. And I had no money. I was living off my parents with no means of repaying them — and I couldn't go to the cinema, for me the worst of all punishment.

So I told mother I was going to Peterhead to see an old friend, where I would stay the night and cycle home the next day. She was terribly worried that I might have another seizure, with no one to help me, especially on the road with a bicycle. But I said I would take my chance; otherwise I would never have a life of my own. She knew I was depressed for want of a job, and that I was missing my companions, so after some deliberation she had to let me go. I dressed myself in the morning and set off on my bicycle down the brae. Mother watched me anxiously until I was out of sight, but I was fairly confident that no harm would befall me.

I spent the afternoon with my friends in Peterhead, a young married couple I had known since my schooldays. In the evening we went to the cinema, where I was greatly inspired by the performance of Lon Chaney in WHILE THE CITY SLEEPS, when he portrayed a sort of modern Kojak detective in a sleazy down-town New York; and I was also greatly taken with the smooth running of the projectors compared

211

with my own nightmare of breakdowns.

I spent the night with my friends in Peterhead, and next day I set out with my bicycle in the country to look for a job on the farms. Quite by chance I met an older man of my acquaintance and he sent me to East Teuchan in Cruden, where Mr. Bruce was looking for a foreman, a position I wasn't really qualified for, but it was a small farm with only one pair of horses and my friend assured me I was quite capable. I was in luck however and I engaged to Mr. Bruce on a weekly basis at seventeen shillings a week, plus food and board, and I would begin work the following Monday. The farmer didn't know he was engaging a potential epeliptic and of course I didn't tell him, I was so eager to get the job. Mother was apprehensive but I was elated with my new prospects and my father didn't seem to mind much; perhaps he would be glad to get me off his hands. He had his own worries because Chapelhall was a hard place to work on and he wasn't finding it easy to cope.

I got on splendidly at my new place. Mr. Bruce was a kind and considerate man who had been a wartime soldier and his wife fed us like gentry on the best food available. Every day we sat down to dinner with a knife and fork as one family, the farmer at the head of the table, and we had morning and afternoon tea-breaks. Mr. Bruce ran a milk lorry to Cruden Bay and he brought back fresh provisions every day. I had never been so well fed in my life before; not even in my mother's kitchen, and I soon forgot the loneliness and frustration of the previous weeks.

At the end of my first week I cycled the seventeen miles home on the Sunday morning and my mother was watching for me at the head of the brae. Mrs. Smart next door said she had never seen a mother in such an anxious state; but though she had family of her own at school she had never seen a grown son in the grip of epilepsy as my mother had done, my jaws locked and foam at my mouth. However, it hadn't happened again so far and I was beginning to gather confidence in the belief that I was cured.

I had only one companion at East Teuchan, a Davie Gatt from Cruden Bay, a haflin about my own age who tended the small dairy herd and we got on together famously. We slept in the small chaumer out in the farm close, and in the long sunny evenings Davie Gatt took me to see his widowed mother in the village, down by the harbour at

BRAIN SCAR

Port Erroll, where she lived in a small cottage on the pier. We also cycled to the pictures in Peterhead and I was back in the old environment I used to share with Bill Kidd. I was enraptured with Douglas Fairbanks in THE IRON MASK; Laura La Plante in SHOWBOAT; Mary Nolan in THE GIRL FROM CHINA; and most of all with the delectable Greta Garbo in WILD ORCHIDS, silent pictures of course but charming in their mysticism and exciting adventure. I suppose I was in love with the young Garbo, so much so that when Davie Gatt took me to see the ruins of Slains Castle I sketched her profile on the inner wall of the battlemented tower overlooking the cliffs, the very spot where Doctor Johnson had said he would not wish for a storm, but if it came, there was no better place anywhere from which he would like to view such a spectacle.

It was about this time that I began to feel a numbing sensation on the left side of my head, just above the scar, and a slight quivering of my lower mandible. It was alarming after this space of time and I was afraid to confide in anyone. Perhaps it would go away. Surely I wouldn't be caught again on the road to Damascus, for I feel sure that Saint Paul suffered from the same malady. So did Julius Caesar, but like Macbeth he was not of woman born so to speak, and wouldn't have suffered any obstetric injury. I have heard it said that anyone afflicted with occasional epilepsy is either very strong or very clever, or both, but I have never made very much of this. Nor did I hear any voice calling to me in my seizure, though the effect of it changed my attitude to life. Gone was the former brooding introvert and the oppression of spirit which assailed me. I became more buoyant and despite fears of recurring attacks my depression lifted as a cloud and revealed the sun. For a whole year I had enjoyed His warmth and glory; living for the sheer joy of simply being alive and well, until this passing cloud again obscured my clearer vision.

I went back to Dr. Yule with my complaint and he prescribed the same mixture, which I took in secret, never telling a soul, not even my mother because of alarming her. Within a week the numbing sensation left me and my jaw muscles ceased to twitch. The scar was dissolving Dr. Yule said; otherwise I would have had another fit. So my skies brightened again, and in the silence of night I secretly thanked God for my deliverance. The spirit of David was in my soul and my living became a psalm of thankfulness.

213

It was hoeing time and by now I was an expert at the job and Mr. Bruce was very pleased with my work; every plant singled and all the weeds scraped away from the drills. Then came hay harvest when I yoked my pair of horses to the mower, something I never did before nor since, and I had the privilege of sitting on the driver's seat, like a real foreman, while the farmer sat on the tilter's seat, where he swathed the hay on to the cutting bar with a long-handled rake.

But there was a destiny shaping my life, with my guardian angel at the crossroads, and in the midst of my contentment he signalled a change. Looking back over fifty years I can see the pattern of my life on the farms, and I can see how important it was for me in making the decision to leave Teuchan, though I wouldn't have guessed it at the time. Yet it is a fact that had I remained at this pleasant little farm for one more week my entire life would have been completely different. For one thing I certainly wouldn't have met the girl I married, the woman who eventually made our marriage one of the hallmarks of my existence, and I would never have written my country life stories, if indeed I would ever have written anything at all in the walk of life which was opened for me, had I cared to take it. I would have learned to drive a motor vehicle while still in my teens, an ability which, in those early days of road transport would have taken me away from the comtemplative life in farming which made writing easier. I would have missed the background that made my rural stories possible. Behind the steering wheel of a lorry the hectic responsibility would have mechanised my formative years, crushing the culture that was slowly taking shape in my mind.

I stayed only one month at East Teuchan. In spite of the excellent food, pleasant working conditions and very agreeable companionship I opted for a situation on a farm almost three miles nearer the cinemas at Peterhead, a factor which has always decided my geographical position while working on the Buchan farms. Districts like New Pitsligo, New Deer, Auchnagatt or Maud were always considered out of bounds, and I usually sought work within seven or eight miles of the coast, where I could cycle easily in the evenings to the picture shows, the only art form apart from literature that I knew anything about.

On the evening that I gave up my job at Teuchan Mr. Bruce was not at home. I got Mrs. Bruce in the kitchen and she was terribly upset. She couldn't understand why I was leaving them. She fed me well she said and the master was kind, what more could I want. He even intended teaching me to drive the milk lorry and raising my pay accordingly. It was a shame to leave now she said when I was doing so well, and the master was pleased with my work. Would I reconsider it?

But it was too late and it had to be or I would have jumped at the chance. I had already engaged to Mr. Mackintosh of Greystone farm, where I had previously worked on leaving school, and as he was also a very kindly man, and because I had fond memories of the place I wasn't going to let him down. They were old neighbours of my parents when they lived at Springhill and were keen to have me back.

Before 1930 was out the giant airship R101 had crashed in France, roasting alive its crew and passengers, but I never managed to get it for my newsreel showings. In fact I was still screening Amelia Earhart on her arrival from Nova Scotia, for I had persuaded Mr. Mackintosh to let me have my cinematograph installed in the green room, just along the passage from the farm kitchen, where the old-fashioned wooden shutters were still on the windows, so that I could close them and have summer evening shows for the family after working hours. Mr. Mackintosh had also allowed me to drive two six-inch nails into the bannister of the loft stair in the barn, where I could rewind my spools and repair broken film. I had new audiences for TWO-STRAW BILL but the mutilation of brittle film continued and I soon lost heart in the whole project. I became utterly disenchanted with the idea of becoming a film exhibitor and the projector stood cold and neglected in the green room for the next six months or so, when I left Greystone for the Kinmundy district.

However, just before the May Term, I was visited by another film enthusiast, also a farm worker, who wanted to buy my cinematograph, provided I wasn't asking too much for it. I let him have it for thirty shillings, the amount it had cost me in carriage to bring it back from Chapelhall of Udny. He took it away in a horse cart and I was glad to be rid of the thing. It was becoming a problem for me when moving on from farm to farm, and as my parents were flitting again I would have to get rid of it in any case, even for scrap.

My participation in the film business had been a bitter disappointment and henceforth I would be content to remain a spectator, though I did enter my name as a projectionist but failed to get an opening. I feel also that this was meant to be, and that my thoughts were to be directed more and more towards literature, preparing me for the great agricultural revolution, when I was to record the dying throes of a social culture that had endured for centuries, and to herald the birth pangs of mechanisation on the land, the only things that posterity may thank me for, which may otherwise have passed beyond memory.

And the brain scar. By then I had almost forgotten about it. I still have the physical scar but the mental aspect of it had gone out of my life. It had served its purpose it seems.